Minutes
to
Midnight

VIOLENCE, COOPERATION, PEACE

AN INTERNATIONAL SERIES

Editors: Francis A. Beer, *University of Colorado, Boulder* and Ted Robert Gurr, *University of Maryland, College Park*

Violence, Cooperation, Peace: An International Series focuses on violent conflict and the dynamics of peaceful change within and among political communities. Studies in the series may include the perspectives and evidence of any of the social sciences or humanities, as well as applied fields such as conflict management. This international book series emphasizes systematic scholarship, in which theory and evidence are used to advance our general understanding of the processes of political violence and peace.

Volumes in the Series

Minutes to Midnight

Nuclear Weapons Protest in America

Frances B. McCrea

Gerald E. Markle

JX
1974.7
.M367
1989
west

VIOLENCE, COOPERATION, PEACE

AN INTERNATIONAL SERIES

SAGE PUBLICATIONS

The Publishers of Professional Social Science

Newbury Park   London   New Delhi

For information address:

SAGE Publications, Inc.
2111 West Hillcrest Drive
Newbury Park, California 91320

SAGE Publications Ltd.
28 Banner Street
London EC1Y 8QE
England

SAGE Publications India Pvt. Ltd.
M-32 Market
Greater Kailash I
New Delhi 110 048 India

Printed in the United States of America

Library of Congress Cataloging-in-Publication Data

McCrea, Frances B.
    Minutes to midnight : nuclear weapons protest in America / by
Frances B. McCrea and Gerald E. Markle.
        p.   cm. — (Violence, cooperation, peace)
    Bibliography: p.
    Includes index.
    ISBN 0-8039-3417-3. — ISBN 0-8039-3418-1 (pbk.)
    1. Antinuclear movement—United States—History.   I. Markle,
Gerald E., 1942-   .   II. Title.   III. Series.
JX1974.7.M367   1989
327.1'74'0973—dc19   89-5847
                                                                          CIP

FIRST PRINTING, 1989

Contents

The four decades of this study link the deaths of grandfather and grandson. This book is dedicated to Marko Banjac (December 10, 1910–April 17, 1945), who was a victim of fascism and war; and to Craig Steven McCrea (March 20, 1969–August 21, 1985), whose short life but long struggle with cancer personified the best of the peace movement and all innocent victims: courage, outrage, perseverance, dignity and hope against all odds.

Preface

One of us grew up in post-World War II Europe, in the aftermath of awful destruction and death; the other in Cold War America, "searching the skies," "ducking for cover," practicing air-raid drills. In the first setting, a revulsion for violence would seem to follow; less obvious is the second setting, though as Todd Gitlin (1987, p. 22) notes, "Under those desks, and crouched in those hallways . . . existentialists were made." These experiences, common to all of our generation, provided the grounding—but not the impetus—for our interest in nuclear weapons protest.

We became interested in the antinuclear weapons movement for several reasons. As students of social problems and social movements, this movement—and particularly the Freeze—posed fascinating questions. We wondered how this massive social movement, in many ways so unlike the protest of the 1960s, had begun, quickly flourished and then rapidly declined. The Freeze seemed like an ideal phenomenon for research: though it was the subject of mass media attention, little scholarly work had addressed the Freeze. As we researched the origins of the Freeze, we decided to broaden our studies. We concluded that to understand the Freeze, one must understand and appreciate the entire antinuclear weapons protest movement. Thus we gave detailed attention to the development of social protest organizations in the post-World War II era, a period largely ignored by today's sociologists.

The antinuclear weapons movement also appealed to us because of its paramount import. We believe that there is no more crucial issue than war and peace in the nuclear era. In his book, *Twentieth Century Book of the Dead*, Gil Elliot (1972) calculated that some 110 million people have died as the result of war and political violence in this century—such a horrible, but abstract and distant calculation! So Elliot carefully and painstakingly supplies a demography of these dead, his attempt to give these massive numbers some meaning. He concludes that human-made death has largely replaced disease and plague as a source of untimely death. "This is the kind of change that Hegel meant when he said that a quantitative change, if large enough, could bring about a qualitative change" (p. 5).

The quality of this particular change becomes clear, he continues, if we connect the total with the scale of death inherent in the nuclear weapons now possessed by the superpowers—hundreds of millions of deaths, the destruction of whole nations and even the entire human race, and all accomplished in a matter of hours. The paramount moral significance of nuclear weapons is inescapable. "If morality refers to relations between individuals, or between the individuals and society," he writes, "then there can be no more fundamental issue than the continuing survival of individuals and societies. The scale of man-made death is the central moral as well as material fact of our time" (Elliot 1972, p. 5).

Yet nuclear weapons were introduced into our world not by some criminal element or illegal conspiracy. Rather they were invented, designed, and produced by our most famous scientists, people widely respected, even revered. How could it be that such horrible destruction was the product of Western civilization's greatest accomplishment? How could it be that science, which in our mythos produces a better world and saves lives, was responsible for this ultimate menace? This dilemma of our world, this central fact of the Twentieth Century, was captured in Max Horkheimer and Theodor Adorno's phrase, the dialectics of enlightenment: the institution of science which produced life-saving vaccines also destroyed Hiroshima and Nagasaki.

The scientist is caught in the middle. Motivated by desires to save, or at least understand the world, the scientist now looks over, and digs deeper into, the abyss. By studying scientists' protest of their own creation—actions unique and unprecedented in history—we hoped to learn more about this horrific and uniquely modern dilemma.

Aside from the obvious but terrible prospect of nuclear annihilation, the nuclear arms race shapes our everyday life—our economy, polity and culture—as does no other issue. How should we confront this issue, let alone try to change it? In studying the actions of protesters, and their successes and failures, we hoped to learn something about how a small group of individuals, with no apparent power base, could challenge a superpower. Thus we hoped to learn something of the struggle for social change in advanced capitalist societies.

Further, we wanted to study antinuclear weapons protest because we have always believed in the righteousness of the cause, the unequaled patriotism (in the best sense of the word) of its advocates, and the clarity of their moral vision. As DeBenedetti (1980, p. 199) has eloquently characterized the American peace subculture:

[It] speaks of forbearance within a culture that has flowered in conquest. It speaks of reconciliation within a society that works better at distributing weapons than wealth. It speaks of supranational authority among a highly nationalistic people who dislike all authority. It speaks to just global order to governing officials anxious for pre-eminence and profit.

We have always supported the peace movement, been active in it as our lives have allowed, and hope to remain active in the future.

Yet our involvement in the movement has been at the periphery, not the center; and this has important implications for this book. We write not as insiders whose personal investments in the movement are huge, whose personal histories overlap, and are an intrinsic part of the story of, movement history. Insiders' unique status gives them great insight. Yet their analyses are more prescriptive and existential than ours. Our stance is from the outside, as bystanders—albeit interested ones—peering toward the center. Moreover, our goal is not to resurrect the movement, though we hope this happens, but in the light of recent social science to understand and critically assess its role in postindustrial America.

Our own motives may not be taken for granted. All scholarship, certainly including our own, ought to be reflexive. Thus as we have struggled with this study, we have questioned the importance of the scholar in social movement activity. In the preface to his fine book, *Rebels Against War*, Wittner (1984) assesses his own contribution to the peace movement by wondering "if anything could be more important than unravelling the mysterious relationship between war and peace." Wittner's answer to his own query was "through books, articles [and] conferences we attempted. . .to apply intellectual energies to ridding humanity of one of its deadliest scourges. We are still at work"(p. viii). Every scholar shares Wittner's hope: that her or his scholarship will make the world a better place. Yet though we share the hope, we do not share the conviction.

We are not sure that clear moral vision and scholarly efforts will help lead to a peaceful world. We do believe, with DeBenedetti (1980), that peacemakers operate more as "pathfinders than power seekers" and that we must continue to "guide forward a subculture of dissent that survives in the certainty that there are working alternatives to the dominant power drive toward national self-aggrandizement" (p. 200).

We recognize that our own reasons for undertaking this study are a complex admixture of professional, scholary and personal motives.

With utmost modesty, and no great expectations of success, we hope that our work may promote greater understanding and help scholars and social activists find ways of promoting disarmament and peace.

Acknowledgments

Because this book reflects our intellectual—and to an extent our historical—biographies, it seems only fair to thank many people: family, friends, former teachers, and colleagues. As they have influenced our lives, so have they shaped this book. Conforming to the task at hand, however, we wish to thank in particular Louis Kriesberg, Ronald Kramer, John McCarthy, Stanley Robin and Rudolf Siebert for reading various early drafts of the manuscript. We gratefully acknowledge their help in shaping our ideas and the final content of this book. For Chapter 3, we appreciate the comments of Allan Mazur and Arie Rip.

We thank Helenan Robin for generously giving us her files on the peace movement and for introducing us to the work of Alain Touraine. We acknowledge Rosalie Robertson, editor of SUNY Press, for making available to us the helpful comments of two referees.

We thank Walter Lynn of Cornell University's Program on Science, Technology, and Society for giving one of us the time and staff support to edit this manuscript. We thank Sue Latham for preparing the index, and Agnes McColley and Sandra Kisner for helping us with our imperfect Word Perfect.

Finally, we gratefully acknowledge a faculty research stipend from Grand Valley State University and a grant from the Institute for the Study of World Politics. Without their generous support, the completion of this research would not have been possible.

Chapter 1

The Rise and Fall of the Freeze

History is full of contradictions, and the early 1980s were no exception. Ronald Reagan, the new President, kept his campaign promise to direct a massive buildup of American military forces. At the same time, the Nuclear Weapons Freeze campaign called for an immediate, mutual, verifiable freeze on the testing, production and deployment of nuclear weapons. Despite Reagan's popularity, support for the Freeze increased dramatically: by 1982 it was active in all 50 states.

On June 12, 1982, in perhaps the largest political demonstration in American history, nearly one million people gathered in New York City to demand an immediate halt to the arms race. Demonstrators included 1960s antiwar activists, pacifists, and anarchists. Yet they were in a small minority. Side by side with them, and overwhelming them in number, were civic leaders, midwestern farmers, nurses, union members, teachers, lawyers, physicians, and religious leaders. They were elderly, middle-age, and young and came from all around the country— a remarkable coalition that gathered in common protest in Central Park.

In the fall of 1982, voters passed a Freeze resolution in 10 of 11 state referenda, the closest the U.S. has ever come to a national referendum on any peace-related issue. On May 4, 1983, the U.S. House of Representatives passed a Freeze resolution by an almost two-to-one majority. By the close of 1983, 23 state legislatures, 370 city councils, 71 county councils, 446 town meetings, 10 national labor unions, 140 Catholic bishops, numerous nationally known academic and other elites, and 150 national and international organizations, including the United Nations General Assembly, had endorsed the Freeze.

The Freeze, though distinct in size and character, was not the first organized movement against nuclear weapons. Protest against the bomb began with the scientists who built it and then sought to bring nuclear weapons under international control. It surfaced again publicly in the late 1950s and early 1960s with the controversy over radioactive fallout from the atmospheric testing of nuclear weapons. Again there was brief protest in the early 1970s against the proposed antiballistic missile system, but this was overshadowed by the massive protest against the war in Vietnam. These movements faded when they seemed to obtain limited objectives.

For almost 40 years the nuclear arms race has continued virtually unchecked, resulting in a global stockpile of about 50,000 nuclear weapons. Yet it was not until the 1980s, in large part because of the efforts of the Freeze movement, that we witnessed a public outcry and the definition of a "new" social problem. Nuclear weapons and the arms race were defined as the greatest peril of our time. A highly publicized and debated television special, "The Day After," depicted the city of Lawrence, Kansas, in the aftermath of a nuclear holocaust. A series of popular books told citizens about the terrible consequences of nuclear war, and what they could do to prevent one. All major news magazines featured the issue in numerous cover stories. For example, *Newsweek*, in its January 31, 1983 cover story claimed, "Arms Control: Now or Never." Many arms control experts interviewed in this story seemed to agree that an historic threshold had been reached: disarmament or annihilation were seen as the choices of the 1980s. Nobel laureate Alva Myrdal (1981) referred to 1983 as the year "when the guillotine falls on Europe" (p. 210).

A proliferation of scholarly books and articles on nuclear issues began to appear in the early 1980s. The history of the atomic bomb,[1] the hydrogen bomb, and the subsequent arms race were reexamined in detail; policies for nuclear strategy and conflict resolutions were proposed and debated; and the psychological impact of "nuclearism" was discovered and assessed. The U.S. Congressional Office of Technology Assessment released a report on the devastating impact of even a limited nuclear war and the concept of "nuclear winter," originated by prominent scientists, was widely debated in scholarly circles.

Despite these claims, the political success of the Freeze was short-lived. By 1984 the Freeze was in decline, and in 1987, after a year of negotiations, the organization lost much of its impetus and identity in a merger with SANE, an older antinuclear weapons protest group. In retrospect, the Freeze appears as if in hyper-time, a postindustrial, uniquely modern flash—startling and enigmatic in its brilliance, equally startling and enigmatic in its disappearance. In half a decade it appeared, placed its mark on the American scene, and in historic time hardly longer than Andy Warhol's fifteen minutes of fame, faded into the background.

To understand the Freeze—both its rise and decline—we need to appreciate its internal structure and dynamics, and its relationship to the larger political structure. Furthermore, we need to view the Freeze not just as an existential phenomenon, but as the latest episode in a long history of peace seeking. History may or may not repeat itself, but there is no way to understand the present without knowing something of the past. In many ways the Freeze faced the same dilemmas, made the same choices, and came to the same fate, as earlier peace organizations.

This book is a sociohistorical analysis of the antinuclear weapons movement. We examine the Atomic Scientists Movement of the 1940s, the Ban-the-Bomb Movement of the 1950s and 1960s, and then focus in particular on the Freeze Movement of the 1980s. We analyze and assess the antinuclear weapons protest activity of the past forty years by addressing the following questions: How did antinuclear weapons protest originate? What has been the nature and dynamic of such activity? Why has it so often floundered? What is the relation between protest activity and social control? Why did a massive social movement not appear until thirty-five years after the atomic bomb? How did the collective definition of nuclear weapons as a social problem arise? How did that definition translate into specific reactions and policies?

To address these questions, we focus on the origins and growth of key antinuclear weapons organizations. We give particular attention to organizational tactics and strategies, organizational dilemmas, funding sources, and the key role of intellectuals as claims makers and movement leaders. We also examine historical contingencies and official responses to protest demands, and how these forces in turn shape movement activity. We have tried to consider these issues deductively and inductively, to interpret antinuclear weapons protest in light of recent social science literature on social movements and social problems, and in turn to use this protest movement as a way of shedding light on the more general issue of the role of social change in post-industrial society.

Chapter 2 presents an intellectual perspective—a synthesis of several sociological theories—that allows us to examine how social movements are founded and fare, how social conditions become defined as social problems, and how historical changes in the political economy have been expressed in terms of social change. From this perspective we consider and assess the antinuclear weapons movement.

Chapters 3 and 4 chronicle the history of the post-World War II antinuclear protest movement. Chapter 3 analyzes the Atomic Scientists Movement and its outgrowth, the *Bulletin of Atomic Scientists*. This social movement was the first attempt by scientists—as scientists—to engage in protest activity. We examine the origins, dynamics, and strategies of the scientist movement and then focus on the *Bulletin* as a social movements organization. Chapter 4 examines protest by non-scientists and their organizations, particularly the United World Federalists and SANE. These organizations, along with traditional pacifist groups, provided the infrastructure and directly presaged the strategy, tactics, and organizational dilemmas of the Freeze movement.

Chapter 5 examines the Nuclear Weapons Freeze Campaign: its origins, growth, and eventual decline. We give particular attention to the infrastructure out of which the Freeze grew, the organizations it created, and the role of the new class and social movements professionals in the Freeze. Chapter 6 assesses the strategy, tactics and organizational dilemmas of the Freeze. We then show how the Freeze was coopted by philanthropic foundations and by the government, particularly Congressional Democrats. The chapter concludes by showing how the Freeze, despite its difficulties, was able to define the nuclear arms race as the paramount social problem of the 1980s.

Chapter 7 presents the conclusions of this research and analysis. We assess the utility of the theoretical synthesis, and discuss the significance of major findings. We conclude with a general discussion of what the antinuclear weapons social movement might teach us about social change in postindustrial society.

Notes

1. The winner of the 1987 National Book Award was *The Making of the Atomic Bomb*, by Richard Rhodes (1986). The book, which Manhattan Project scientist and Nobel Laureate I.I. Rabi called "an epic worthy of Milton," is written in a scholarly format and is replete with technical details, yet is accessible to the general reader.

Chapter 2

Social Movements in Postindustrial Society

Before we turn to the antinuclear weapons protest movement, we need some guidelines to help us sort through the vast detail of history, to help us see what is meaningful, what is significant. So many accounts are possible, yet few would serve our aims. Our choices regarding theory and method, and what we hope to accomplish with them, are discussed in Appendix A to this book.

We propose to follow the advice of Scott McNall (1979) in developing a theory that would guide our work, illuminate dark corners of the world, and look beneath society's respectable veneer to expose those forces that limit human freedom. Let us be clear from the outset: we are not developing a theory for the purpose of testing some series of hypotheses. Our notion is that theory is, as C. Wright Mills (1959) wrote, a form of imagination, a way of making sense of things.

The kinds and types of questions we are posing are not ones normally asked by American sociologists. Positivists, whose interests tend toward cause rather than process, cross-sectional and formalistic analysis rather than historical, have typically not addressed such questions. In the United States, nonpositivist sociologists, particularly social constructionists and phenomenologists, have faced some of these issues, particularly the importance of "claims making" in the creation of a new social problem. Yet the limitations of that approach, particularly in regard to its extreme relativism, have caused a floundering among social problems theorists. Resource mobilization theorists have also addressed some of these issues. Yet their case studies focus mainly on organizational issues, leaving aside larger trends in political economy.

Sociologists from Europe, especially those influenced by the Frankfurt School, and their American followers have examined in detail some of these issues. As Kivisto (1984) has written:

> The form and content of advanced industrial societies, as well as the malcontents and discontents they have generated, has necessitated a reconceptualiza-

tion of contemporary modes of domination and the potential for social movements to coalesce and challenge such domination. It has further led to a
rethinking of the nature of social movements, including, in some instances,
an analysis of their self-reflexive capabilities (i.e. their ability to 'learn' by
linking critique to action). (p. 355)

Yet the work from this school of thought is often highly abstract, and
difficult to relate to an empirical case study.

We propose a synthesis of these various approaches that will allow a
deeper understanding of the dynamics of antinuclear weapons protest,
and also shed light on the general role of social movements in postindustrial society. In this chapter, we examine the relationship between
social problems and social movements by placing claims making and
resource mobilization in the historical context of late capitalism. By
analyzing the role of the "new class" in social movements, we hope to
show that claims *making* is not a random, ahistoric phenomenon; rather
we focus on claims *makers* and show that they are strategically located
historical actors. Moreover, claims making occurs in an organizational
context that is influenced by effective mobilization of resources. The
mobilization of these resources, in turn, is best understood from a class
conflict perspective. Such an approach should allow a concomitant
analysis of micro-level claims making, organizational level resource
analysis, and macro-level class analysis. To do this we discuss certain
relevant aspects of social constructionism, resource mobilization, and
new class theory.

Social Constructionism

The social constructionist perspective, variously referred to as social
definitionist or subjectivist, offers a way to understand how social
problems are created that is decidedly different from previous
positivistic views.[1] To the constructionists, what makes a condition
problematic depends not on objective reality, but on the political process through which powerful interest groups are likely to impose their
definitions of reality. Thus social problems are the result of enterprise,
and the products of certain people or groups making claims based on
their particular interests, values, and views of the world (for a review
of social constructionist approach to social problems, see Schneider,
1985).

Malcolm Spector and John Kitsuse have most fully developed this perspective in a 1973 article and their 1977 book, *Constructing Social Problems.*[2] They defined social problems as "the activities of groups making assertions of grievances and claims with respect to some putative conditions" (Kitsuse and Spector, 1977, p. 9). Objective conditions, so-called "facts," became theoretically irrelevant in explaining the nature and existence of a social problem. The goal of the theorist, in this view, is to account for collective definitions of reality. Harmful conditions (e.g., slavery in Antebellum South) are often ignored by ruling elites; and some harmless or even nonexistent conditions (e.g., witchcraft in Salem, Massachusetts) become defined as social problems.

Throughout the 1970s and 1980s, the social constructionist position came to dominate both theoretical and empirical studies of social problems. Moreover, the constructionist position attracted key social movements scholars. As early as 1963, Joseph Gusfield argued that definitions of social problems often resulted from symbolic battles "between opposed systems of moralities, cultures and styles of life" (p. 173). Armand Mauss (1975) went even further, standing traditional functionalist logic on its head. Rather than viewing social movements as the result of social problems, Mauss explored the crucial role of social movements in creating, through new collective definitions, a social problem:

> No social condition, however deplorable or intolerable it may seem to social scientists or social critics, is inherently problematic. It is made a problem by the entrepreneurship of various interest groups, which succeed in winning over important segments of public opinion to the support of a social movement aimed at changing that condition. (p. xvi)

Despite its utility, the social constructionist view has two severe limitations. First, its extreme relativism means that objective conditions are considered theoretically irrelevant. Yet to claim that objective conditions are irrelevant to social problems theory ignores dialectics, the impact of historically produced structures on subjectivity. As Gusfield (1983) stated: "Process without substance is like a bath without water; it is a fine container, but there is nothing in it. . .it delimits knowing a great deal apart from current definitions" (p. 3).

Even more, as Woolgar and Pawluck (1985) have noted, there is a tension between the way the world is socially constructed and its existential reality. On the one hand, the natural world, especially in the form of a social context, gives rise to alternative accounts of what "is"; on the other hand, these accounts, definitions, and claims are said to be "constitutive" of reality. Furthermore, constructionism demands that sociologists suspend both common sense commitments about what social problems are (e.g., undesirable conditions), and their own scientific judgments about which claims and definitions about these putative conditions are true. The latter of these demands, as Schneider (1985, p. 224) has pointed out, is especially difficult for sociologists to achieve.

The second problem with constructionism arises out of its micro and often ahistorical orientation. Given its attention to individual actors, political change is difficult to assess, and power—though implied—is an underdeveloped concept. Not all claims are equal. Rather, the importance given to a claim is a function of the power of the claimant. As Schneider (1985) stated: "We need a clearer understanding of precisely how participants' activities affect the viability of claims and definitions" (p. 225).

Resource Mobilization

Resource mobilization developed at the same time as, but independently of, social constructionism. Partly as a reaction to the traditional "strain" theories[3], but also as a way of making sense of the extraordinary social protest activities of the 1960s, resource mobilization theory became the dominant social movements' perspective of the 1970s (see Olson, 1965; Tilly, Tilly, and Tilly, 1975, 1981; and Gamson, 1975; for a review, see Jenkins, 1983). Resource mobilization draws on conflict, interactionist, and economic models, assuming that conflict is an inherent feature of all societies, and that discontent is ever present for deprived groups. Yet collective action is rarely a viable option for deprived groups because of lack of resources and the threat of repression by dominant groups and political elites.

When deprived groups do mobilize, it is usually due not to increased discontent, but to interjection of external resources such as leadership, money, and organizing skills coming from outside the aggrieved social base. Mobilization theorists view participants as formally rational, purposeful actors who weigh the consequences of their actions. They see protest activity as emerging from social interaction processes, both interpersonal and group interaction. The emphasis is not on the psycho-

logical state of participants or the mass of potential movements supporters, but on the processes by which individuals and organizations
mobilize resources. Movement success is more likely when there is a
combination of sustained elite support, and tolerance and/or disunity
among the polity. Rather than assuming the permeability of the political system, resource mobilization theorists see polity response as problematic—an important variable for movement success or failure.

Three concepts—resources, mobilization, and social control—are
crucial to this perspective. Resources can be material such as jobs,
income, supplies, facilities, and media services; or they may be non-
material, such as legitimacy, authority, moral commitment and skills,
and knowledge. Mobilization is the process by which aggrieved groups
assemble and invest resources for the pursuit of group goals. Social
control refers to the same process, but from the point of view of the
incumbents or the group being challenged. The interaction between
mobilization and control processes generates the dynamic elements of
conflict and collective behavior. Whereas the political system is generally viewed as closed, the social system of conflict is seen as an open
system. Over time, actors may expand the conflict, drawing more
groups into the arena, committing ever more resources to one or the
other side (Oberschall, 1973, pp. 28-29).

TACTICS AND ORGANIZATION

Social movement organizations have a number of strategic tasks. In
addition to mobilizing supporters, they also need to neutralize and/or
transform mass and elite publics into sympathizers. Dilemmas frequently occur in the choice of tactics and organizational modes, because what may achieve one goal may conflict in achieving another.
William Gamson (1975) has made the most systematic attempt to
evaluate the success or failure of social movements in terms of strategy,
tactics, and organizational modes. Gamson conceptualized success on
two dimensions: the provision of tangible benefits that meet goals
established by the movement organizations, and the formal acceptance
of the movement organization by its main antagonists as a valid representative of a legitimate set of interests. From this two-by-two scheme,
movement outcomes fall into four categories: full success, cooptation
(acceptance without benefits), preemption (benefits without acceptance), and failure.

In an analysis of the successes and failure of 53 randomly selected
movement organizations active in the U.S. between 1800 and 1945,

Gamson found that: (1) Single issue groups were far more successful than multiple issue groups, but this difference disappeared when he controlled for attempts by challenging groups to displace or destroy their antagonists. (2) Groups that used either violence or direct-action tactics such as strikes, boycotts, civil disobedience and other "unruly" forms of protest were more successful than groups that used conventional political tactics. (3) Bureaucratic and power-centralized forms of organizations were more successful than decentralized, grass-roots organizations. Centralized power groups were less likely to experience factionalism, or the creation of splinter groups. Moreover, bureaucratic organizations and centralized power were statistically independent, and cumulative in their effects of success. (4) Large groups, with peak membership greater than 100,000, were more likely to gain acceptance—but not more likely to gain new benefit—than smaller groups. (5) Groups which offered selective incentives also had a higher success rate.

Yet "public interest" movements whose beneficiaries are defined in terms of broad publics, rarely can offer selective incentives to their members. This is what Mancur Olsen (1965) called the "free-rider" problem: why should rational self-interested individuals work for a social movement when they benefit, regardless of their input, from its success? To overcome the free-rider problem, social movements must offer "collective incentives of group solidarity and commitment to moral purpose" (Jenkins, 1983, p. 537). For such groups, a well articulated movement ideology thus seems essential to generate solidarity and moral commitments. Gerlach and Hine (1970) have argued that any decentralized movement with a minimal division of labor has similar problems of solidarity, and thus needs an overarching ideology to be effective.

Anthony Oberschall (1973) has drawn attention to the importance of coalition building for movement success. Many social movements tend to be short-lived because they fail to solve the central problem of "cementing together an organizational network." Moreover, an organizational base and continuity of leadership are necessary for any sustained movement. Rapid mobilization, he concluded, occurs only through the recruitment of "blocs of people who are already highly organized participants" (p. 125). These contentions are supported by Olsen's (1965) suggestion that small groups often "triumph over numerically superior forces. . . because the former are generally better organized and active" (p. 128). In others words, small well-organized groups able to form coalitions appear to have a greater likelihood of success.

Mayer Zald and Roberta Ash (1966) formulated a series of propositions concerning the growth, decay, and change of social movement organizations. They point out that social movement organizations do not remain static entities, but change according to both external and internal conditions; and they make an important distinction between exclusive (those with rigorous membership requirements) and inclusive organizations (those with minimal membership qualifications). External factors such as the ebb and flow of sentiments in the larger society, and the existence of similar or competing organizations, are most likely to affect inclusive groups. The inclusive group is more likely than the exclusive group to participate in coalitions and mergers. With regard to internal processes, Zald and Ash suggest that the poorer the short-run chances of attaining goals, the greater the problem of maintaining a movement. Other interests and incentives will serve to weaken the membership base, especially as the organization must replace or routinize the original charismatic leadership.

To illustrate, inclusive social movement organizations attempting such broad goals as disarmament should encounter organizational problems, unless their goal is reached in the short run. The same would not be true for exclusive organizations. Consequently, we would expect that when there is a campaign for disarmament or global justice extending over several decades, it would be backed by exclusive organizations; when the goal is short-term, such as a nuclear test ban or a freeze on weapons, the main support should come from inclusive organizations.

ENTREPRENEURIAL MODEL

The resource mobilization perspective—with its main focus on organizational aspects, tactics, and strategies employed by protest groups—has little to say about the emergence of social movements. A notable exception is John McCarthy and Mayer Zald's (1977) entrepreneurial model of social movements.

Central to the entrepreneurial model is the key role of movement professionals and issue entrepreneurs, individuals who earn their living in the employ of social movements organizations and whose primary task is to define issues addressed by movement activity. These actors may create "grievances" and the appearance of widespread grass roots support. According to McCarthy and Zald

> there is always enough discontent in any society to supply the grass roots support for a movement if the movement is effectively organized and has at

its disposal the power and resources of some established elite group. For some purposes we may go even further: grievances and discontent may be defined, created and manipulated by issue entrepreneurs and organizations. (1977, p. 1215) (Emphasis added)

Entrepreneurial theory thus highlights the importance of elite involvement in the emergence of social movements; deprivation and grievances, the focus of traditional social movements theory, are given as secondary or background components.

Entrepreneurial theory also posits an amelioration of the free-rider problem by focusing on "conscience constituents" from the wealthy, and the affluent middle class. Their role is opposite that of free-riders: conscience constituents contribute resources but are not part of the aggrieved group, and thus do not benefit directly from the movement success (McCarthy and Zald, 1977). Contrary to the classical model, McCarthy and Zald contend that the membership or mass base of a social movement does not provide the bulk of resources; moreover, leaders of modern social movements operate independently of membership during the earliest stages of organizational growth. In fact, social movements are becoming increasingly professionalized:

> The functions historically served by social movement membership base have been taken over by paid functionaries, by the "bureaucratization of social discontent," by mass promotion campaigns, by full-time employees whose professional careers are defined in terms of social movement participation, by philanthropic foundations, and by government itself. Moreover an affluent society makes it possible for people devoted to radical change and revolution to eke out a living while pursuing their values. (McCarthy and Zald, 1973, p. 3)

Professional social movements are characterized by (1) a leadership that devotes full time to a movement, (2) a large proportion of resources (particularly from foundations) originating outside the aggrieved group that the movement claims to represent, (3) a very small or non-existent membership base, (4) attempts to impart the image of "speaking for potential constituency," and (5) attempts to influence policy toward that same constituency (McCarthy and Zald, 1973, p. 20).

The entrepreneurial model has received empirical support from studies of deprived groups such as farm workers (Jenkins and Perrow, 1977) and welfare recipients (Jackson and Johnson, 1974). Entrepreneurs had come to these causes after training in the civil rights and student movements, causes that had become factionalized. Their role was crucial since both movements were centered among groups with few resources, minimal political experience, and little prior organization. The model best fits movements generated by uniting previously factionalized groups. Major movements do not appear to emerge from de novo manufacture of grievances by entrepreneurs. Rather, "entrepreneurs are more successful by seizing on major interest cleavages and redefining long standing grievances in new terms" (Jenkins, 1983, p. 531).

The strongest support for the McCarthy-Zald theory has come from studies of public interest movements that came to prominence in the 1970s. A majority of these were founded by energetic entrepreneurs acting without significant increases in grievances (Berry, 1977). For example, the environmental movement was formed by a few natural scientists and policy makers who redefined traditional conservationist concerns into ecological terms, and pursued goals in the name of broad, diffuse, disorganized collectivities such as the general public or the middle class consumer (Schoefield, Meier, and Griffin, 1979; Wood, 1982).

Despite this support, the entrepreneurial theory has raised a number of problems and questions, particularly relating to the role of external funding, the involvement of the middle class, and the behavior of elites. For most of the 1960s movements, the roles of external resources "were reactive, not initiatory, and were not consistently beneficial" given the long-term aims of the movement (Jenkins, 1983, p. 535). Most funds were mobilized by moderates and used to capture movement leadership from more radical elements. Even more problematic is middle class and student involvement in the various movements of the 1960s and 1970s. By focusing on economic changes that facilitated movement involvement (e.g., discretionary income and schedules), the theory ignored changing cultural values. The middle class "participation revolution" was rooted in a shift toward "postmaterialist" values, which emphasized moral concern for the plight of the less fortunate. McCarthy and Zald also undervalued the impact of elite behavior. When elites challenged postmaterialist values by manipulative acts or outright rejection, the middle class rallied around the very movements which advocated these values.

Other questions, particularly those germane to the theoretical development of this study, also must be addressed. Who are these issue entrepreneurs, conscious constituents, and "established elites" who seem to be taking an increasingly significant role in social movements?

Under what conditions do elites become involved in social change efforts; i.e., which issues receive elite backing? What brings about divisions among elites, leading some to support new social movements? Resource mobilization has posed but not answered these larger questions. Zald and McCarthy (1979, p. 245) conclude that a perspective on the long-term development of elite divisions in modern welfare states, as well as an understanding of elite relations with governmental apparatus, seems necessary to provide the theoretical backdrop to an understanding of modern social movements. In other words, the study of social movements must move beyond a "recent narrowness" and "be nested within broader perspectives upon politico-historical processes" (p. 245).

New Class

We believe that a perspective in which intellectuals[4] are defined as "new class" may provide partial answers to the questions left unresolved by resource mobilization. Whether intellectuals or intelligentsia comprise a new social stratum or a "class" in the Marxist sense has been the subject of considerable debate (for a review, see Gella, 1976; Walker, 1979). However, virtually all analysts agree that a profound change has taken place within the old middle class of western societies. The increase in white collar workers accompanied by the overproduction of university graduates has caused the rise of an educated, but unpropertied non-business oriented generation. Moreover, this group—despite its relatively high economic position—has been deeply involved in most of the leftist social movements of the 1970s.[5] In response to this anomaly of upper-middle class liberalism and dissent, many scholars have turned to new class theory.

New class theories (for a review, see Brint, 1984) have been articulated by both neoconservative analysts (Kristol, 1978; Ladd, 1978) and leftists (Ehrenreich and Ehrenreich, 1977; Gouldner, 1979). To neoconservatives, the new class is powerful and bad, determined to undermine free enterprise and the moral fiber of society. In this view, the popularity of adversarial culture reflects a unique combination of elitism and envy, the former derived from superior education, its presumed cultural superiority, and its disavowal of material wealth; the latter is derived from its lack of real power to control society.

Leftist thinkers agree with much of this analysis, though their evaluation of the new class is not so hostile. They emphasize the cultural and ideological bases of class divisions rather than the divergent economic interests of the old and new classes. According to these theorists, new class efforts are aimed at safeguarding or extending privileges tied to mental skills or knowledge-based authority; these interests often conflict with the profit-seeking interests of the business elite.[6]

GOULDNER'S NEW CLASS

Drawing on a neo-Marxist perspective,[7] particularly on the works of critical theorists, Alvin Gouldner focuses on the transformation of liberal capitalism or industrial society to late capitalism or post-industrial society. Advanced industrial society is characterized by general affluence, mass higher education, mass communication, an interventionist state, a growing public sector and a concomitant shrinking private sector, and most importantly, a production process that increasingly depends on high technology and specialized knowledge. In late capitalism, continued expansion and profit more and more depend on revolutionizing the production process. The old moneyed class must reproduce its capital with maximum efficiency by rationalizing the productive and administrative processes. But this rationalization is increasingly dependent on the efforts of intellectuals and technical experts, the producers of cultural capital. Thus it is inherent in its structure that the old class must bring a new class into existence.

In *The Future of Intellectuals and the Rise of the New Class*, Gouldner (1979) maintains that conditions of late capitalism have created a new class of intellectuals whose privileges are grounded in their education, knowledge, culture, and specialized language. They constitute a cultural bourgeoisie who appropriate privately the advantages of an historically and collectively produced cultural capital (p. 19). Yet this new class, according to Gouldner, is not homogenous; rather it is sometimes characterized by intra-class conflict between humanistically oriented intellectuals and technically oriented intellectuals, whom he termed "intelligentsia."[8] The social position of humanistic intellectuals in a technocratic society becomes more marginal and alienated, whereas the intelligentsia, particularly those in the private sector, frequently aligns itself with the ruling class. It is vital to understand that the privileged and advantaged, not simply the suffering, come to be alienated from the very system that bestows privilege upon them. The members of the new class experience a status disparity between their "high culture," and lower deference, repute, income, and social power, which leads to relative deprivation.

Although the new class remains subordinate, its capacity to overcome the resistance of the old class (be they business or party leaders), is considerably greater than that of other subordinate classes. By virtue of its specialized knowledge of the forces of production and means of administration, the new class already has considerable de facto control over the mode of production, which gives it considerable leverage to pursue its interests.

The main struggle, though, is not over money or property, but rather over knowledge and values, that is, the power to manage society. By virtue of their "higher morality," as they see it, members of the new class assume the roles of judges and regulators of the normative structures of contemporary societies. As Alexander Gella (1976, p. 18) has noted, their liberal education

> has exposed them to systems of ideas as contrary to the value structures of capitalism as was 19th Century liberalism to the prevailing. . .feudal system. . . .Their social role is becoming as crucial for the shape of modern civilization as was the social role of the industrial proletariat for the development of revolutionary ideologies in the 19th Century.

In their struggle to gain control over the management of society, the new class cultivates alliances with oppressed groups, speaks on their behalf, and critiques the ruling class in order to sharpen class conflict and delegitimize the existing order:

> Short of going to the barricades the New Class may harass the old, sabotage it, critique it, expose and muckrake it, express moral, technical, and cultural superiority to it, and hold it up to contempt and ridicule. The New Class, however, does not seek struggle for its own sake. . .it is concerned simply about securing its own material and ideal interests with minimum effort. (Gouldner, 1979, p. 17)

Gouldner has clearly been influenced by Jurgen Habermas' emphasis on language as a tool in demystifying society. Through critical discourse, the distinctive language behavior of the new class, the traditional authority of the ruling class is undermined. In the culture of critical discourse, claims and assertions may not be justified by reference to the speaker's social status, but must rest on the merit of arguments presented. This has the consequence of making all authority-referring claims potentially problematic. As Gouldner (1985) wrote in *Against Fragmentation*, a book published after his death:

> The credit normally given to the claims of those with worldly success, to the
> rich and powerful, now needs to be hidden if not withdrawn, because it comes
> to be defined as illicit and unworthy. [Critical discourse] is alienating and
> even radicalizing because it demands the right to sit in judgment over all
> claims, regardless of who makes them. (p. 30)

The new class, trained in critical discourse, thus becomes a speech
community. By exposing existing inequalities and by unmasking distorted communication, the new class has contributed to ushering in a
"legitimation crisis" for the ruling class. This legitimation crisis may
become behaviorally manifested in social protest and social movements (Friedrichs, 1980).[9]

HABERMAS' HISTORICAL MATERIALISM

Jürgen Habermas, generally recognized as the contemporary leader
of the "Frankfurt School" of critical sociology, has written widely on
the problems of late capitalism. In his reformation of historical materialism, Habermas argues that human societies evolve along two separate
but interrelated dimensions: development of the forces of production,
and development of normative structures of interaction or integration.
Corresponding to each is a mode of knowledge or reason: technical-
instrumental to the former, and moral-practical to the latter (Habermas,
1975b; Held, 1978).[10]
The implementation of these two types of knowledge results in new
productive forces and new forms of interaction and integration. Thus
Habermas' theory of social evolution encompasses stages of development not only for the mode of production (similar to Marx), but also for
normative structures.[11] Conditions of late capitalism are particularly
problematic. In advanced industrial societies, technical-instrumental
rationality has come to dominate practical-moral reasoning to the point
where most social phenomena become defined in technical terms.[12]
Habermas identified two related trends of Western capitalism that have
led to this technocratic consciousness: increased state interventionism
in both the economic and social spheres, directed toward stabilizing
economic growth, and the increasing interdependence of research and
technology, which has made science the leading force of production
(Habermas, 1971; for a review see Giddens, 1977).
In contrast to liberal or early capitalism, the "political" and "economic" are no longer easily separable, and the old form of legitimation,
based on the ideology of "fair exchange," has become obsolete. The

legitimation system of advanced capitalism tends to become a technocratic one, based upon the capabilities of elites to manage or program the economy and culture.

In his 1975 book, *Legitimation Crisis*, Habermas argues that technical-instrumental rationality has not been able to solve the contradictions of advanced capitalism. Increased need for state intervention in the economic sphere has not eliminated the class struggle, but rather has displaced it from the economic to the political arena. It has become increasingly apparent that the economy is not regulated by a neutral market mechanism, but by state actions that favor the old ruling class. These partisan actions are leading towards a legitimation crisis, the withdrawal of support or loyalty by significant segments of the population. The state cannot fall back on traditional modes of integration such as religion or custom, since scientific rationality has undermined those. Large segments of society have been exposed to liberal education and critical discursive reasoning; this in turn has fostered more participatory and egalitarian expectations.

Habermas sees the emergence of new emancipatory social movements based on practical-moral reasoning, where the main struggle is directed against technical-instrumental domination. He takes a Parsonian stance in specifying the central criterion for judging progressive, emancipatory social movements. Only movements having universal interests, rather than particularistic ones, are qualitatively new and progressive. He rejects the working class as leading such movements; his theory of rational discourse and communicative ethics (1981, 1984) points toward a key role for intellectuals. However, so far Habermas has been unwilling to specifically name the new subjects (leaders) of emancipation.

TOURAINE'S CRITICAL ACTION THEORY

Alaine Touraine, a French sociologist and originator of the phrase "post-industrial society," is becoming increasingly well-known among British and American scholars. Consistent with action theory, Touraine views society as the ongoing accomplishment of social actors. Social protests and social movements are the key mechanisms through which society creates itself.[13] Collective action can be studied by focusing on the consciousness of the actor, the "other" against which "self" and identity form, and the collective definition of the situation. Social movements then can be seen as processes of collective will-formation which mediate between received social structure and possible new forms of social order (Eyerman, 1984, pp. 76-78).

In *The Voice and the Eye* (1981), an analysis of contemporary social movements, Touraine posits that class conflict is manifested in social movements (for reviews, see Gamson, 1983; Grayson, 1984; Kivisto, 1982; Nagel, 1983). Each historical era is characterized by a major social movement. The period of merchant capitalism in Europe was characterized by struggles centered on demands for the extension of political and legal rights. In industrial society, the primary movement was the labor movement which struggled over economic and work related issues. In the transition to postindustrial society (the current stage of development), the labor movement no longer plays a progressive, innovative, and unifying role. Because of shifts in the forces and relations of production, the actions of workers have become fragmented and largely defensive, or incorporated and coopted into established patterns of power and authority (Eyerman, 1984). Particularly in the U.S., workers have been coopted by consumerism, and the labor movement has been institutionalized through unionism.

In basic agreement with Gouldner and Habermas, Touraine depicts postindustrial society[14] as characterized by scientific and technological domination, and state interventionism. Means-end or instrumental rationality no longer remains confined to just the technical execution of labor, but moves to the administrative-managerial level, and finally to the institutional level, resulting in a "programmed" society (Touraine, 1983). The state or "ruling apparatus" increasingly becomes the locus of domination:

> [t]he state's new role. . .has less to do with integration than it did in the past, and more to do with domination; it has become an instrument of power rather than order; a mobilizer of resources, a manipulator of privileges, feelings and political support. (1976, pp. 215-216)

The emergent social movements in postindustrial society are anti-technocratic in nature. They center on gaining control over the dissemination of information from the ruling apparatus of society. These struggles are less concerned with the organization of work than with the management of systems of communication. Production and accumulation of knowledge take on a new importance. Thus educational institutions, particularly the university, come to play a key role in social change. In the same way that the workers movement drew its strength from skilled workers in a trade, the new antitechnocratic movements draw on a fraction of liberal educated professionals and intellectuals. They speak in the name of knowledge against an apparatus that seeks to use knowledge to serve its own interests, and ally themselves with those forced to the sidelines of existing power relationships (Touraine, 1981, p. 22). Touraine maintains that the antinuclear power/ecology movement is the first important manifestation of the antitechnocratic movement.

Touraine appears less reluctant than Habermas to specify the role of intellectuals in social movements. He even urges sociologists to become social change agents. In his method of "sociological intervention," he sees the role of sociologists not as "free-floating intellectuals" or as a "political avantgarde", but as advisors to incipient social movement groups, by making visible to activists the social relations masked by order and domination and distorted by ideology (Touraine, 1981, p. 139). Touraine thus gives a privileged status to sociologists, reminiscent of Comte and Durkheim and equally difficult to justify.

Toward a Synthesis

In probably the best empirical evaluation of new class theory, Brint (1984) conducted a multivariate analysis of data from the General Social Survey. He concluded that important historical changes have occurred in the relationship between class and ideology in the United States. When compared to survey data from the 1930s and 1960s, his data indicated that the educated professional-managerial strata are "more liberal than they once were, and that larger pockets of dissent exist within these strata than previously" (1984, p. 58). Though theorists have, according to Brint, exaggerated the levels of new class dissent and even liberalism, they have "performed an important sensitizing function" (1984, pp. 58, 60). By calling attention to higher white collar dissent, and by "dramatizing this development through the use of class conflict imagery, they have paved the way for analysis of this important modification in the relation between class and ideology" (1984, p. 60).

For the purposes of this study, we define new class as an elite social category consisting of humanistic and technical intellectuals who produce cultural or knowledge capital. Members can be distinguished by their advanced degrees and include scientists, engineers, lawyers, physicians, social workers, educators, social scientists, and so on—a substantial number of whom find their careers in the expanding public sector rather than the private.

The concept of new class has been widely criticized, both in definition and application (Telos, 1981-82; Walker, 1979). We do not claim that the new class is homogeneous, that all members think or act in predictable ways. Moreover, in the analysis of any data, strict operationalization is difficult at best. We use the concept of new class not in any reified way, but rather as a sensitizing, heuristic device. In this sense, new class is no better—but also no worse—than such ideas as upper, middle, and working class, concepts that have been enormously useful in the social sciences.

Our thesis is that characteristics of advanced capitalistic society have created a new class that increasingly comes in conflict with the old ruling class over the management of society. This conflict is mediated by the emergence of professional change agents (predominately members of the new class) who mobilize resources and engage in claims making. Their efforts, consistent with left ideology, focus on four areas of social change: (1) movements demanding more government control over the private sector, such as consumer and environmental protection movements (2) antitechnocratic movements, such as the antinuclear power movement (3) movements for personal liberation, such as abortion, gay and civil rights movements and (4) movements characterized by their international rather than nationalistic nature, such as movements for global peace, disarmament, and world government.

One prominent feature of these postindustrial movements is, in the words of resource mobilization theorist Mayer Zald (1987, p. 323), "a heavy dose of expert opinion." With increasing regularity, the manipulation of options and consequences, causes and costs, requires "extensive knowledge of esoteric subjects, unavailable to even relatively well-educated laymen." In modern society, he continues, "experts play a role in defining facts and issues for many movements," and increasingly such movements "become battles over expert definitions, and the ability of parties to command expertise becomes an important part of the power equations."[15]

Since the main production site of expertise and cultural capital is the university (as the factory is for material capital), the new class is concentrated in academe, either as students or teachers.[16] Those who leave academe upon completion of their education frequently enter one of the professions. This spatial concentration in academe and the close communication links through professional associations, journals and conferences, allow for the emergence of a distinct new class ideology.

Professionalization also gives members of a profession self-control over the socialization and credentialing process, further contributing to a shared ideology and a concomitant weakening of ruling class control. Shared grievances, collective interests, and common values and beliefs, all lead to a questioning and critiquing of the existing order. Awareness of relative deprivation (in terms of repute, power and income) increases alienation from the ruling apparatus. Ideology, relative deprivation, and alienation are not independent of each other, but rather feed on each other and escalate critique of, and conflict with, the ruling class.

As Gouldner (1979) has suggested, the social position of humanistic intellectuals in a technocratic society becomes more marginal and alienated than that of technical intelligentsia, producing an intra-class conflict. Although these intra-class tensions exist, the education of all intellectuals has a cosmopolitanizing influence, with a corresponding distancing from parochial interests and values. In other words, their interests tend to shift from the particular to the universal. To intellectuals, nationalistic concerns often become secondary to global issues.

The efforts of the new class to discredit the old class have contributed to a legitimation crisis. Widespread dissatisfaction and distrust of government and ruling groups are conducive to the emergence and polarization of a number of issues that challenge the established order. But issues in and of themselves do not lead directly to action. Often some precipitating factor provides the spark to mobilize the action process. For example, the precipitating factor for the mobilization of the civil rights movement was the arrest of Rosa Parks for refusing to move to the back of a bus. The findings of President Kennedy's Commission on the Status of Women led to the creation of NOW, an organization that gave the women's movement its start (Freeman, 1973). We would assume that the greater the saliency of an issue to new class concerns, the more likely that a precipitating factor will motivate members of the new class to take leadership roles in the mobilization process.

The growth of the new class has created a pool of intellectuals whose discretionary resources can be allocated to social movement activity. Discretionary resources are time, money, knowledge, and skills, which can be easily re-allocated and thus are not fixed and enduringly committed. Although the members of the new class usually devote large amounts of their time and energy to their careers, they can rearrange their work schedules to fit the needs of socio-political action. Also, students at colleges and universities (the Lumpenintellectuals?) have the flexibility to engage in social action.

A parallel development along with the growth of the new class has been the establishment and growth of foundations. The structure of estate tax laws has led capitalists to establish foundations. In the United States, though dating back to the nineteenth century, the major growth of foundations has occured since 1940. The massive increase in foundation assets (approximately 1500 percent between 1930 and 1962) has become a fertile source for social movement support. Along with foundations, churches have also begun to allocate greater amounts to social action projects. This increase is noted not only among Northern liberal churches, but also among more conservative Protestant churches such as the Southern Baptist and American Baptist. This increased foundation and church support has created career opportunities for full-time social change agents, making it possible for members of the new class to assume issue-related leadership without financial sacrifice. As these staff positions multiply, the necessity of linking a career to a single movement or organization is reduced (McCarthy and Zald, 1973, p. 12).

These new funding opportunities have led to the professionalization of social movements and independence from mass support, but have also created a new dependence. Churches, philanthropists, and foundations are involved in a new web of social control. We would agree with McCarthy and Zald that established institutional sectors would not support radical professional social movement organizations for any length of time. Rather, the effect of established institutions' backing of movement organizations is to direct dissent into legitimate channels and limit goals to ameliorative rather than radical change.

Once full- and part-time social change agents and an organizational structure emerge, their task is to magnify an issue through resource control. Through manipulation of the mass media, particularly television, organization leaders are able to create the impression of widespread activity and grievance. Successful claims making will increase foundation support and draw adherents and constituents to the issue, making a collective definition of a new social problem more likely.

In the following chapters, we attempt to use this synthesis to understand the antinuclear weapons protest movement. Before proceeding, we should point out that one study has examined the key role of intellectuals in the British antinuclear weapons movement: Frank Parkin's 1968 book, *Middle Class Radicalism*.

Parkin's book is a study of the social basis of support for the Campaign for Nuclear Disarmament (CND), the major British antinuclear weapons movement. Parkin demonstrates that "one of the seemingly vital prerequisites for the establishment of a political mass movement is the leadership and support of an intellectual stratum" (1968, p. 93). His survey data show that sympathies for CND were particularly strong among the new generation of postwar intellectuals, especially many of the most celebrated writers and artists of that period. Parkin's principle finding, reflected in the anomaly of his title, is that the idea of middle class radicalism is a contradiction in terms. Middle class social movements will generally pursue ameliorative, rather than radical, goals. Although intellectuals may be radical in their critique, their actions are not. Given their position in the establishment, they have too much to lose.

In accounting for intellectual activism, Parkin rejected the various classical theorists such as Mannheim, who claimed that "the fanaticism of radicalized intellectuals should be understood. . .[as]. . .a psychic compensation for the lack of more fundamental integration into a class" (1960, p. 141). Similarly, he rejected Michels, who claimed that intellectuals' "tendency toward extremism arises. . .from the nature of mental work which can be easily dissociated from reality, so making its practitioners unreliable political advocates" (1968, p. 121).

Yet the explanation Parkin advocated suffers in that it was written before social constructionism, resource mobilization or new class were articulated in their current forms. Though Parkin focused on intellectuals, he is little concerned with their various claims making activities. Moreover he sees intellectuals operating as individuals, rather than as part of an organizational context, as members, rather than as movement leaders engaged in strategic and tactical debate. Nor does he account for the historical increase in numbers of intellectuals, from a small elite group to a large stratum or class. Nonetheless Parkin does emphasize the intellectual's attraction to radicalism in terms of the analytic abilities and critical attitudes which are a part of intellectual training. "Those who live by the exercise of intellect," he concluded (1968, p. 96), "are felt to be less able or willing than others automatically to endorse existing values and the status quo."

The synthesis developed here points toward the importance of intellectuals engaged in critical discourse to undermine the legitimacy of the present system. Intellectuals should also be found in key leadership positions in movement organizations, making claims and mobilizing resources to bring about disarmament. Furthermore, there should be a discernable trend toward movement professionalization and increased foundation support, leading to an emphasis on conventional political tactics and strategies. Finally, a pre-existing organizational structure and communications network, along with energetic issue entrepreneurs, should account for the mass social movement that emerged in 1980.

Notes

1. The positivistic view, also called objectivist or absolutist, holds that social problems are objectively given, intrinsically real, and because they exist independent of values, lend themselves to scientific analysis. This position is perhaps best explicated by Manis, who defined social problems as those conditions identified by scientific inquiry as detrimental to human well-being (1984, p. 25).

2. This perspective can also be traced through Peter Berger and Thomas Luckmann, Alfred Schutz, Edwin Husserl, Max Weber's action theory, and ultimately to Friedrich Hegel's *Phenomenology of the Mind.* In the social problems literature, social constructionism goes back at least as far as Waller (1936). In 1971 Herbert Blumer called for a reconceptualization of social problems as "products of a process of collective definition" rather than "objective conditions and social arrangements" (1971, p. 298). Rather than studying whether or not something is really a harmful condition, Blumer called for sociologists to "study the process by which a society comes to recognize its social problems" (1971, p. 300).

Following this logic, Kitsuse and Spector eschew the positivistic vision of the sociologist as a technical expert whose moral vision supercedes that of other people studied. In their view, this stance is empirically problematic, morally infused, and grossly presumptuous. Rather the sociologist's task is "to account for the emergence and maintenance of claims making and responding activities" (1973, p. 415).

3. The central concern of traditional theories, based on functionalist and pluralist assumptions, was to explain why individuals participate in protest or other collective behavior. The major formulations—mass society theory (Kornhauser, 1959), relative deprivation (Gurr, 1970), rising expectations (Davis, 1962), and collective behavior theory (Smelser, 1962)—all point toward a sudden increase in individual grievances generated by "structural strains" and rapid social change. Sources of strain, according to Smelser, include new knowledge, deprivation, disharmony between ideals and reality, and the rise of new values and expectations. Though strain is not a sufficient condition—his value-added model also includes structural conduciveness, generalized beliefs (loose ideologies), precipitating incidents, mobilization, and social control—it receives the major emphasis.

Traditional theories also share the assumption that movement participation is relatively rare, discontents are transitory, and actors often irrational, alienated, and marginal to society. "The beliefs on which collective behavior is based," according to Smelser (1962, p. 8), "are thus akin to magical beliefs." In *Social Systems* (1951a) Parsons refers to social change agents as "'utopian deviants' who make trouble for established groups." In *Theories of Society* (1951b) he wrote that "[S]train. . .is manifested by a series of symptoms of disturbance showing the psychological marks of irrationality." In short, social movement activities were seen as extensions of more elementary forms of collective behaviors such as riots or panic.

If groups do have legitimate grievances, charismatic leaders will emerge out of these disorganized and anomic masses, who then will organize and focus protest. The resources required to mount collective actions are assumed to be broadly distributed and shared by all sizeable groupings. The political system is perceived as pluralistic and potentially responsive to organized groups. If movements succeed, it is due to efforts of the social base; if they do not, it is because they lacked competent leaders, were unwilling to compromise, or behaved otherwise irrationally.

4. The sociology of intellectuals and intelligentsia has a long and venerable history. With its origin in Russia and Poland in the nineteenth century, the term "intelligentsia" has been used "to designate groups or strata of educated but unpropertied people" (Gella, 1976, p. 9). "In every society," wrote Mannheim (1936, p. 10), "there are social groups whose task is to provide an interpretation for the world and that society." We call these "intelligentsia." The term "intellectual," which is now often used interchangeably with intelligentsia, was coined by Clemenceau in 1898 to describe the group of prominent defenders of Dreyfus (Nettl, 1969, p. 25).

5. No comparable evidence exists, according to Brint (1984, p. 31) "of an equivalent rise in 'New Right' adversarial and anti-establishment sentiments" among college educated professionals and managers. Neoconservatives are, of course, from the professional-managerial strata, but their politics are characterized by centrist, rather than radical right, positions. Support for the anti-establishment right (e.g., the Moral Majority) hardly ever comes from the professional and managerial strata, but rather from blue collar workers, small business people, and farmers—more from southern and rural, than northern and urban, areas.

6. New class membership has been delineated in a variety of ways, though—most interestingly—not correlated in any consistent way with the political ideology of the analyst. The most inclusive definition of membership has been put forth by the Ehrenreichs. According to them, new class, or what they call the "professional-managerial class" includes all human service professionals, all social and cultural specialists, all technical professionals, and all mid-level salaried managers in both the public and private sector. Kristol's new class is the least inclusive, being confined entirely to social and cultural specialists with advanced degrees, along with top salaried managers in the public sector. Between these extremes are Ladd and Gouldner. Ladd's view is similar to the Ehrenreichs, but excludes those with less than a B.A. degree. In Gouldner's view, new class is composed of those who hold college diplomas in the social and cultural specialties, or in the technical professions.

7. Some leftists are extremely critical of the concept of new class. According to Piccone, the editor of the neo-Marxist journal *Telos*, new class theorists did nothing more than dig up

the ruins of earlier theories of intellectuals. . . provide them with dubious new intellectual underpinnings (e.g., sociolinguistics) and reinvent the class struggle, this time resulting not in a dictatorship of the proletariat, but in the equally suspect and unlikely rule of intellectuals. (1981, pp. 115-116)

Yet rather than being activists, Piccone (1981) characterizes intellectuals as safely packed away within the academic mothballs of colleges and universities. . .or held in reserve as consultants or cheap researchers for both the bureaucratic and industrial apparatus. Exiled into academic irrelevance. . .most intellectuals. . . disintegrate into narrow professionals and experts prostituting their skills to whatever funding agency happens to engage their services. (p. 117)

8. This intra-class conflict is particularly salient in academe, where humanistic and technical intellectuals struggle over control of curricula and distribution of rewards.

9. Anthony Oberschall (1973, p. 48), writing from a resource mobilization perspective, also contends that when a regime's legitimacy is in question, social protest and upheaval is more likely.

10. The technical and practical are derived from the Greek philosophical distinction between "techne" and "praxis." The technical is in the area of work, science and the economy, and refers to narrow, rational processes designed to gain control over the environment and material conditions. The practical is in the sphere of human development, and can be reached only through human discourse and interaction, in which subjectivity and reflexivity are the main components. Thus culture, morality, and identity are formed by practical discourse. The reader may recognize these themes in the work of George Herbert Mead.

11. These stages reflect patterns of increasing reflexivity and a movement from particular to universal beliefs (themes also found in Parsons' work). For Habermas, normative structure progresses from myth through religion, philosophy, and ideology. For the future, Habermas holds open the possibility of communicative ethics, where justice and equality are achieved through practical-moral reasoning. Thus the history of the human species can be reconstituted as the history of humanity's increasing capacity for emancipation from the vicissitudes of both environmental and personal conditions (Held, 1978). But there is no guarantee of progress; the potential for crisis and regression are always present.

12. Critical theorists have pointed out that technical-instrumental rationality has led to scientism, where all social problems tend to be seen as technical problems to be solved through technical means. This technological imperative prevents seeking moral and political solutions to social problems. For example, the problem of peace is recast as a technical problem to be solved with ever more technically sophisticated weapons. The "dialectic of enlightenment" (Horkheimer and Adorno, 1972) is that the rationality of science may ultimately result in irrationality—nuclear holocaust.

13. Touraine's work is not easily categorized; he has been variously labeled as an "anti-functionalist," a "neo- or post-Marxist," a "left Durkheimian" and an "action theorist." His work strongly resembles that of contemporary critical theorists. However, because he integrates Weber's action theory, Touraine might be best classified as a critical action theorist (for a review of his works, see Eyerman, 1984; and Kivisto, 1984).

Touraine rejects approaches that see social protest as dysfunctional or arational. In this regard, his orientation is similar to resource mobilization theory and critical Marxist perspectives.

All share the following common characteristics: they view movements as rational responses to institutionally embedded discontents and their chances for success are determined by the organizational and ideological resources they are able to muster, which in turn depends to a significant degree on the political strategies pursued. (Kivisto, 1984, p. 361)

14. Touraine does not postulate a complete rupture between industrial and post-industrial society. In more recent work, he suggests that postindustrial society can be viewed, at least in part, as a hyperindustrial society. Thus he appears to agree with critics who believe it more useful to speak about advanced industrial societies rather than supplantation of industrialization (Kivisto, 1984, p. 358).

15. Though Zald (1987, p. 327) recognizes the role of new class in post-industrial social movements, he does not emphasize their import. Rather he lists three sociodemographic bases for such social movements—the increasing population of aged, the changing racial-ethnic composition, and the growth of female-headed households. Zald also lists four transformations of class and status—the purported growth of the Yuppies, the growth of a new class of professionals and highly educated who are critical of established values, (i.e., the new class), the movement to the Sunbelt, and the emergence of prosperous fundamentalist Protestants (p. 327).

16. One measure of the growth in the number of intellectuals is enrollment in institutions of higher learning. Enrollment in private colleges and universities was 147,000 in 1900 and had risen to 1,540,000 in 1960; enrollment in public colleges and universities increased from 91,000 in 1900 to 2,210,000 in 1960 (Gouldner, 1979, p. 106). The baby boom greatly accelerated this trend. The number of college degrees, graduate and undergraduate combined, doubled between 1956 and 1967. The proportion enrolled in public institutions rose particularly fast. Yet as Todd Gitlin notes: "The elite universities still trained gentlemen, but increasingly the gentlemen were being trained as managers and professors, not bankers, diplomats and coupon-clippers with a taste for higher things" (1987, p. 21).

Chapter 3

The Atomic Scientists Movement
and the *Bulletin*

The nuclear era began at the close of World War II. The atomic bomb, developed to defeat the Nazis, but dropped on an enemy of a different race, had concluded that most terrible war. And though very few Americans had prior knowledge of the bomb, its carnage moved even few Americans to protest this new era of advanced weaponry. On August 8, 1945, a poll found that only 10% of all Americans opposed the use of atomic bombs on Japanese cities, while 85% approved. A December 1945 poll revealed that 23% wanted to use "many more [atomic bombs] before Japan had a chance to surrender." Only 4.5% "would not have used any atomic bombs at all" (Wittner, 1984, p. 129).

Among the first protesters against the atomic bomb were some of the scientists who designed and built it. After the explosion of the first bomb at Alamogordo in 1945, scientists at all Manhattan Project sites, principally Oak Ridge, Los Alamos, and Chicago, advocated international control of nuclear weapons. Only when one considers both the public's indifference or even enthusiasm toward this new weapon, and the historic role of the scientist, can the uniqueness of this protest be fully appreciated.

This chapter and the next, as well as Appendix B, are intended to place the Freeze in an historical perspective. Appendix B is an historical exegesis that attempts to show the long and venerable history of peace-seeking in the United States prior to World War II. We are impressed with this history, both for the perseverence of its key actors, and for what it teaches us about the protest activity that followed the destruction of Hiroshima.

Chapters 3 and 4, though intricately related, are split for the purpose of exposition. This chapter chronicles and analyzes the Atomic Scientists Movement and its outgrowth, the *Bulletin of the Atomic Scientists*. Given our theoretical perspective, we examine the origins, dynamics, strategies, and tactics of the scientists' movement, and then focus on the *Bulletin* as a social movement organization. We assess the role of key intellectuals and their attempt to define nuclear weapons as a social problem.

Atomic Scientists and Politics

The traditional role of the scientist is to remain isolated from social and political protest movements. The atomic bomb changed all that. Manhattan Project scientists, having "known sin" (in Robert Oppenheimer's words), became convinced that American nuclear weapons policy would lead to Armageddon. "In spring 1945, this conviction led some scientists to an attempt. . .to interfere *as scientists* with the political and military decisions of the nation" (Rabinowitch, 1956, p. 2).[1] This so-called Atomic Scientists Movement was "The first large confrontation of scientists and politicians in American history, and perhaps the only sustained organized political activity by science as such in world history" (Strickland, 1968, p. 2). Though the movement was short-lived, out of it came the Federation of American Scientists and the *Bulletin of the Atomic Scientists*, a magazine advocating arms control and disarmament for more than four decades.

The Atomic Scientists Movement (for comprehensive histories, see Smith, 1965; Strickland, 1968) was a two-stage phenomenon: (1) the reaction of elite Manhattan Project scientists to the Truman administration's Atomic Energy Bill in the fall of 1945, and (2) the attempted mobilization of the entire scientific community and many liberal groups to support Senator Brien McMahon's atomic energy bill (later amended and passed as the Atomic Energy Act of 1946). Even though the movement never involved more than a very small percentage of scientists, at most between 2 and 3% of all physicists and chemists, it affected the institutional structure of American science and the ingression of science into government policy (Strickland, 1968). Following this short-lived movement, scientists never again reverted to their pre-war detachment. Leaders in scientific organizations advocated a new social responsibility, and a new sub-culture of government science-advisers arose to form an elite within an elite.

To understand the origins of the Atomic Scientists Movement and the *Bulletin*, the activities of scientists at the Metallurgical Laboratory at Chicago are by far the most important. The "Met" Lab had been organized in 1942 with groups transferred from Columbia and Princeton universities to pursue research on nuclear reactors. For several reasons these scientists emerged as protest leaders (Simpson, 1981). Unlike other Manhattan Project sites, the Metallurgical Lab at Chicago was part of a major university and thus had resources—a sympathetic university administration, social scientists, theologians, and so on—unavailable elsewhere. Indeed, Robert Hutchins, President of the University of Chicago, contributed $10,000 from a special educational fund to the nascent movement. Moreover, he encouraged sociologist Edward Shils, anthropologist Robert Redfield, and others to establish "An Office of Inquiry into The Social Aspects of Atomic Energy," thus creating important cross-disciplinary allegiances within the university elite. Chicago scientists also had access to the news media of a large metropolitan area. In addition, at the conclusion of World War II, Chicago scientists remained at their university jobs, whereas scientists at other Manhattan sites dispersed.

The University ambience of the Met Lab contrasted sharply with the Oak Ridge Lab, which was staffed principally by DuPont scientists: "There was an appreciable gulf between those accustomed to the directed efficiency of industrial research and those who throve in the more chaotic atmosphere of academic laboratories" (Smith, 1965, p. 15). This difference between Oak Ridge and the Met Lab is reminiscent of Gouldner's distinction between the intelligentsia in the private sector and the intellectuals in the public sector.

At the conclusion of World War II, two topics dominated discussion among Manhattan Project scientists (especially at Chicago's Metallurgical Laboratory): the urgent need for international control of atomic energy, and the deleterious effects of secrecy upon the growth and development of science (Smith, 1965, p. 128). Having been unable to convince the Roosevelt administration of the need to bring the scientists of allied countries (particularly the Soviet Union) into the top secret Manhattan Project, sharing this information now seemed imperative to prevent a terrifying arms race.[2] Problems of domestic control of atomic energy appeared less important and urgent to these scientists.

The situation changed dramatically when the Truman administration introduced its War Department bill to establish an atomic energy commission. Opposition to the May-Johnson bill, as it came to be known, and domestic control became the great preoccupation of atomic scientists. It brought about the unification of scientists from the various Manhattan sites into the Federation of Atomic Scientists and its almost immediate expansion into the Federation of American Scientists (Smith, 1965, p. 128).

The May-Johnson bill contained strict security provisions over scientific research, focused more on weapons than on peaceful use of atomic energy, gave the military a great deal of power, and had nothing to say about international control. The security provisions and military control evoked furor among atomic scientists who were still rancorous over the military administration of the Manhattan Project. They perceived the bill as a threat to science itself because the broad language might even be applied to what was taught in the classroom. As Strickland (1968, p. 4) has pointed out:

> The reaction to the May-Johnson bill was indeed so strong that it shifted attention largely from the issue of international control of atomic energy to the issue of secrecy and thence to domestic legislation generally.

The scientists' eleven month struggle over atomic energy legislation involved two basic strategies: (1) a lobbying campaign aimed at officials in Washington, and (2) a publicity campaign aimed at harnessing public opinion. These tasks fit in with their ordinary roles as educators and their liberal ideology, a belief that people would act wisely once presented with the "facts". Convinced that the release of the atom meant a qualitative change in weaponry and international relations, they made a number of prophetic claims. Though many of these fell on deaf ears, less than two decades later their ideas and phraseology permeated the claims put forth by the various groups in the peace movement, and were repeated by the Freeze Movement 40 years later.

According to atomic scientists, the Truman administration suffered from "a most deadly illusion" in its belief that the U.S. could retain its monopoly over atomic weapons" (Pringle & Spigelman, 1981, p. 39). Secrecy and mistrust of the Soviet Union, in the scientists' opinion, would lead only to a costly and upward spiraling arms race which could end in total annihilation. In May of 1945, three months before the Hiroshima bombing, Leo Szilard had met with Secretary of State James F. Byrne:

> When I spoke of my concern that Russia might become an atomic power, and might become an atomic power soon, if we demonstrated the power of the bomb and if we used it against Japan, his reply was, "General Groves tells me that there is no uranium in Russia." (quoted in Weart and Szilard, 1978, p. 184)[3]

Although the scientists in the movement were often factionalized, they were unified by three related themes which became the slogans of their campaign: (1) there is *no secret* of the atomic bomb; (2) there is *no defense* against it; (3) there must be *international control* of atomic energy. The "no secret" slogan was based on the scientists' belief in the universality and discoverability of scientific facts, and thus the impossibility of a long-term U.S. monopoly on the atomic bomb. The "no defense" claim was based on the conviction that nuclear bombs were a revolutionary new weapon which would render warfare obsolete and change diplomacy, lead to an arms race, and bring about the demise of the nineteenth century notion of national sovereignty. And finally, because there is no complete defense against atomic weapons, immediate sharing of data would lessen already existing suspicion and help convince other countries of the peaceful intentions of the U.S. Only a sharing of data and personnel, international ownership of raw materials and weapons, in short "international control" of atomic energy, according to these scientists, would prevent an arms race and allow the world to avoid a nuclear holocaust.

The struggle over the May-Johnson bill intensified, particularly over the issue of civilian vs. military control of domestic atomic energy. Most scientists made the tactical decision that this issue needed to be settled before international control could be considered. Seizing on the emotional issue of military control, Senator Brien McMahon introduced his bill. It placed less emphasis on secrecy and more on peaceful use of atomic energy; but most importantly, the bill asserted civilian control over atomic energy.

The atomic scientists rallied behind the McMahon bill and worked to defeat the May-Johnson bill. Their insistent lobbying and all-out publicity campaign led to the eventual passage of the McMahon bill (Smith, 1965; Strickland, 1968). Yet after a lengthy Congressional battle, the final draft came to resemble the original May-Johnson bill. When the bill was signed into law as the Atomic Energy Act of 1946, the compromise Vandenberg Amendment provided that a military liaison committee be attached to the Atomic Energy Commission. The scientists had achieved far less than they had hoped, and indeed had come away from their first Congressional encounter badly bruised.

At the same time, during the spring of 1946 when the battle over the energy bill reached its peak, the State Department released the Acheson-Lilienthal report, later revised and known as the Baruch Plan. This was an attempt (however feeble) to reach an agreement with the Soviet Union over atomic weapons. Most of the scientists had been preoccupied with the domestic energy bill until it was passed by Congress in July. Belatedly, they turned their attention to the Baruch Plan and international control of atomic energy, the issue they originally had thought most important.[4]

Ironically, scientists then found there was little they could do. Because negotiations were conducted within the United Nations, their lobbying tactics were difficult to implement. Moreover, in terms of their informational campaign, they had no way to influence the Soviet Union. Perhaps most importantly, the Scientists Movement was exhausted. It had operated at a very high pitch for almost a year; now its issues and ideology had become more opaque (Strickland, 1968, pp. 134-135). Scientists could not agree on whether "international control" meant that uranium must be internationally owned, or whether international cooperation and information sharing was enough, or whether it was necessary to establish a world government.

Following the U.S. atomic test in the Bikini Islands, the Soviet Union rejected the Baruch Plan. The chill of the Cold War set in, and the Scientists Movement all but collapsed. In retrospect, at least two reasons may be cited for the scientists' failure to realize their intentions. First, scientists were politically naive. They thought that education, both public and in the form of lobbying, would replace ignorance with enlightenment and therefore bring about disarmament; and second, scientists, despite speaking against the bomb, nevertheless wanted to take scientific credit for its making, and in so doing advance their careers (Strickland, 1968, p. 9). We will return to this latter point in some detail in Chapter 7.

Two Moral Entrepreneurs

Of those most active in the Scientists Movement, and who continued to work for peace, two Met Lab scientists in particular stand out (in Howard Becker's 1963 term) as moral entrepreneurs: Leo Szilard for his brilliance, vision, and energy, and Eugene Rabinowitch for his determination and perseverance in making the *Bulletin of the Atomic Scientists* the standard-bearer for scientists in the peace movement.

Leo Szilard is generally recognized as one of the most profoundly original thinkers of the twentieth century. He made significant contributions to various fields of physics and biology, as well as American political life. Born in Hungary in 1898, he received his Ph. D. in Germany in 1922. His dissertation established the relationships between entropy and information, foreshadowing modern cybernetic theory (Feld, 1976). He patented inventions that led to the development of nuclear particle accelerators and, with Albert Einstein, an electromagnetic pump which is today a crucial component of nuclear reactors. In 1933, with the rise of Hitler, he left Germany for Britain, where his research contributed to the discovery of nuclear fission.

Szilard had a dramatic personality. Even as a child, according to his own account, he had "predilection for saving the world" but understood that "it is not necessary to succeed in order to persevere" (Weart and Szilard, 1978, p. 3). His political style was unique among leading scientists (Strickland, 1968, p. 24). He did not address himself prophetically to the general public, as did Linus Pauling; nor did he work within the government, as did Oppenheimer and Edward Teller. Rather he was forever creating "schemes, cliques and ephemeral groups modelled after H. G. Wells idea of a benevolent open conspiracy" (Shils, 1964).

Szilard's fear of the Nazis led him to author the famous Einstein letter to Franklin Roosevelt, which led to the Manhattan Project. The horror unleashed by the bomb compelled him to devote his life to its control. He was the moving force, the original energy, behind the Atomic Scientists Movement and the establishment of the *Bulletin*. In one of the first issues of the *Bulletin*, Szilard (in language consistent with Becker's image) called for a "crusade" to control atomic weapons. Discouraged with the narrow educational focus of the *Bulletin*, he founded Scientists for a Livable World (later renamed Council for a Livable World), which directly funds political candidates who sympathize with the cause of disarmament. He also helped found the International Pugwash Conferences on Science and World Affairs, a series of annual meetings designed to promote international (and particularly Soviet-American) cooperation on issues relating to nuclear weapons.

The other moral entrepreneur, Eugene Rabinowitch, was born in Russia in 1901 and received his Ph. D. in Germany in 1926. In 1933 he worked with Niels Bohr in Copenhagen, coming in 1935 to the United States to work on solar energy at the Massachusetts Institute of Technology. He joined the Met Lab in 1942, eventually becoming a senior chemist on the Manhattan Project. From 1947 to 1968 he was a Professor of Botany and Biophysics at the University of Illinois, after which he became Professor of Chemistry and Director of the Center for Science and the Future of Human Affairs at SUNY Albany until his death in 1973.

Under the umbrella of the Federation of Atomic Scientists, and particularly the Atomic Scientists of Chicago, Rabinowitch and Hyman

Goldsmith, also a Manhattan Project scientist, began writing and editing the *Bulletin*. After Goldsmith's death in 1949, the *Bulletin* increasingly became the product of Rabinowitch—his intelligence, his opinion, and most of all his perseverance. Though Rabinowitch maintained a full-time academic career, and published a three-volume treatise on photosynthesis, his devotion was to the *Bulletin*. As a long-time colleague and former managing editor of the *Bulletin* told us:

> The magazine was Eugene's life. Though he maintained his work as a scientist in Chicago, he took the *Bulletin* to bed with him and got up with it in the morning. He really lived a life of wanting to find some way of making science good for people. (Adams, 1983)

Rabinowitch's role in Pugwash was also seminal. He helped organize, and drew the agenda for, the first few conferences. Because he spoke Russian, he was able to mediate and promote cooperation between Soviet and Western scientists (Feld, 1984, p. 5).

Though Szilard and Rabinowitch led the crusade to control nuclear weapons, they disagreed over tactics and strategies. Rabinowitch was committed to the long, slow process of education to bring about the new climate of public opinion necessary for control of nuclear weapons. Szilard, on the other hand, "maintained that the whole educational program was not worth a few well-chosen contacts in Washington" (Smith, 1965, p. 292). In his eulogy to Szilard, Rabinowitch reaffirmed his own commitment to education, stating that Szilard did not believe in the slow process of enlightening public opinion; he was out to save the world from nuclear death by conspiracy, rather than waiting for its salvation by education (Rabinowitch, 1963, p. 19).

A Social Movement Organization

The first issue of *Bulletin of the Atomic Scientists of Chicago* was published in December, 1945. Scientists at other sites suggested a name change to "Bulletin of the Federation of Atomic Scientists," with each site contributing articles and sharing costs. The Chicago group refused, though they did drop the "Chicago" from their title in March of the following year. Though closely connected, the *Bulletin* never became the official organ of the Federation. Its independence was resented, and

Rabinowitch began signing his editorials so that they would not be mistaken for official Federation positions (Smith, 1965, p. 296). By 1948 the *Bulletin*, in order to obtain tax exempt status, had formally separated from the Chicago scientists, proclaiming itself an organ of "The Educational Foundation for Nuclear Science, Inc."

For this analysis, we conceptualize the *Bulletin* as a social movement organization (McCrea and Markle, 1988). As McCarthy and Zald (1977) have shown, SMOs attempt to convert various resources into political action for social change. Toward that end some produce mass demonstrations, some might lobby Congress, and others might provide information and analysis for educational purposes. It is in this last category that the *Bulletin* belongs. Through the printed word it exists as a claims-making organization calling for social change.

The *Bulletin* is a formal organization, officially governed by a Board of Editors, Board of Directors, and Sponsors. Most of these positions are held by elite academics who lend prestige to the organization and aid in fund raising, but contribute little to the *Bulletin*'s day-to-day operation.[5] The editor-in-chief contributes a monthly column that sets the *Bulletin*'s moral and political tone; but since Rabinowitch's death, even this position has been remote (and geographically removed) from the day-to-day operations of the magazine.

Since 1961 the *Bulletin* has had a managing editor who acts as the equivalent of an SMO executive director. From 1961 to 1968, and from 1978 to 1984, that editor was Ruth Adams. We characterize Adams as a social movement professional. Prior to rejoining the *Bulletin*, she served as Vice President of the Council for a Livable World, Council member of the Federation of American Scientists, and Executive Director of the Chicago office of the American Civil Liberties Union. Her successor, Len Ackland, was a *Chicago Tribune* reporter with extensive academic and movement experience. He holds a Master's degree from the Johns Hopkins School of Advanced International Studies, and was active in the International Voluntary Services during the Vietnam War.

The *Bulletin* gathers relatively little data about itself, making quantitative assessment difficult. From 1980 to 1985 circulation varied inconsistently between 20,000 and 25,000. However, Adams had no data on how many subscribers were individuals rather than libraries, nor did she know anything of subscriber demographics. During this same time period, between one-fifth and one-third of all income was raised from private donors and foundation grants (*Bulletin of the Atomic Scientists*, 1985). In 1987 the *Bulletin* employed a staff of 10 people.

52   MINUTES TO MIDNIGHT

STRATEGY AND TACTICS

Rabinowitch's overwhelming commitment to education, rather than
direct political action, strongly shaped the *Bulletin*. The strategies of
the *Bulletin* to bring about the control of nuclear weapons were stated
on the first page of its first issue:

> 1. To explore, clarify and formulate the opinion and responsibilities of
> scientists. . .
> 2. To educate the public to a full understanding of the scientific, technologi-
> cal and social problems arising from the release of nuclear energy.

These strategies did not change significantly over time. In a 1974
statement of purpose the editors reaffirmed their initial goals and
strategies, maintaining that the *Bulletin* provided "a forum for informed discussion. . .in the spirit of detached analysis." Articles were
to "avoid political partisanship" and assure "a wide and responsible
representation of views on all controversial questions." In short, the
Bulletin saw as its mission "to help scientists clarify the issues for
themselves, and to help public policy makers reap the benefit from their
dialogue" (*Bulletin of the Atomic Scientists*, 1974, p. 2).

To carry out this dialogue, the *Bulletin* turned to the most famous
scholars and politicians of the time. Articles by Albert Einstein and
Bertrand Russell, David Lilienthal and Archbishop Cushing, Michael
Polanyi and Talcott Parsons gave prestige and authority to the *Bulletin*.

During the *Bulletin*'s initial years, almost all of its articles dealt with
the international control of nuclear weapons, and indeed this focus has
remained the raison d'etre of the magazine. When it became clear that
the *Bulletin*'s goal was not to be accomplished quickly, its scope
broadened to include various global and humanistic issues. Under
Rabinowitch's leadership, third world problems and environmental
issues received considerable attention. By 1951, articles on world
hunger, the population explosion, and urban problems had appeared. In
1969 and 1971, special issues were devoted to China and the energy
crisis respectively. Topics ranging from space exploration to the debate
over recombinant DNA also received the *Bulletin*'s attention.

Rabinowitch was the editor and the heart of the journal for 28 years
until his death in 1973. His successor was Bernard Feld. He had been
an assistant to Enrico Fermi and Szilard in the Manhattan Project. Later
he was active in the Council for a Livable World and, at the time of his
appointment as editor, was Secretary General of Pugwash and Professor of Physics at the Massachusetts Institute of Technology.

Under Feld's leadership the magazine followed Rabinowitch's example. Upon his retirement in 1984, Feld reflected:

> Some have argued that we should limit our contents to nuclear arms control, while avoiding such distracting issues as environment, development, international scientific cooperation and so forth. At the other extreme we have been admonished for being too much concerned with day-to-day practical issues, showing insufficient interest in the broad philosophical questions that, in the long run, will decide the fate of the human species. My response to both criticisms is: amen! (Feld, 1984, p. 4)

Even so, Feld's monthly editorials were more narrowly focused than Rabinowitch's: almost all dealt directly with the arms control issue.

From 1985 until his death in 1987, Harrison Brown became the third editor-in-chief of the *Bulletin*. He also played a key role in developing the bomb and was "good friends with [Rabinowitch and Feld] on the Manhattan Project in Chicago" (Brown, 1985, p. 3). Although a distinguished chemist, Brown's interests ranged far beyond traditional science. His 1946 book, *Must Destruction Be Our Destiny*, detailed the threat presented by the introduction of nuclear weapons in the U.S. military arsenal, while his 1954 book, *The Challenge of Man's Future* dealt with the problems of economic development, hunger, and population growth.

Upon becoming editor, Brown immediately addressed a basic strategic issue:

> We must ask: Where do we go from here? What should we do? What can we do?. . . .These are the major questions which the *Bulletin* should address. . . . It seems to me that our goals should be much broader and the discussions should involve substantial portion of the world community, including developing nations. (1985, p. 4)

Yet broadened goals did not signal strategic changes. Echoing Rabinowitch, Brown called for the *Bulletin* to examine and explore— that is, to continue claims making—rather than to act in some other way. In this sense the *Bulletin* has never deviated, and continues to excel in its carefully defined role.

PARADOXICAL SUCCESS

For more than forty years the *Bulletin* has not missed a single issue. It has been unflagging in its attempts to halt the arms race. Even as nuclear arms proliferated and became more powerful, and their control became more elusive, the *Bulletin* persevered. During any time this would be noteworthy; but during the McCarthy era, when the country was consumed by paranoia of communism and there was no popular support for disarmament, the *Bulletin*'s perseverance was exemplary.

In accordance with its strategy of exploring, clarifying, and formulating the opinion and responsibilities of scientists, the *Bulletin* has regularly provided national and international links among scientists. Foremost in this effort has been its strong support of the Pugwash conferences. The *Bulletin* has also provided a forum for the dissemination of controversial opinion. For example, an article by Bertrand Russell that had "been refused by five American periodicals of wide circulation" (1946, p. 19) was published by the *Bulletin*. In pursuing the proper responsibilities of scientists, the *Bulletin*'s excellence has been recognized. A feature article, which elucidated the ways in which U.S. government officials falsified documents to allow Nazi scientists into this country, was awarded the prestigious Investigative Reporting Award for the best magazine article of 1985.

The *Bulletin* has also served as a media resource. As the former managing editor told us:

> I think our other success has been working with the press, they use us all the time, for help in tracking down stories, finding someone who is willing to speak on issues, and so on. . . . But most importantly we are successful because we still exist. (Adams, 1983)

The *Bulletin*'s most powerful tactic is its dramatic symbol: the doomsday clock which appears on the front cover of every issue.[6] Midnight represents the nuclear holocaust. The time shown on the clock, which varies in accordance with its view of international tensions, is intended to show how close the world is to nuclear midnight. The clock is intended to reflect major shifts in international relations, rather than ephemeral changes reported in daily headlines. Thus in 38 years it has had only 12 settings.[7] Decisions to move or not to move the clock are made by the board of directors based on the editor's recommendation. The *Bulletin* views its clock not only as an authoritative measure of objective conditions which move the world further from, or closer to, nuclear holocaust, but also as a tactic to mobilize public concern. Normally ignored by the press, and virtually invisible to the public, the *Bulletin* achieves international notice when it changes the setting of the clock. "When [the clock] moves," says Feld, "the world takes notice" (1984, p. 4).

The *Bulletin*'s success is paradoxical. In Rabinowitch's own words, the *Bulletin*'s "measure of success is also a measure of failure" (1966a, p. 3). Had the *Bulletin* achieved its goal, disarmament, its existence would no longer be necessary. As early as 1951 the *Bulletin* had expressed despair over its failure:

> What then have we to show for five years of effort, except the relief of having "spoken and saved our souls"—and the doubtful satisfaction of having been right in our gloomy predictions. (Rabinowitch, 1951, p. 5)

The sources of the *Bulletin*'s success—highly-visible and well-connected scientists—have also become the sources of its limitation. The scientific mode of thought, so successful in naturalistic investigation, has certain limitations in the political arena; similarly the expert role, a prerequisite of good science, often proves a double-edged sword outside the confines of the laboratory. Thus the *Bulletin* drew strength from its scientists, but may have suffered from scientism and elitism.

> We may say that scientism is present where: people draw on widely shared images and notions about the scientific community and its beliefs and practices in order to add weight to arguments which they are advancing, or to practices which they are promoting, or to values and policies whose adoption they are advocating. (Cameron and Edge, 1979, p. 3)

Scientism is an ideology which may be used as a resource to: (1) "Capitalize on authority in order to make discourse more persuasive, [and] in so doing. . .reinforce and consolidate that authority" (1979, p. 3); and (2) "colonize territory where scientific language, techniques, approaches, models and metaphors. . .have been previously thought inapplicable" (1979, p. 6). More specifically, we use scientism to denote the belief that social problems may be solved through scientific (instrumental) reasoning.

By training and philosophy, the *Bulletin* scientists believed in the power of science to solve social problems. As Rabinowitch wrote in 1966:

> I . . . believe in science as a powerful influence for human escape from the dead-end of international strife. . . . If I did not believe in this role of science, I would not have devoted much of my time in recent years to *The Bulletin of Atomic Scientists* and the Pugwash Conferences. (1966a, p. 2)

Thus, in our view, Rabinowitch fell into the trap of scientism. Science, from which the nuclear age arose, was supposed to lead to disarmament as well.

Instrumental reasoning calls for scientific detachment. According to this logic, facts speak for themselves; thus disagreement ought to be resolved on the merits of scientific argument. Yet the issues that these scientists were addressing clearly demand moral and political judgments. Thus the scientists' dilemma, especially since the bomb, was to choose between scientific detachment and education, in which they were trained, or direct political action. *Bulletin* scientists by and large chose the former.

Scientism and elitism often go together. The roots of elitism among atomic scientists go deep. In 1930 Szilard had written of the need for a youth organization—a "Bund"—to guide Germany's future. In a vision similar to Plato's, he dreamed:

> If we possessed a magical spell with which to recognize the "best" of the rising generation at an early age. . . . Then we would be able to train them to think independently, and through education in close association we would create a spiritual leadership class with an inner cohesion which would renew itself on its own. (quoted in Weart and G. Szilard, 1978, p. 24)

From its inception, the Atomic Scientists Movement struggled with the issue of elitism. The Los Alamos component of the movement favored direct political action, and organized at least one large public rally. Strickland caricatured this group as "the Children of Light who would finally do in the politicians," albeit by "apply[ing] the scientific method to social problems." The Chicago group opted for a different strategy, caricatured as: "Jesuits in the Imperial Chinese Court, fascinating the rulers with their technology" (1968, p. 64).

From its first issue, the *Bulletin* was a magazine for and by scientific elites. Thus according to Shils, the *Bulletin* has installed itself "into the conscience and intelligence of the upper levels of American public life [whose] influence has radiated outward toward the whole politically interested population" (1964, p. 14). Conversely, Bernard Feld proudly maintained:

> The *Bulletin*'s main asset, however, is that relatively small groups of devoted supporters—many of whom have been involved since our beginnings—upon whom we can always depend, in time of crisis, for both moral and financial help. (1984, p. 4)

The *Bulletin* has never reached the public to a significant extent. It was the *Bulletin*'s strategy (perhaps wishful thinking) that a scientific dialogue on nuclear issues would somehow motivate public action. Being full-time academic scientists rather than journalists, they were unable (or unwilling) to translate this dialogue into lay language. Indeed, they showed little interest in who their readers were, or in reaching them in greater numbers.

Elites can give a journal prestige and longevity, yet their contributions are problematic. Famous scientists owe their success, at least in part, to the system. As such they may be unlikely agents of social change. As one Berkeley physicist maintained:

> As for the dreams of a bold leadership role for science in our threatened world, I conclude that the veterans of the old guard are not likely to do anything significant, no matter how good their intentions. They have been spoiled by too much success. (Schwartz, 1969, p. 42)

Conclusion

The *Bulletin*'s goal was to promote disarmament through heightened public awareness. In sociological terms we may say that their strategy was to define a new social problem. During the *Bulletin*'s forty years, the world has changed greatly: various anti-war and civil rights movements have developed; the peace movement has evolved considerably; and the role of science in society has expanded dramatically. In the midst of all this change, it is difficult to isolate the *Bulletin*'s achievements. Yet the *Bulletin*'s continuity through the printed record offers some hope—and some data—for analysis.

According to traditional theories (e.g., Smelser, 1962), the principal determinant of social problems and social movements is structural strain. Strain, the threat of nuclear war, has been with us for more than forty years. From this point of view, the doomsday clock can be seen as a measure of strain (for other objective measures of strain, see Kriesberg, 1986). The closer the clock moves to midnight, the more we ought to observe social movement activity and social problem definition.

From 1947 to 1953 the clock moved closer to midnight. And from 1953 to 1960 it was set at two minutes to midnight, the closest setting of its history. Yet during that time strain seemed to lead not toward social movement activity, but rather toward intensified cold war. Proposals for fallout shelters, advice to "duck and cover," and the

Kennedy "missile gap" were expressions contrary to the goals of the *Bulletin*.

As the next chapter shows, beginning in 1957 the American peace movement became active again. Yet it was not until 1980, with the *Bulletin* clock set *back* to seven minutes, that the extensive Freeze Movement for disarmament—not a "marginal factor in American politics, but an important participant, a serious contender for power" (Wittner, 1984, p. 277)—emerged.

Traditional theories cannot explain why a massive antinuclear weapons movement appeared 35 years after the initial appearance of strain. Resource mobilization theory offers a better explanation. Empirical studies from this perspective have shown that political agitation, narrow focus, civil disobedience, effective manipulation of the mass media, and coalition building are necessary for social movement success—all tactics and strategies that *Bulletin* scientists did not consistently follow.

Our contention is that scientism and elitism isolated the *Bulletin*, diminishing its effectiveness in defining nuclear weapons as a social problem. Its exclusive educational strategy further limited its political effectiveness. As a journal of science, the *Bulletin* has always been somewhat isolated from other peace groups. Most histories of the contemporary American peace movement fail to mention the *Bulletin*, or do so only in the context of its founding and the Atomic Scientists Movement (see, for example, Wittner, 1984). The *Bulletin* has never created formal links with other social and political groups that share their goal of disarmament. For more than four decades the *Bulletin* has called for, and waited for, public action. Yet when there arose a mass social movement to control nuclear weapons in the early 1980s, the *Bulletin* had no formal ties to it. Although the *Bulletin* has run several articles on the Freeze Movement, and although Bernard Feld personally endorsed the Freeze, the *Bulletin* has never editorially endorsed the Freeze nor been a moving force behind it.

To us, the *Bulletin* seems to live in the past—in the excitement, the romance, the incredibly ironic "sin" of the Manhattan Project and the horror of Hiroshima. Its three editors-in-chief were all products of Manhattan. Indeed, the *Bulletin* has always covered its own history rather extensively, including the entire December, 1985 issue devoted to its 40th anniversary.

To summarize, the *Bulletin*'s educational nature, detachment, elitism, and isolation led to a separation of theory and practice. The *Bulletin* analyzed and elucidated a problem; then waited for something to happen, though how it was to happen, and by whom, they never specified. Ruth Adams, longtime managing editor, told us that young people are so busy acting that they do not have time to read. Perhaps it is fair to say that "older people" were so busy thinking and reading that they did not have time to (or were in some way disinclined to) act. It seems clear to us that both theory and action, the classical components of praxis, are necessary for meaningful social change.

Notes

1. In the United Kingdom, eminent scientists such as Julian Huxley and Nobel laureate J.D. Bernal had by the early 1930s raised the issue of "the social function of science." By the late 1930s Bernal and other elite scientists had formed the Association of Scientific Workers, which issued a Marxist analysis opposing entry into World War II (MacLeod and MacLeod, 1976). Even in the United States there was protest activity prior to World War II. In 1938 Robert Oppenheimer and others organized the American Association of Scientific Workers, a leftist counterpart of the British organization. The Manhattan Project led not only to increased protest, but to increased political integration as well: "certain branches of science became increasingly regarded by politicians and by scientists as being of great military, economic and hence, political significance" (Mulkay, 1976, p. 455; see also Gilpin,1962, Ch. 1).

2. In 1945, Nobel laureate Eugene Wigner wrote that as early as 1939:

[w]e did hope for another effect of the development of atomic weapons in addition to warding off eminent disaster. We realized that, should atomic weapons be developed, no two nations would be able to live in peace with each other unless their military forces were controlled by a common higher authority. We expected that these controls, if they were effective enough to abolish atomic warfare, would be effective enough to abolish all other forms of war. This hope was almost as strong a spur to our endeavors as was our fear of becoming the victims of the enemy's atomic bombings. (quoted in Rhodes, 1986, p. 308)

Thus, according to Wigner, many of the themes that dominated the postwar discussion of nuclear arms control were long anticipated by the atomic scientists.

3. At that same meeting, Byrnes had supplied another reason for dropping the atomic bomb on Japan. In Szilard's recollection:

He was concerned about Russia's postwar behavior. Russian troops had moved into Hungary and Romania, and Byrnes thought it would be very difficult to persuade Russia to withdraw her troops from these countries, that Russia might be more manageable if impressed by American military might, and that a demonstration of the bomb might impress Russia. I shared Byrnes' concern about Russia throwing around her weight in the postwar period, but I was completely flabbergasted by the assumption that rattling the bomb might make Russia more manageable. (quoted in Weart and Szilard, 1978, p. 184)

4. The Baruch plan which was presented to the Soviets appears, at least from hindsight, fatally flawed and bound to fail. Based on the assumption of America's long-lasting atomic monopoly, the plan was presented as a self-righteous take-it-or-leave-it proposition, with no basis for negotiation (Pringle and Spigelman, 1981, pp. 52-53). Bernard Baruch, the 74-year old Wall Street speculator who was chosen to present the proposal to the Russians, had modified the original Acheson-Lilienthal report quite drastically. As a capitalist, Baruch vehemently objected to the idea of international ownership of all uranium mines, and would only place processed uranium under such control. The ore itself, and the mines and plants to refine it, would remain in private hands. The Baruch Plan was to be implemented in separate stages over a period of fifteen years. In the first stage, Baruch proposed a worldwide survey and inspection of uranium sources, especially in Soviet bloc countries. This move would have forced the Soviets to play their only card, their unknown uranium sources, before the U.S. was prepared to make any concessions. Moreover, the plan did not require the United States to stop making bombs during the early stages. Perhaps the most extreme part of the Baruch proposal, which was interpreted by the Soviets as nuclear blackmail, involved a U.N. stockpile of atomic bombs to be dropped on any country that joined the new agency and failed to obey its rules (Pringle and Spigelman, 1981, p. 54).

5. In 1985, for example, the new chairman of the board was the Director of the John Sloan Dickey Endowment for International Understanding and former Provost of Dartmouth College; and a new member of the board was the Dean of Physical Sciences at the University of Chicago.

6. Ironically, it was Edward Teller ("father" of the hydrogen bomb) who in 1947 created the symbol. By 1973 he had resigned from the Board of Directors and in the 1980s, as a supporter of President Reagan's "Star Wars" program, has called the *Bulletin* a "propaganda instrument."

7. Originally set at 7 minutes, the clock was moved forward to 3 minutes to midnight in 1949 when the Soviet Union exploded its first atomic bomb. In 1953, with the development of the hydrogen bomb by both the U.S. and U.S.S.R., the clock was moved forward again, this time set at 2 minutes to midnight. This setting, the closest the clock has ever come to midnight, remained unchanged for 7 years. In 1960 the clock was set back again, to 12 minutes, following the signing of the Partial Test Ban Treaty. Five years later, in 1968, the clock was advanced 7 minutes to reflect the proliferation of nuclear weapons to other countries. One year later, with the ratification of the nuclear non-proliferation treaty, the clock was set back to 10. In 1972 the clock was again set back, this time to 12, after SALT 1 was ratified. After SALT failed to make progress, and India joined the nuclear club, the clock was moved forward, in 1974, to 9 minutes. In 1980 the clock advanced to 7 minutes because of "irrationality of national and international action" leading to increased danger of nuclear war (Feld, 1984 p. 3). In 1981, after the U.S. elections and the administration consideration of limited nuclear war, the clock was advanced to 4 minutes to midnight. Once again, in 1984, the clock was moved forward to 3 minutes—this time as a result of the Euro-missile crisis. Finally, in 1988, with the negotiation of the INF treaty, the clock was set back to 6 minutes to midnight.

_____

Chapter 4

Ban the Bomb

Scientists were not the only ones to protest against the atomic bomb. Immediately after Hiroshima, intellectuals and other peace activists wrote, organized, and militated against nuclear weapons. Some belonged to pacifist groups such as the American Friends Service Committee or the Fellowship of Reconciliation, which had historically opposed war; others formed new groups, the most important of which was the National Committee for a Sane Nuclear Policy (SANE).

This chapter, which follows in chronology Appendix B, examines the development of the post World War II antinuclear weapons movement. Our method is to use three histories, Charles DeBenedetti's (1980) *The Peace Reform in American History*, Lawrence Wittner's (1984) *Rebels Against War*, and Milton Katz's (1986) *Ban the Bomb* as our basic accounts. As indicated, we supplement this material with secondary sources and, for the post-1955 period, some of our own analysis. Of the many histories that could be written on this subject, of the various social constructions that the present imposes on the past (see Markle and McCrea, forthcoming), these three accounts seem particularly prescient.

Our goal is to let these accounts interact with our theoretical perspective, and to give some context to what later peace groups experienced: to the ideals which moved them, to the dilemmas which vexed them, to the defeat which all to often faced them. Given our interest in resource mobilization and new class, we focus on the role of key organizations, the importance of intellectuals as leaders, and the professionalization of the movement. Our contention is that key organizations, particularly United World Federalists and SANE, with the support from traditional pacifist groups, provided the infrastructure and in some ways directly presaged—in strategy, tactics, and organizational dilemmas—the Freeze Movement.

The Postwar Years

According to Hodgson (1976), four great facts dominated international politics in the postwar years. The first was the atomic bomb. The second was the rise of the Soviet state, aggressively led by Joseph Stalin. The third was the sheer strength of the United States. And the last was the relative weakness and war weariness of all other nation-states.

World War II brought about a profound shift in public mood. The war just fought was widely viewed as a just war, in which the forces of evil had been defeated by the forces of good. The Nazis and their world view—hatred, violence, and Aryan supremacy—had, in the view of most Americans, been defeated by the superior military strength of the United States. Although the U.S. victory spurred some intellectuals and pacifists to work for disarmament, it ironically fostered among a vast majority of Americans a virulent nationalism and feelings of moral superiority. This superiority was "taken to be a permanent quality which not only explains past victories, but also justifies the national claim to be the lawgiver and arbiter of mankind" (Curti, 1964, pp. 730-731).

Along with this new nationalism came the belief that America's world position depended on power found through armament.[1] Coupled with this was a profound change in foreign policy towards the Soviet Union. As Marshall Shulman has noted, "within the space of a few months there was a massive turn-around in U.S. policy, from a period of collaboration with the Soviet Union as the 'gallant ally'" who had "contributed heroically and with great loss of life to the defeat of the Nazi armies," to one of distrust and confrontation (1987, p. 15).[2] The Truman Doctrine of 1947 not only provided $400 million in aid to Greece and Turkey, but also pledged to resist Soviet expansionism and Communist insurgence anywhere in the "free" world.

In the immediate postwar years, both the United States and the Soviet Union were expansionist powers. Even worse, the leaders of the two countries:

> [H]eld a political philosophy as the truth. Each believed that in the end their truth must prevail universally. Each believed that history was on their side. It could only be a matter of time before two systems, each justified in its own view by political morality and historical necessity, came into conflict. (Hodgson, 1976, p. 25)

In these times, the message of peace was likely to fall on deaf ears. Yet the atomic bombing of two Japanese cities, extreme acts even in the context of military history, served as a catalyst to mobilize once again the peace community—a small current within the larger flow of history. In addition to the atomic scientists, two other groups—traditional pacifists and world federalists—became active in the immediate postwar years.

REVIVAL

With the close of the war, traditional pacifist groups lost their "outlaw status" (Wittner, 1984, p. 15), and began to recoup their fallen prestige. In 1946 the Nobel Peace Prize was awarded to Emily Green Balch of the Women's International League for Peace and Freedom; the next year, the prize went to the American Friends Service Committee (AFSC). In the period from 1945 to 1948, to use Wittner's (1984, p. 151) phrase, the peace movement experienced a "mild revival."

More successful than either pacifist or the atomic scientists in organizing a social movement in these years were the world federalists (see Yoder, 1972). Certain that atomic weaponry had changed the very nature of international politics, a coalition of various world federalist groups pursued the idea of bringing about a democratic world government. In 1946, fifty-three of sixty-five candidates for the Eightieth Congress who answered a questionnaire approved of changing the United Nations into a world federation with a majority rule legislation. A Gallup Poll of the same year found that 52 percent of the American public favored the liquidation of all national armed forces, and the concomitant establishment of an international police force; only 24 percent opposed this idea.[3]

In February of 1947, representatives of sixteen separate federalist groups held a convention in Asheville, North Carolina, resulting in the merger of most of them under the name of "United World Federalists For World Government With Limited Powers Adequate To Prevent War." Its platform was to work towards strengthening the United Nations into a world government. The growth of the new organization was dramatic. With 600 chapters in 1948, the UWF budgeted an additional $550,000 to establish a chapter in every U.S. community. By 1949 there were 45,000 dues-paying members in 720 local chapters (Yoder, 1972, p. 100). In June of that year some 8,000 people attended a UWF rally; Supreme Court Justice William O. Douglas and other speakers supported a Congressional resolution to develop the United Nations into a true world federation.

The UWF leadership was composed of various intellectuals—writers, professors, and other professionals—all of whom had supported World War II. A study of its social composition revealed that members tended to be Protestants from liberal denominations, residents of eastern metropolitan areas, and relatively well-to-do—though few were business people (Peck, 1947, p. 38). A typical UWF activist, according to Wittner (1984, p. 141), was Grenville Clark, author of the Selective Service Act of 1940 and, in the postwar years, an advocate of world government. As historian Dexter Perkins (1952, p. 113) observed, although world government proponents were "not very powerful numerically," they were "a part of that elite opinion which deserves to be regarded as of more importance than mere numbers suggest."

Proponents of world government were split over how much power such an organization should be able to exercise. "Minimalists" argued for merely enough power to prevent war, whereas "maximalists" claimed that a world government, to be effective, had to have enough power to ensure political and economic justice. Among the proponents of the maximalist position, headed by University of Chicago President Robert Hutchins,[4] were such prominent academics as Law School Dean Wilber Katz and anthropologist Robert Redfield of the University of Chicago, dean of the Law School James Landis, Harvard University professor of religion William Hocking and Union Theological Seminary's Reinhold Niebuhr. Hutchins argued that "If we wish to be saved, we shall have to practice justice and love" and subordinate "Americanism to Humanity." Redfield agreed by proclaiming "The price of peace is justice" (quoted in Wittner, 1984, pp. 172-173). Despite these pleas the UWF decided to adopt a minimalist position by calling for a world government of limited powers, adequate to prevent war. Its first president was Cord Meyer, Jr., Yale graduate and Pacific War hero; and one of its vice-presidents was Norman Cousins, editor of the *Saturday Review*.

From its peak in the late 1940s, the UWF quickly and precipitously declined. Criticism came from within and without, from left and right. Pacifists like A.J. Muste and Bayard Rustin, a black Quaker, were quick to point out that the world federalist position suffered from the same inconsistencies as the atomic scientists'. Whereas atomic scientists told of the horrors of the atomic weapons while continuing to build and develop them, world federalist   riticized American foreign policy but accepted its underlying principle—military deterrence. As UWF president Cord Meyer, Jr. proclaimed: "Until this world federation is established. . .we must maintain our defensive military strength." To clarify his point he added, "I think we have to follow a policy of military preparedness now, given the fact that other nations are" (quoted in Wittner, 1984, p. 175).[5] The irony of this position was not lost on its critics—simultaneous support for the arms race and a world government. If atomic warfare would bring catastrophe, then why prepare for it?

Though criticism from the left may have hurt the UWF, it was criticism from the right that proved fatal. Directly presaging the later troubles of SANE, the UWF had to face the issue of communism. Even before the period of McCarthyism, Norman Cousins, later President of the UWF, was giving anti-Communist speeches. "Although he was the spokesman for a movement based on the theoretical ability of people to live peace," charges Yoder (1973, p. 108), "he flaunted as patriotic credentials the fact that he could not communicate with communists." And in 1952, Cousins essentially agreed with the validity of McCarthy's red-baiting:

> There could be no more ghastly irony than is presented today by those who in the name of Americanism are actually helping to prepare this country for the eventual triumph of communism. (quoted in Yoder, 1973, p. 107)

With the onset of the Korean War, the world government movement began to crumble. Prior to 1950, twenty-three state legislatures had passed resolutions in favor of world federalism; by late 1951, sixteen of those resolutions had been rescinded. In 1951, the UWF had 40,000 members and an income of $180,000; within five years, it had 17,000 members and an income of $65,000 (Yoder, 1973, p. 105). Many world federalists supported the Korean War, rationalizing it as a United Nations action. Cord Meyer and Thomas Finletter left the UWF, the former to join the CIA, the latter to pursue a law career and eventually become Secretary of the Air Force.

Why the dramatic decline of the UWF? In his critical essay, Yoder concluded that the UWF failed because of characteristic weaknesses on the part of American liberals:

> Tragically paralleling the larger movement in which American liberals became conservatives . . . a well-financed, intelligent, internationalist peace movement succumbed to an obsolete and ignorant nationalism by sacrificing its ideals "for the duration" upon the alter of expediency, committing organizational suicide in the name of American pragmatism. (1973, p. 112)

COLD WAR AND NADIR

The Cold War relegated the peace movement to insignificance. From 1950 to 1956, the movement "consisted of little more than a small band of isolated pacifists" (Wittner, 1984, p. 228). Yet while the peace movement had retreated from political action, its intellectual vitality remained unbroken. In the dark days of the early 1950s, the best of the pacifist thinkers subjected the ruling apparatus to critical reexamination and sought to develop political alternatives. The result was an incisive critique of American political and economic structure. As early as 1950 Lewis Mumford, in an article titled "In the Name of Sanity," wrote, "In the United States reason is cowed by governmental purges" and "criticism and dissent. . .are identified as treason." He called for a renewed critical analysis of the U.S. economic, technological and foreign policies to restore "sanity" and rationality (1950, p. 7).

In 1951 the AFSC published an in-depth foreign policy analysis entitled "Steps to Peace", which stimulated considerable excitement in intellectual circles. This Quaker analysis condemned the Truman Doctrine of "containment and its assumption that military force is the only language understood by the Community high command," an assumption which has "virtually dominated American foreign relations." The report claimed "Our insecurity stems from rapid expansion of Russian influence, but we should recognize that a major reason for this expansion is the economic appeal of Communism." A foreign policy aimed at "impressing a handful of men in the Kremlin" and subordinating the problems of a "billion Asians" and "half a billion Europeans" is a policy that is "doomed to failure." As an alternative, the AFSC urged an end to the arms race, strengthening the U.N. into an effective world government, and a worldwide struggle against poverty (AFSC, 1951, pp. 9-64).

The most sophisticated and widely read policy analysis was "Speak Truth to Power," published by the AFSC in 1955. In a pointed indictment of military power, the report stated that a working peace required fundamental attacks upon world poverty, an end to colonialization, the development of a world organization, and disarmament (AFSC, 1955). Instead of acting on these requirements, noted Robert Pickus, who initiated the study, political leaders only give lip service to these goals, and instead the United States government continues in its "lust for power," continues the arms race, and supports "undemocratic governments dedicated to the maintenance of the status quo." If the United

States truly wished to emerge as the champion of global justice, it must throw off its commitment to organized violence (Pickus, 1955, pp. 6-8).

Critical of the foreign policies of both the United States and the Soviet Union, pacifist intellectuals began to advocate a "Third Camp." The Third Camp, explained A. J. Muste, stood for a radical pacifist revolutionary movement which would work for the destruction of militarism, the overthrow of colonialism, the elimination of "racial and national discrimination," the abolition of poverty, the emancipation of Russians and Americans from the "regimes which. . .exploit them and harness them in the service of global atomic war," and the "liberation" of the total human person from those economic, political and technological forces which "deprive him of his essential dignity and the possibility of self-realization" (Muste, 1954, pp. 1-11).

Yet these were voices in the wilderness, their analysis overwhelmed by Cold War rhetoric. The Cold War was fostered by historical circumstances that made peace-related work a frustrating endeavor for the modern peace movement and disarmament unlikely.[6] It grew out of— and was the logical extension of—the "national security state." Termed by DeBenedetti (1980, p. 138) "the most profound development in American Politics between 1941 and 1961," national security concerns—developed as a response first to Nazism and then to Communism—became an excuse to extend military power abroad and minimize dissent at home. With the passage of the National Security Act in 1974, national leaders prepared the country to secure the postwar peace through a bureaucratized state-security system. Between 1950 and 1953, U.S. military expenditures quadrupled, while the level of civilian defense related personnel doubled. The FBI experienced continued expansion, while the CIA "grew six-fold into an independent government agency commanding manpower and budget far exceeding anything originally imagined" (DeBenedetti, 1980, pp. 155-156).

The domestic counterpoint of American foreign policy was McCarthyism. Citizens who emphasized nonmilitary cooperation toward a more just world appeared as threats, and "came to be viewed as subversive," a view that plagues the peace movement to this day (DeBenedetti, 1980, p. 138). It was Senator Joseph McCarthy's genius to promulgate not only a fear of Russians abroad, but a fifth column of American spies at home. In the opening prayer of the U.S. Senate in 1952, evangelist Billy Graham, following McCarthy's lead, warned of "barbarians beating at our gates from without and moral termites from within" (quoted in Wittner, 1984, p. 214). In the logic of McCarthyism, pacifism was equated with Communism. According to the American Council of Christian Laymen, the Fellowship of Reconciliation (FOR) was a "radical pacifist group using Christian terms to spread Communist propaganda," and the War Resistors League (WRL) was a sponsor of "numerous Communist-controlled movements" (quoted in Wittner, 1984, p. 218).

McCarthy reserved particular wrath for advocates of world government, or "one-worlders," as he referred to them, seeing little distinction between their position and Communism. Local and federal government agencies often acted on this conclusion. In February of 1953, *Newsweek* reported that loyalty investigators were asking would-be government employees if they had ever been members of the United World Federalists. During the same year the State Department directed U.S. overseas information centers to remove Clarence Streit's *Union Now* from their shelves, and Senator Pat McCarran introduced a bill to bar funds to agencies promoting a one-world government. Representative Lawrence Smith of Wisconsin summed up the prevailing mood when he noted that world government was "just as dangerous as the communism we are figthing" (quoted in Wittner, 1984, pp. 221-222).

In such a climate, peace advocates were ill-suited for long and continuous struggle. According to a 1949 analysis, "pacifists are drawn chiefly from the ranks of comfortable, respectable people," most commonly from the teaching profession, who are

> more interested in their particular field of study, their family, their record collection, their correct and genteel friends than they are in challenging people to think anew on the great issues of war and peace. (quoted in Wittner, 1984, p. 211)

In the context of the Cold War, advocacy of peaceful coexistence had become at best utopian, at worst treasonable. Clearly the period of 1950 to 1956 represents the nadir of the peace movement. "In this strange half-life," in Wittner's (1984, p. 213) eloquent description,

> The remnants of the historic movement witnessed their struggle against war, formulating radical alternatives to American military policy and serving as prophets in the Cold War wilderness. Yet rarely had the prospect seemed so bleak and their witness so hopeless.

THAW AND BREAKTHROUGH

After the Korean War ended and Senator McCarthy was discredited by the Army-McCarthy hearings in 1954, the remnants of the peace movement began to stir from their frozen inactivity. Yet it needed an issue around which to mobilize itself and reach the public. Unexpectedly, a galvanizing issue presented itself when a U.S. H-bomb test explosion accidentally scattered radioactive dust on twenty-three Japanese fishermen. FOR called for an immediate test ban. "No nation," it claimed, "has the right for purpose of military experimentation to inflict this horror upon innocent and defenseless multitudes" (quoted in Wittner, 1984, p. 240). "If there is still a peace movement left in America," challenged journalist I. F. Stone, "this must be its platform. . .no more tests" (quoted in Katz, 1986, p. 14).

In the November 1954 issue of the *Bulletin*, physicist Ralph Lapp presented the first detailed description of the dangers of fallout.[7] This article set off a series of claims and counterclaims between antinuclear activists and policy makers (for a summary, see Kopp, 1979). Attempting to allay public fears, the U.S. Civil Defense Administration published a pamphlet claiming that "fallout is nothing more than particles of matter in the air" (quoted in Wittner, 1984, p. 240). An Atomic Energy Commission Report, finally released to the public in February of 1955, confirmed the *Bulletin*'s analysis of radioactive fallout.

In July of 1955, Albert Einstein and Bertrand Russell joined this debate by issuing an eloquent appeal for disarmament. Signed by other renowned scientists, including Americans Herman Muller and Linus Pauling (Nobel laureates), and Frederic Joliot-Curie of France and Leopold Infeld of Poland, the appeal attempted to break out of the instrumental reasoning which had dominated the debate and reassert a moral practical reasoning. The text began:

> We are speaking on this occasion, not as members of this or that nation, continent or creed, but as human beings. . .whose continued existence is in doubt.

and concluded on the same humanistic note:

> Shall we. . .choose death because we cannot forget our quarrels? We appeal, as human beings, to human beings: Remember your humanity and forget the rest. (quoted in Pauling, 1958, pp. 158-159)

Within a week, fifty-two Nobel laureates issued a statement endorsing the Einstein-Russell appeal.

In 1956, Democratic presidential candidate Adlai Stevenson made the test-ban a central issue in the election campaign. Though Stevenson found it a poor political issue in a nation committed to a national security state, Cousins and other activists had enough political clout on this issue to shape Stevenson's behavior.

It was a small group of professors at Washington University, including biologist Barry Commoner, who convinced Cousins that milk supplies were being contaminated with strontium-90. Shortly thereafter, Cousins persuaded highly respected and revered humanitarian physician Albert Schweitzer to speak out against nuclear testing. On April 24, 1957, Schweitzer made his famous "Declaration of Conscience." His statement produced a powerful reaction throughout the world.[8]

Linus Pauling, assisted by Barry Commoner, drew up a petition calling for an immediate international agreement to halt nuclear testing. Almost 3,000 American and 8,000 international scientists signed the petition, which was released to the press in June of 1957. Startled by this unexpected challenge to their authority, government officials fought back. Pauling was subjected to a Congressional investigation. The Atomic Energy Commission announced that an atmospheric test ban was not technically feasible, because underground explosions could not be detected beyond a maximum distance of 250 miles. Following protest from the scientific community, the AEC raised the maximum distance to 2,300 miles. In 1958, Edward Teller, "father" of the hydrogen bomb, and Albert Latter of the Rand Corporation, wrote in the February 10, 1958 issue of *Life* magazine that radiation "need not necessarily be harmful—indeed, it may conceivably be helpful."

In 1957, despite the activity precipitated by the fallout issue, the peace movement remained on the defensive, still ravaged and overwhelmed by Cold War McCarthyism. In that year, Congressman Francis Walter of Pennsylvania called Linus Pauling a Communist; and Representative Lawrence Smith of Wisconsin called Norman Cousins a Communist dupe. Smith appealed to the American people not to "let the superficial, disputed fear of radioactivity blind us to the greatest threat of all—atheistic Communism" (quoted in Katz, 1986, p. 20). Nor was red-baiting confined to government officials. Sociologist Nathan Glazer (1961, p. 291), asserting sympathy but writing as a strong critic, claimed that in 1957 "the peace movement was, in the eyes of many (and in some measure a reality) a creature of Russian foreign policy."

But this time not even red-baiting could make the issue disappear. Antinuclear activists understood that radiation was one topic that touched a sensitive nerve in the American people. The year 1957 signalled a breakthrough for the peace movement. Liberal organizations like the Federation of American Scientists, United World Federalists, American Friends Service Committee, the Women's International League for Peace and Freedom, the Fellowship of Reconciliation, and the World Council of Churches were all speaking out against nuclear testing. All that was needed was a central organization to coordinate a national campaign. Out of this need came the National Committee for a Sane Nuclear Policy, whose history is so crucial for understanding the later Freeze Movement.

SANE

FOUNDING AND PURPOSE

On April 22, 1957, several members of the American Friends Service Committee, along with leading pacifist A.J. Muste of the Fellowship of Reconciliation, met to discuss the future direction of the peace movement. Two important strategic decisions were made: to focus on nuclear testing rather than broader issues of disarmament, and to operate through a three-fold organization. The three groups were to consist of (1) an ad hoc liberal nuclear-pacifist organization which would be more "educational and conventionally oriented," later known as SANE, (2) an ad hoc radical pacifist, direct action oriented organization that would become the Committee for Non-Violent Action, and (3) the older peace organizations such as AFSC and the Women's International League for Peace and Freedom (WILPF) which, while maintaining their identities, would focus on the nuclear testing issue, thus providing support to the two ad hoc organizations (Katz, 1980, p. 22).

In June of 1957, prominent intellectuals met at the Overseas Press Club in New York to form the Provisional Committee to Stop Nuclear Tests. That September the group renamed itself, at Erich Fromm's suggestion, the National Committee for a Sane Nuclear Policy (SANE). Fromm, a refugee from Nazi Germany and a leading intellectual of the Frankfurt School, having watched one power overcome by mass madness, insisted that the American public must first "recognize the revalidation of simply saving sanity."

According to Fromm, the "normal drive for survival" had been overwhelmed by the Cold War and the public's lack of fear of the arms race was a "symptom of a kind of schizophrenic indifference...characteristic of our age" (quoted in Katz, 1986, p. 24), a mass pathology very similar to the "psychic numbing" popularized by Robert Jay Lifton and Richard Falk in their 1982 book, *Indefensible Weapons*. As all Frankfurt intellectuals, Fromm was convinced of the liberating potential of language and the importance of naming things correctly to "demystify" distorted reality. The role of intellectuals and informed citizens, according to Fromm, must be to "Bring the voice of sanity to the people."

The nascent group grappled with the multiple versus single issue over how to best influence national policy. Some members wanted a broad attack on the problem of disarmament; others preferred a quiet approach to policy makers. Catherine Cory, a Friends organizer, convincingly argued that "the man on the street becomes paralyzed at the complexities of 'general disarmament.'" In calling just for an end to nuclear bomb tests, she continued, "at last we have an issue that the average Joe understands" (quoted in Katz, 1986, p. 24). Like the Freeze more than twenty years later, SANE thus began as a single issue organization.

SANE started out, as the Freeze later would, as an informal national committee aimed at educating the American people, and stimulating a great debate over a single nuclear issue. But it soon became apparent that there was a need for a more formal national organization with finances and full-time personnel available. At the first organizing meeting in October 1957, Norman Cousins of the United World Federalists and Clarence Pickett, secretary emeritus of the AFSC, became the first cochairs; and Homer Jack, a Chicago Unitarian minister, volunteered to serve part-time until a full-time executive secretary could be hired. Trevor Thomas from AFSC was hired as the first full-time executive secretary. When Donald Keyes was hired as its full-time executive director, SANE was well on its way to becoming what John McCarthy and Mayer Zald have called a professional social movements organization.

The single most important individual, or moral entrepreneur, in the history of SANE was Norman Cousins. On the night after the atomic destruction of Hiroshima, Cousins, then the young editor of the *Saturday Review*, composed one of the most famous editorials in American history: "Modern Man is Obsolete." Published twelve days after Hiroshima, it declared that the atomic bomb "marked the violent death of one stage in man's history and the beginning of another." The "new age" created a "blanket of obsolescence not only over the methods and products of man but over man himself." In the editorial, which reached an estimated forty million readers, Cousins (1945) concluded that,

> There is one way and only one way to achieve effective control of destructive atomic energy and that is through centralized world government.

Born in 1912 and educated at Columbia University Teachers College, Cousins was to become a key tactician and visionary of the peace movement. In addition to his opposition to nuclear weapons, as editor of the *Saturday Review* he campaigned against the indiscriminate use of "miracle drugs," the harmful side-effects of fluoridation, and American involvement in Indochina; he also campaigned for substantial commitment to space exploration. Although a peace liberal, Cousins was not a pacifist. He had supported World War II, first as a member of the editorial board of the Overseas Bureau of the Office of War Information, and from 1943 to 1945 as editor of *U.S.A.*, a wartime government information journal for distribution abroad (*Current Biography*, 1977).

A political activist as well as an intellectual, Cousins was president of the United World Federalists from 1952 to 1954; ten years later he was president of the World Association of World Federalists. In the mid 1960s, Cousins was stricken with a rare and supposedly incurable collagen disease that paralyzed most of his body. Designing his own "holistic" treatment of Vitamin C injections and "positive emotions," Cousins recovered completely and told his story in a best-selling 1979 book, *Anatomy of an Illness*, which made him a guru of the holistic health movement.

As cochairs of SANE, Cousins and Pickett agreed that the new organization should focus on what was seen as the most strategically compelling issue—nuclear testing. As Pickett wrote, this issue "gave anxious citizens from varied backgrounds a single meaningful issue on which to act" (quoted in Wittner, 1984, p. 244). Presaging strategy later adopted by the Freeze movement, Cousins was particularly concerned that SANE be independent from partisan politics, involve the clergy in the moral issues of nuclear testing, and promote a scientific understanding of issues surrounding nuclear testing.

The statement of purpose of the newly formed organization, written by the organizing committee, including Pickett and Cousins, listed among its goals "developing public support for a boldly conceived and executed policy which would lead mankind away from nuclear war and toward peace and justice." To achieve this goal, "the immediate cessation of all nuclear weapons tests by all countries" was proposed, "enforced through a United Nations monitored agreement" (Katz, 1986, p. 26). The statement also included the functions of the National Committee: to serve as a rallying point and clearing house; to prepare and print informational materials and distribute films; to issue public statements, sponsor visits with major policy making leaders, and call conferences; to encourage the formation of local committees; and to stimulate other national organizations to take a stand on disarmament.

One of SANE's first and most successful tactics toward mobilizing public support, which proved to be a milestone in the history of social movements organizations, took place on November 15, 1957. On that day, SANE placed a full-page advertisement in the *New York Times* that proclaimed: "We Are Facing A Danger Unlike Any Danger That Has Ever Existed. . . .." The statement was a call for moral-practical reasoning reminiscent of the Russell-Einstein appeal.

Written mainly by Cousins, the ad set disarmament arguments in a broadly humanistic framework. "We are not living up to our moral capacity in the world," it said. In our desire for bigger incomes, bigger televisions and bigger cars, "we have been developing our appetites, but we have been starving our purposes." To face the problems of the world we must redirect our loyalty: "The sovereignty of the human community comes before all others." To achieve these goals the ad called for a moral awakening. "All that is required is to redirect our energies, rediscover our moral strength, redefine our purpose." The ad did call for Americans to press their government for an immediate suspension of nuclear testing. Yet the major themes and interest of the ad were clearly focused on moral, universalistic issues.

Though many liberals signed the petition accompanying this ad, Eugene Rabinowitch of the *Bulletin* and other prominent scientists withheld their signatures, objecting to its purportedly emotional prose. Although such language was colorful, Rabinowitch felt that the scientist's task was to engage in instrumental analysis and thus "help replace qualitative attitudes with quantitative judgments" (quoted in Katz, 1986, p. 28).

Although the advertisement drew mixed reactions from the public, with some labelling members of the national committee "Communists," the overwhelming response was positive. SANE received thousands of letters and donations. The $4,700 cost of the ad was quickly recovered, and supporters all over the country placed reprints of the original *Times* ad in 32 different newspapers; SANE received 25,000 requests for reprints of the statement.

SANE was totally unprepared for this response. Indeed, the organization had not been formed to promote or even invite a grass-roots membership. Yet as thousands of letters arrived, SANE leaders redesigned the organization. By the summer of 1958, membership had grown to about 25,000, organized into some 130 chapters. "Powerfully SANE swept into a vacuum in the American peace movement," according to Katz (1986, p. 29), "energizing people to politically relevant action on specific issues of the arms race."

Yet this grass-roots image is only partially correct. Some liberals with no previous attachment to the peace movement did join SANE; however it drew its main source of strength from existing peace movement groups. As Nathan Glazer (1961, p. 290) obseved, SANE was a coalition of two major groups that had their origins in older issues: world government and traditional pacifism. Prominent SANE spokespersons Norman Cousins, Oscar Hammerstein, and Walter Reuther had all been officers in United World Federalists. SANE's first full-time executive director, Donald Keyes, had also been on the UWF staff. A considerable number of SANE leaders were moderate pacifists such as Clarence Pickett, Robert Gilmore, and Norman Thomas; more radical pacifists like A.J. Muste gave initial support, but later became critical of the organization for its mainstream tactics and liberal ideology. From its beginnings, SANE took pains not to appear radical: "pragmatic, not absolutist" (Katz, 1986, p. 30).

An early analysis of SANE membership also indicates considerable social and geographic unevenness. According to Sanford Gottlief, later Executive Director of SANE, the organization "recruited from the business and professional middle class" (quoted in Hodgson, 1976, p. 276). Almost eighty percent of responses and contributions came from New York, along with other eastern and a few California locations. Full page ads in the *Wichita Beacon* (circulation 100,000) elicited one contribution of only $8.00; ads in Buffalo, Indianapolis, Minneapolis, New Orleans, Dallas, and San Antonio drew no contributions (Katz, 1986, p. 30). Despite these problems and eastern concentration, SANE became the largest and most influential nuclear disarmament organization in America.

THE FALLOUT ISSUE

After its initial success, SANE continued its moderate strategy of education with numerous *New York Times* advertisements as its primary tactic. Most importantly, however, SANE decided to focus on the fallout scare, and did so by devoting its considerable resources to a test-ban treaty. This was a fateful, two-edged strategic decision for SANE. Although the fallout issue galvanized public opinion, it became an environmental rather than a disarmament issue for most Americans—a problem that could be eliminated by underground testing.

SANE's second ad, which appeared on March 24, 1959, in the *New York Herald Tribune* (a departure from the *Times* norm) was entitled "No Contamination without Representation." Taken from an editorial published earlier by Cousins in the *Saturday Review*, it charged that the American tests were poisoning the atmosphere of the entire world. "We do not have the right," the text claimed, "nor does any nation—to take risks, large or small, for other peoples without their consent." Civil rights leader Martin Luther King, Jr. enthusiastically endorsed and signed the ad, but critics claimed it was too emotional and pitched to exploit people's fears and anxieties. Others, like Lewis Mumford,[9] thought SANE should engage less in education and more in action—a theme that would later haunt the Freeze Movement.

After the Soviet Union announced a unilateral halt to nuclear testing, SANE urged the Eisenhower administration to follow suit. SANE organized a 19 day rally in New York, its first foray into direct action. On April 11, 1958, SANE leaders placed another full-page ad in the *New York Times*. It was not subtle. Half the page showed a mushroom cloud under the caption: "Nuclear Tests Are Endangering Our Health Right Now." The ad closed on an urgent note:

We must stop the contamination of the air, the milk children drink, the food we eat. While there is still time, let us come to life on this issue and take the moral initiative.

The ad was yet another attempt to assert moral-practical reasoning over instrumental rationality. However, several signers of the two earlier ads refused to endorse this ad because of its moralistic and frenzied tone (Katz, 1986, p. 32).

Public opinion, if swayed, was not entirely won over. In an article titled "How sane is SANE?", the April 21, 1958 edition of *Time* magazine accused Pauling and other signers of the ads of being Communists. Under their pictures ran the caption: "Defenders of the unborn. . .or dupes of the enemies of liberty?" In a Gallup poll (1972, pp. 1541, 1552-1553) in April of 1958, the American people rejected by a two-to-one margin a unilateral halt to nuclear testing, though almost half believed that continued testing would harm future generations.[10]

In June of 1958, the United States joined the Soviets in a moratorium on nuclear testing; both nations agreed to meet in Geneva to begin negotiations for a test ban treaty. SANE rallied to build support at home for the Geneva talks. During 1958 and 1959, SANE gathered thousands of signatures on petitions in support of a test ban treaty. It also arranged for nineteen world figures, including Eleanor Roosevelt and Martin Luther King, Jr., to address an appeal to the negotiators. Published as a full-page ad in the *New York Times* on October 31, 1958, "To The Men At Geneva" stressed the issues of fallout and nuclear proliferation.

SANE did not anticipate the difficulty of obtaining a test ban, let alone a partial test ban. John McCone, head of the Atomic Energy Commission and later director of the CIA, pressed to resume testing to develop the desired "clean" bomb; SANE published another full-page ad. Titled "Mr. Eisenhower, Mr. Khrushchev, Mr. Macmillan, The Time is Now!" this February 13, 1959 *New York Times* ad declared that "the political judgements of the Atomic Energy Commissions and the Defense Department provide dangerous counsel for Americans and the World." Fifty-eight members of prominent American elites, including Nobel Prize winning scientists H.J. Muller, Linus Pauling, and Harold Urey, and psychologist Gordon Allport, signed the ad.

Following this ad, SANE conducted a month-long "spring campaign," inaugurated with an Easter demonstration in New York and several other American cities. Cosponsored by AFSC, the demostrations were patterned after Britain's "Ban the Bomb" marches started by the Campaign for Nuclear Disarmament (CND).[11] As part of this campaign, New York SANE used one particularly effective tactic—a Times Square window display with Geiger Counter and literature on the dangers of fallout—to illustrate the fallout problem. A loudspeaker told the passing crowd: "Strontium-90 falls to the earth like rain. It can cause leukemia, cancer and bone disease." An estimated 40,000 people per day visited the display (which also challenged passers-by to an electronic computer game of tic-tac-toe), taking away 80,000 pieces of literature. Six thousand people signed a petition advocating a test ban. The *New York Post* and the *Nation* carried several feature articles on the display, and the Committee gained national television exposure on the "Today" show (Katz, 1986, p. 38).[12]

In another full-page ad in the *New York Times* on August 13, 1959, titled "Humanity Has A Common Will And Right To Survive," SANE claimed that the hearings had ignored the high level of radiation in the food supply. "More dangerous than nuclear fallout," the statement declared in an indictment of instrumental reasoning, "is the psychological fallout that blinds men to the peril and drives nations to seek solutions to world problems in ways that threaten world disaster." Among the sixty-nine signers were such well-known academics as C. Wright Mills and David Riesman, author Tennessee Williams, and actor Steve Allen. During this period SANE grew rapidly. By the close of 1959 it had 150 local committees organized in many cities, including chapters in Canada and Puerto Rico. Joining SANE had become chic and popular. In Hollywood, Steve Allen hosted the first chapter meeting in the Beverly Hills Hotel.[13] Within a few days such well-known actors as Marlon Brando, Kirk Douglas, Gregory Peck, Milton Berle, and Henry Fonda had joined, raising $5,000 for National SANE (see Katz, 1986, p. 74). The National Committee had become financially stable, paid off most of its debt, and raised and spent $50,000 on behalf of its program. During 1959 alone, SANE had run three full-page ads in the *New York Times*, distributed 202,000 pieces of literature, issued twenty-five action memos and placed spokespersons on more than fifty television and radio programs (Katz, 1986, p. 42). All these efforts had paid off. A Gallup (1972, p. 1643) poll taken in mid-November of 1959 showed that an overwhelming seventy-seven percent of those asked wanted "the agreement to stop testing H-bombs extended for another year." SANE exaggerated this public sentiment by claiming in another full-page ad on February 8, "Three Out of Four Americans Favor a Ban on Atomic Testing" (*New York Times*, 1960, p. 8).

FROM CRISIS TO TREATY

In May 1960, at the height of its influence and prestige, SANE held a major rally in Madison Square Garden, planned to coincide with the Eisenhower-Khrushchev summit. Speakers who addressed a crowd of 20,000 included Cousins, Eleanor Roosevelt, former Republican presidential nominee Alfred Landon, governor of Michigan G. Mennon Williams, and Walter Reuther of the UAW. Telegrams from Senators Hubert Humphrey, Jacob Javits, and Adlai Stevenson praised SANE. On the West Coast, the Hollywood chapter presented "An Evening with Harry Belafonte," attended by a sell-out crowd of 6,600 people (Nation, 1960, p. 482; Glazer, 1961, p. 290).

Yet this rally was the beginning of troubled times for SANE. On the eve of the rally, Senator Thomas J. Dodd of Connecticut, a strong opponent of the test ban, demanded that SANE purge their ranks of Communists (Glazer, 1961, p. 292).[14] Senator Dodd's primary target was Henry Abrams, the Garden rally organizer, a former leader of the American Labor Party and an activist in the 1948 campaign of Henry Wallace. Though there was no evidence that Abrams had ever belonged to the Communist Party, he refused on principle to tell Cousins whether or not he was a Communist. Cousins, very much concerned with "respectability," fired Abrams.

Dodd's charges, and Cousins reaction to them, initiated a crisis within SANE. Three national board members resigned in protest, including Robert Gilmore of the AFSC and Linus Pauling. A. J. Muste—the most prestigious of American pacifists and leading figure in FOR and the Committee for Non-Violent Action—severely criticized Cousins, and was particularly bitter over the fact that certain SANE leaders had met with Dodd's staff (Glazer, 1961, p. 293). To Muste, Dodd's accusations on the eve of the Madison Square Rally amounted to nothing less than sabotage and political blackmail at a time when the controversy over nuclear testing had reached a critical point.

The issue of communism had once again exercised a perverse influence on the peace movement. As executive director Homer Jack declared: "Ironically, SANE helped continue what it was supposed to be fighting against: McCarthyism and the Cold War Hysteria" (quoted in Katz, 1986, p. 62). About one-half of all chapters refused to adopt new anti-Communist charters—as demanded by Cousins—and were thus expelled from the organization. In retrospect, it is clear that SANE lost some badly needed support from radical pacifists and the emerging New Left. In the final analysis, the peace movement was, and continued to be, vulnerable to red-baiting.

Yet SANE's work for a nuclear test ban treaty, which was stalled after almost three years of negotiations, had become more urgent than ever. On August 13, the Soviets built the Berlin Wall, and two weeks later broke the three-year moratorium on testing. SANE immediately released a statement condemning this Soviet move and at the same time urged the United States not to follow suit. Yet SANE's plea was to no avail, as the United States almost immediately announced its own plans to resume testing, though for the time being only underground.

When it appeared that the test ban talks were all but dead (even though meetings were still perfunctorily held), President Kennedy gave a dramatic speech before the United Nations General Assembly. Using almost the same phrases that Seymour Melman—SANE board member and professor of economics at Columbia—had used a short time earlier, Kennedy challenged the Soviet Union to a "peace race" instead of an "arms race." He further announced his commitment to total disarmament, called for a strengthened U.N. and a negotiated settlement on Berlin (Katz, 1986, p. 69).

Encouraged by the President's apparent commitment to peace, SANE assumed leadership in pressing for the establishment of the U.S. Arms Control and Disarmament Agency, which Congress approved in September of 1961. At the same time, pressure mounted on Kennedy to resume atmospheric testing. Giving in to testing advocates, headed by Edward Teller and Pentagon officials, Kennedy announced on March 2, 1962 that the U.S. would resume atmospheric testing.

SANE responded by placing another series of full-page ads in the *New York Times*, focusing again on the fallout issue. The most brilliant and tactically successful, published April 16, 1962, showed a large picture of a grave looking Benjamin Spock peering down on a small child. The caption read: "Dr. Spock is worried." A few months earlier, Benjamin Spock, famed pediatrician and author of one of the all-time best sellers, *Baby and Child Care*, had sent SANE a donation and was quickly recruited as a national sponsor. In the text, Spock said: "I am worried not so much about the effects of past tests, but the prospects of future ones." Given that the tests were damaging children's health, he called the testing debate "a moral issue."

The impact of the ad was tremendous. It was reprinted in 700 newspapers worldwide. *Time* and *Newsweek* wrote articles on the ad, posters of it were widely displayed, and 25,000 reprints were distributed across the country (Katz, 1986, pp. 72-76). The usual reason cited for the ad's phenomenal success is the presence of America's most famous physician. Yet another reason, it seems to us, may be equally important. William Bernbach, SANE board member and partner in the prestigious Doyle, Dane, and Bernbach Advertising Agency, had offered his services to produce the ad. Under Bernbach's direction, Spock's original statement, which he had spent one month writing, was reduced from 4,000 words to some 200; the ad's visual content—minimal in previous SANE ads, was increased to three-quarters of a page: a sober, reflective Dr. Spock now spoke to the American people. This ad, and those immediately following, show that SANE had become more than ever a professional social movement organization with the wherewithal to mobilize impressive resources.

On July 5, 1962 SANE published another full-page ad. This one showed a bottle of milk with the poison label of a skull and crossbones. The caption read: "Is this what it's coming to?" The ad emphasized the threat to health by iodine-131, a claim that drew angry protests from the dairy industry (Katz, 1986, p. 77). The following month, Graphic Artists—a new chapter that would include such famous artists as Jules Feiffer and Ben Shahn—designed for SANE the famous "pregnant woman" poster. The caption read "1 Million unborn children will be born dead or have some gross defect because of Nuclear Bomb testing." The poster also appeared on thousands of subways and train platforms. On April 7, 1963, following the Cuban missile crisis,[15] SANE continued to press the fallout issue by publishing another tactically clever ad in the *New York Times*. Signed by over 200 dentists, the full-page ad showed three laughing children, captioned "Your children's teeth contain strontium-90."

Within the Kennedy circle, Cousins' personal influence was considerable. Indeed, he played a role in breaking the test-ban deadlock. At Secretary of State Dean Rusk's behest, Cousins met with Nikita Khrushchev at his Black Sea retreat, followed by a White House meeting with President Kennedy. A few days later, Cousins wrote a letter to Kennedy urging him to address the peace issue at his planned commencement address at the American University in Washington, D.C. Kennedy responded with a landmark speech in favor of detente, characterizing peace as "the necessary rational end of rational men," and appealing to the Soviets to join in relaxing tensions. The Soviets responded favorably; and on July 25, 1963, the U.S. and the U.S.S.R. signed a test ban treaty, albeit one that still permitted underground testing.

The treaty still needed a two-thirds vote of approval by the Senate; and SANE leaders threw themselves into the final campaign to secure ratification. Heading those opposed to ratification were Edward Teller and General Thomas Powers, chief of the Strategic Air Command. After a two month struggle, the Senate approved the treaty on September 24, 1963, capping for SANE a six year battle against atmospheric testing. President Kennedy then acknowledged Cousins' role in securing the treaty (Katz, 1986, p. 86).

As might have been expected, after the ratification of the partial test ban treaty, the tide of peace activism began to ebb. Nuclear testing, widely perceived as an environmental and health issue rather than one of disarmament, was now a non-issue. Because of their tactical decision to stress the fallout issue, SANE leaders had failed in defining nuclear weapons themselves as a social problem. Furthermore, many Americans assumed that their government was making progress in resolving the Cold War disputes with the Soviets, a perception later reinforced by the Nuclear Non-Proliferation Treaty of 1968, the Strategic Arms Limitation Treaty (SALT) of 1972, and a variety of other Great Power agreements. Nuclear pacifists, in particular, grew more "respectable" and merged in many instances into the liberal wing of the Democratic Party. SANE as an organization decayed, while older pacifist groups like WRL, WILPF and FOR "held up somewhat better, although they lost momentum" (Wittner, 1984, p. 280).

VIETNAM AND DECLINE

In the years after the 1963 treaty, American nuclear testing—conducted underground where the U.S. enjoyed a technological advantage—greatly accelerated, producing the most destructive weapons in human history. Peace activists, who had worked so diligently to halt the nuclear arms race, were either lulled into a false security or increasingly sidetracked by other concerns such as civil rights and the war in Indochina.

At SANE's sixth annual conference in 1963, two issues dominated: a proposed merger with the UWF, and the 1964 elections. Merger with UWF was attractive, given Cousins' and other SANE leaders' activities in both organizations. Moreover, the two organizations had many of the same policies, and perhaps more importantly, both were suffering from declining local activities and disinterest after the Test Ban Treaty. Yet there were important differences between the two groups as well. SANE had a much shorter history that UWF, and was less democratic in its decision-making; moreover, SANE had focused on a single issue in contrast to the UWF emphasis on more general and distant goals. Though the merger never occurred, the debate—both point and counterpoint—presaged the eventual SANE-Freeze merger of 1987.

The second issue, SANE's role in electoral politics, was also one that later plagued the Freeze. It was the position of Sanford Gottlieb, newly appointed political action director, that carried the day. Gottlieb, whose influence over the contemporary peace movement has been enormous, has all the qualifications for new class membership and for identification as a social movements professional. He received his B. A. from Dartmouth, and his doctorate in political science from the University of Paris. He later served as Executive Director of SANE, Executive

Director of New Directions, and visiting fellow at the Center for Theology and Public Policy. During the height of the Freeze Movement, he was Executive Director of United Campuses to Prevent Nuclear War (UCAM). In 1986 he became a senior analyst at the Center for Defense Information. At the 1963 meeting, Gottlieb argued "SANE will have to operate at two levels: as a political pressure group, and as a force within at least one of the two major political parties" (quoted in Katz, 1986, p. 90). Indeed, in the 1964 elections, SANE not only supported but worked for Lyndon Johnson—who was perceived as a peace candidate—and a variety of Congressional candidates.

Though SANE was an early opponent of the Vietnam War, the organization was perceived as conservative and overly cautious by more radical groups. After many antiwar groups started demanding the immediate withdrawal of American troops, SANE continued to press for only a negotiated settlement. Moreover, its opposition to the war was always respectable and "straight." "In middle class America," according to Gottlieb, "the neatly dressed, well groomed and restrained simply have greater acceptability, and their acceptability is 'transferrable' to the realms of ideas." To recognize this, he concluded, "is not to make value judgments about appearance, but to understand how to communicate" (quoted in Katz, 1986, p. 98).

Gottlieb may have been a political realist, but new leftists characterized SANE liberals as having a "style of politics which emphasizes cocktail parties and seminars rather than protest marches, local reform movements and independent bases of power" (quoted in Gitlin, 1987, p. 86). To liberal Kenneth Galbraith, longtime SANE activist, "the unearthly light of a handful of nuclear explosions would signal [Western civilization's] return to utter deprivation." New left poet Allen Ginsberg characterized the bomb in different terms: "America when will we end the human war?/Go fuck yourself with your atomic bomb." As Gitlin (1987, p. 86) summarizes:

> Galbraith's bomb was the threat to the affluent society, While Allen Ginsberg's was its extension. . . . Was the problem of nuclear weapons rooted in bad political-military strategy or a fundamentally wrong-thinking civilization? Galbraith's Bomb and Ginberg's, the reformist and the radical challenge, later quarreled for the imaginative possession of the ban-the-bomb movement.

Caught in a fierce battle between liberal and radical thinking, SANE clearly represented the former and thus "became the negative role

model for the New Left" and was seen as an apologist for the establishment (Katz, 1986, p. 99).

By 1967, SANE was severely divided over tactics concerning its
Vietnam opposition. Spock, who was then cochair, advocated increased
social protest and direct action; others, particularly Cousins, emphasized the "policy change" approach. By the close of the year,
Cousins and executive director Donald Keyes resigned because to them
the "committee had strayed too far to the left." Benjamin Spock, on the
hand, resigned because he felt SANE needed to cooperate with more
leftist peace organizations to "enhance SANE's efforts" (quoted in
Katz, 1986, p. 108). Sanford Gottlieb became the new executive director; and with that move SANE's middle-of-the-road position and commitment to electoral politics prevailed. According to Gottlieb (1972,
p. 8):

> The Right (in the peace movement) didn't know what the radicals thought and
> more importantly felt, and the Left was so busy emoting that they stopped
> thinking in this period. Ultimately, SANE's middle position triumphed.

In October of 1967, SANE became the first national organization to
advocate removing Johnson from office and became the leader of the
"Dump Johnson" campaign. In January of 1968, the SANE national
board voted to support the Eugene McCarthy presidential campaign.
By 1969, with Nixon in the White House, most SANE leaders agreed
that the Vietnam issue "must receive the major emphasis until the war
is ended." Reflecting this change from its original goal, SANE dropped
the word "nuclear" from its name and officially became SANE: A
Citizen's Organization for a Sane World (Katz, 1986, p. 129).

Yet SANE did not remain totally unconcerned and inactive in opposing the nuclear arms race after 1963. Worried that America's bombing
of Vietnam could escalate into a nuclear war, SANE placed a full-page
ad in the *New York Times* on July 22, 1965. The ad depicted a cockroach
in the middle of a blank space with the caption: "The winner of World
War III."

In early 1968, SANE set up a sub-committee to study the antiballistic
missile issue. The result was the famous ad and poster first published
on March 24, 1969 in the *New York Times*. The ad, captioned "From the
people who brought you Vietnam: The antiballistic missile system,"
depicted Edward Sorel's satirical drawing of four generals and one
Pentagon official lighting an ABM in the War Room in Washington.

The ad "became the most successful advertisement in recent history for a political cause," and was widely reprinted and used to illustrate articles on the military-industrial complex. The *Wall Street Journal* ran a front-page article entitled "People With a Cause (and money) Now Find It Pays To Advertise" (Katz, 1986, p. 129). SANE distributed 250,000 handbill-sized reprints and 5,000 large posters. Two Democratic Congressmen used this SANE ad in their newsletters critiquing the defense budget and the military-industrial complex (SANE World, 1969, p. 3). Using this resource, SANE lobbied to defeat the ABM authorization bill, and in May of 1969 sponsored a national conference for academics on ABM and the militarization of American society (Katz, 1986, p. 132).[16]

By the mid 1970s, SANE was suffering a severe financial crisis. Since American troops had left Vietnam, SANE, like other peace organizations, experienced a rapid decline in membership until it reached a low of 6,000. For the first time in SANE's history, payrolls were missed on several occasions and payments on loans could not be met. Since 1973, SANE had discussed merger with UWF, Clergy and Laity Concerned, and Council for a Livable World. In 1976, Gottlieb attempted to merge SANE with New Directions, a citizens lobby group working on a wide variety of global issues. Rebuffed by his national board, Gottlieb resigned from SANE to became arms control and disarmament director for New Directions.

Gottlieb's departure marked a low point for SANE. By July, 1977, the budget had a deficit of $28,830 with $32,373 still outstanding in loans (Katz, 1986, p. 137). The outlook for the new executive director, David Cortright, could not have been more bleak. Like his predecessor, Cortright had impeccable credentials as a member of the new class and a social movement professional. After graduating from Notre Dame in 1968, Cortright was drafted into the army, where he helped found GIs United Against the War in Vietnam. He later studied for three years at the Institute for Policy Studies, there writing a book, *Soldiers in Revolt*. Before joining SANE he was selected as a Fellow of the Robert F. Kennedy Memorial to study the problems of youth in the military. As the new Director of SANE Cortright managed, with the aid of an anonymous donor, to survive for the next couple of years until the "freeze" issue brought new life to the organization.

Under Cortright's leadership, SANE continued to emphasize two goals—nuclear disarmament and economic conversion. During the late 1970s, SANE worked closely with the National Campaign to Stop the

B-1 Bomber, to ratify the SALT II Treaty, and to defeat the MX missile system. At the same time, SANE pushed for national legislation on economic conversion. An economic conversion bill was drafted in 1977, mainly by cochair Melman and board member Lloyd Dumas, and introduced in Congress in 1978. SANE sought cooperation from labor groups and others in supporting the bill. SANE received a major boost in March of 1979, when William Winpinsinger, president of the million member Machinist Union (IAM), became cochair of SANE along with Melman. It was hoped that this move symbolized an emerging labor-peace alliance (Katz, 1986, p. 149). Yet with the American hostage crisis in Iran, the Soviet invasion of Afghanistan, and the defeat of the Carter administration, hopes for a speedy passage of economic conversion legislation were dashed. But better times lay ahead for SANE as the Freeze Movement developed in the 1980s.

The close of the 1970s marked a time to assess SANE's achievements. SANE was founded, as was the Atomic Scientists Movement and the *Bulletin*, and later the Freeze, on the basic premise of liberalism: that dialogue, facts and effective communication can set right a policy that has gone wrong. SANE limited its direct action tactics to persuasion and protest. It made no attempt to use noncooperation or civil disobedience because government, it was believed, was responsive to the people's will. Yet the question remains whether liberalism was and is appropriate for transforming the Cold War and the arms race into a lasting peace.

As Katz (1986, p. xii) maintains, "This strategy balanced between advocacy and acceptability accounts for both the organizations' strengths and weaknesses." By being effective and skilled advocates, SANE became the center of action for nuclear pacifists and liberals. It deserves credit, at least in part, for the establishment of the Arms Control and Disarmament Agency in 1961, the partial Test Ban Treaty of 1963, and the "Dump Johnson" coalition of 1968. Yet the same liberal strategy and tactics also limited its vision and curtailed its impact within both the peace movement and American politics. In its consuming desire to remain respectable, SANE spent too much energy fighting radicals within their own movement, thus ironically adopting a key part of the right wing agenda. In eschewing radicalism for respectability, SANE attempted to build a broad coalition. What it got was indeed broad, but also shallow—a following hardly committed to a long and difficult struggle. In the final analysis, SANE failed at its most important task: though it was able to define fallout as an environmental and health problem, it was never able to define nuclear weapons as a social problem.

More than any organization in the history of the peace movement, SANE presaged the Freeze. To study its organizational dilemmas, its strategic and tactical debates, is—in retrospect—disturbing. For the Freeze faced many of the same issues which had challenged and troubled SANE. Though in some respects history may have repeated itself, the Freeze was also unique in many ways. To this story we now turn.

Notes

1. The writings of newspaper columnist Walter Lippmann epitomized this change in American thought. International law, justice, morality, and disarmament were all chimeras; "we must consider first and last the American national interest," he wrote (1945, pp. 84-85). The moral drawn from the war by the "new realists" was that peace was contingent on national strength, a philosophy later resurrected in the extreme by the Reagan administration.

2. According to polls in mid-1945, fifty-five percent of all American respondents named the United States as the nation that had contributed most toward winning the war; even though in Britain, polls showed most chose the Soviet Union and only 3% so designated the United States (Wittner, 1984, p. 103).

3. This apparent contradiction between the desire for an imperial America, and the wish for some sort of world federalism once again demonstrates the dialectical nature of culture.

4. In August 1945, University of Chicago President Hutchins established an "Institute for World Government," pointing to its "symbolic" value given the University's key role in inaugurating the atomic age. Thereafter, the new Committee to Frame a World Constitution, headed by Hutchins, developed the "maximalist" position and made the University of Chicago the stormy center for elite intellectuals debating the question of world government.

5. In the 1950s, UWF adopted increasingly conservative positions, until they became virtually indistinguishable from official government policies. Norman Cousins, then vice-president of UWF, told a radio audience in 1952 that "America represents the hope of men everywhere" (quoted in Wittner, 1984, p. 224).

6. The cold war demonstrates once again the dialectics between economic and cultural/ideological factors. Except for the families who experienced the tragic death or wounding of a loved one, most Americans benefited from the dramatic economic revitalization brought about by the war. In 1940 the gross national product stood at $90 billion; by 1944 it had reached $200 billion. Corporate profits rocketed to the highest in history and unemployment fell to an all-time low. Dividends increased tremendously and the stock market boomed (Nelson, 1946, p. 216). Enthused by the wartime bonanza, leading corporate executives were instrumental in establishing the military-industrial

complex (see the ground-breaking work of Mills, 1956, and Domhoff, 1967). For example, Charles E. Wilson, then president of the General Electric Corporation (later head of General Motors and Secretary of Defense under Eisenhower), suggested an alliance of business and the military to maintain "a permanent war economy" (Coffin, 1964, p. 162). To accomplish this goal, Wilson urged that every corporation employ a former military officer to serve as a liaison to the Pentagon—a policy put into practice during the 1950s (Cook, 1961, p. 285).

7. Scientists had long known that extreme and deadly radiation would accompany an atomic blast. In 1941 Karl Compton, in a report to the "Uranium Committee" (predecessor to the Manhattan Project), had written of the possibility of "the production of violently radioactive materials. . .carried by airplanes to be scattered as bombs over enemy territory." Even if the bomb turned out to be less than the anticipated super-weapon, according to a report written later that year, the destructive effects on life of the bomb's radioactivity "may be as important as the explosion itself" (quoted in Rhodes, 1987, pp. 365, 386).

8. Ironically, Schweitzer's statement might have gone virtually unnoticed in the United States—the American press generally ignored it—had it not been for an official government reply. Willard Libby, Atomic Energy Commissioner, claimed the Schweitzer appeal was not based on the latest scientific evidence and that the slight risk of fallout was more than offset by national security needs. It was Libby's response, more than Schweitzer's appeal, which caused the ensuing furor.

9. As early as 1946, Mumford had questioned the sanity of a nuclear arms race. In an article titled "Gentlemen: You Are Mad" he wrote:

> The madmen are planning the end of the world. What they call continued progress in atomic warfare means universal extermination, and what they call national security is organized suicide. There is only one duty for the moment: every other task is a dream or a mockery. Stop the atomic bomb. Stop making the bomb. Abandon the bomb completely. Dismantle every existing bomb. Cancel every plan for the bomb's use. . . . Either dethrone the madmen immediately or raise such a shout of protest as will shock them into sanity. (pp. 4-6)

10. Using the term "unilateral" was confusing because the Soviets had already stopped testing. Yet again we see this ambivalence among the American people: prepare for war, but pursue peace.

11. Though contact between SANE and CND seems to have been limited, Homer Jack of SANE went to London in 1958 to help organize the campaign to protest Britain's explosion of its first H-bomb. CND wished to model itself after SANE in mapping a strategy directed towards influencing established figures. Though led by members of elites, such as Lord Russell, the CND was able to align itself with the labor movement, and through massive demonstrations became a powerful force in British politics (Myers, 1978).

12. The debate on the dangers of fallout continued. On May 5, 1959, a special Congressional Committee on Radiation began a four-day series of hearings on the hazards of fallout. It concluded that future testing in the atmosphere would soon lead to dangerous levels of strontium-90 in the bodies of everyone on earth. But when the report was referred to the AEC's General Advisory Committee, it concluded that the risk of radiation from fallout was very slight, amounting to less than five percent of natural radiation exposure and exposure from medical x-rays combined. SANE took strong

exception to this conclusion, and demanded the hearings be reopened so that critics of testing could present their case.

13. The site of this meeting, as with so many other gatherings, challenges the image of peace seekers as politically and culturally marginal.

14. Ironically, Dodd was a friend and neighbor of Cousins, and also a former member of UWF. As we noted in our treatment of the UWF controversy, Cousins had long been concerned about not appearing soft on Communism. In 1958 he had asked the FBI to furnish SANE with the names of any subversives who might attempt to infiltrate the local committees. Cousins was not alone in this concern: earlier in 1960, Norman Thomas had warned SANE's Executive Committee to "face up to the Communist issue" (quoted in Katz, 1986, p. 47).

15. This Super-Power confrontation demonstrated the political impotence of the peace movement in responding to a major political crisis. As Moscow and Washington moved along a collision course over the emplacement of Soviet missiles in Cuba, SANE and WILPF leaders urged Kennedy to halt the U.S. naval blockade of the island, remove U.S. missiles from Turkey, and submit the entire dispute to the U.N.. Kennedy ignored this advise, bringing the world to its closest brush with self-destruction. The Cuban missile crisis exposed the meager political influence of the peace movement, but also gave "new force to the criticisms raised by emerging New Left" spokespersons "that the issue of nuclear testing was distracting peace seekers" from the more important issues of Third World interventionism and the drive for nuclear supremacy (DeBenedetti, 1980, pp. 168-169).

16. When the Nixon administration began to discuss the possibility of fighting a "limited" nuclear war, SANE responded with another full-page ad in the *New York Times* on June 2, 1974 (p. 23), titled "From the people who brought you Inflation: Humane Nuclear War." Using the same war room scene employed in the 1969 ABM ad, this ad alerted readers to the dangers of a "limited" nuclear war plan—a counterforce strategy of targeting Soviet missiles that purportedly would limit civilian deaths—and to the connection between military spending and inflation.

Chapter 5

The Freeze:
Origins, Growth and Decline

In just seven years, the Freeze went full cycle. Beginning with Randall Forsberg's "Call to Halt the Nuclear Arms Race" in 1980, a massive and diverse social movement developed: by 1982 it had achieved impressive grass-roots organization, almost instantaneous national visibility, and surprising electoral victories. By 1986 the Freeze was in disarray: its national staff was reduced from 20 to 6; its Executive Director (only the second in its history) was fired after 18 months in office; and in 1987 the organization officially merged (some said it was subsumed) with SANE.

How might we account for the brief and volatile history of the Freeze? Pam Solo (1988) and Douglas Waller (1987), both movement insiders, have attempted to combine advocacy with analysis. Their books have great "insider" strengths and insights, but seem more interested in reforming the movement than analyzing it. Other scholars have attempted to combine their own advocacy and experience with a sociological perspective, generally resource mobilization.[1] As some of the sociologists admit, their works suffer from a tension between the academic and the advocate: is the purpose to understand, or to advance, the movement? Moreover, if the purpose is the latter, authors are prone to an ahistorical analysis, asserting that in any given year, the movement would advance or save itself by choosing one particular tactic or strategy rather than another.[2]

Our goal in this chapter and the next is to assess the Freeze—to understand its unprecedented successes and almost predictable failures. This chapter presents an overview of the Freeze in more or less chronological order. To understand its origins and growth (as well as its decline), we emphasize in particular the infrastructure from which the Freeze grew, the new movement organizations which characterized it, and the expression of the Freeze as part of the larger struggle of the new class. The following chapter is organized around key analytic themes, emphasizing particularly its internal contradictions and its relationship to the larger political structure. More specifically, it considers the role and import of external funding, the strategic and tactical dilemmas of the Freeze, and its social control and cooptation by the authorities.

Origins

With the close of the Vietnam war, and the economic recession which followed it, the mood of the country shifted toward the right. Yet the peace movement was beginning to appeal to new constituencies. During the 1970s, the women's movement grew in size and influence. The new feminists, not unlike their predecessors in the Suffrage movement, defined male violence and warfare as dangerous reflections of masculine culture and as a hindrance to women's equality. As a result, educated middle-class women assumed an increasing role in peace efforts (McAllister, 1982; Wittner, 1984, p. 294).

An unexpected source of support came from organized labor. As peace groups emphasized guns vs. butter issues, and as increasing unemployment made these issues more salient, some labor unions retreated from their previously hawkish line. Leaders such as the Machinists' William Winpinsinger denounced the arms race and called for a reordering of national priorities. Even some old guard labor leaders no longer automatically supported military initiatives. These trends towards a peace/progressive coalition were bolstered by the formation of the Democratic Socialist Organizing Committee (DSOC), which broke away from the defunct Socialist Party. Under the leadership of Michael Harrington, DSOC, and the organization it created, Democratic Socialists of America, made important progress in drawing together peace, labor, women's and racial justice activists.[3]

In 1976, the War Resisters League (WRL) organized a Continental Walk for Disarmament and Social Justice from Vancouver to Washington D.C. Their literature read: "Since 1945 we. . .have been preparing death for ourselves. . .[and] for future generations," the "death of nuclear annihilation." March leaders emphasized that "the case for disarmament must be taken to the people, town by town," and that the need to replace weapons systems with useful jobs and services must be explained (quoted in Davidon, 1979, pp. 31-32).

ANTINUCLEAR POWER

As these developments took shape below the surface of American political debate, one issue did capture public attention—the hazards of nuclear power. The early antinuclear power movement consisted mainly of environmentalists who focused on the ecological effects of nuclear power production, and scientists who were concerned with the safety of reactors. These groups either ignored nuclear weapons or assumed that they were needed for national security (Davidon, 1979; Mitchell, 1981). Many antiwar activists, on the other hand, had accepted nuclear power as desirable or irrelevant to opposition of nuclear weapons. Thus the two strains of the antinuclear movement initially operated quite independently of each other (Daubert and Moran, 1985).

One group that was influential in both strains was the Union of Concerned Scientists (UCS). Originally organized in 1968 by a small group of MIT scientists in opposition to the proposed antiballistic missile (ABM) system, the UCS turned its attention to research on safety problems of nuclear power reactors. In 1971, the UCS released a report claiming that the Atomic Energy Commission's safety program was seriously flawed, and that the Emergency Core Cooling System might not prevent accidental melt-downs (Mitchell, 1981).

This information, made into a public issue by Ralph Nader's national organization Critical Mass, galvanized many grass-roots groups into protesting at various nuclear power plants. The formation in 1976 of the Clamshell Alliance, engaged in direct action protest against the twin reactor nuclear power station in Seabrook, New Hampshire, served as the prototype organization for many similar alliances in the vicinities of local nuclear installations. One analysis of the environmental movement estimated that by the late 1970s, the number of grass-roots antinuclear groups had reached 1,000 (Wood, 1982). At the national level, such organizations as Friends of the Earth, Critical Mass, and the Sierra Club worked for restrictions on nuclear power plant development. Nuclear power became for many activists a symbol for a corporate-dominated, overcentralized, environmentally insensitive, inhumane society threatening human survival (Mitchell, 1981).

As early as 1975, some groups had attempted to make the "nuclear connection" between power and weapons (Davidon, 1979; Nelkin, 1981). The Rocky Flats Action Group, organized by the AFSC in 1974, staged protests at the nuclear weapons (not power) plant at Rocky Flats, near Denver, Colorado. The first demonstrations in 1975 brought out only 25 protestors, but by 1979 that number had reached 15,000 (Nelkin, 1981).

Also in 1975, the Union of Concerned Scientists drew up a Scientists' Declaration on Nuclear Power signed by 2,000 prominent scientists. This document, widely distributed, warned of the dangers of weapons proliferation and urged the President and Congress to suspend nuclear power plant exportation and reduce domestic construction. Increasingly, claims were advanced that catastrophic nuclear reactor accidents are possible, that proliferation of nuclear weapons is facilitated by the spread of nuclear power technology to other countries, that increasing numbers and kinds of nuclear weapons make nuclear war more likely, and that alternative energy sources such as sun, wind, geothermal, and vegetation are safe, renewable, and abundant (Davidon, 1981).

Yet there was considerable resistance to joining power and weapons issues. Strategic and political considerations discouraged nuclear power activists from taking on nuclear weapons. They believed that it was fundamentally difficult to mobilize a constituency on issues relating to national defense and foreign policy, issues perceived as too abstract or off-limits for public criticism. Activists in the peace movement feared that nuclear power issues would dilute and undermine the cause of disarmament, as well as attracting public criticism. Even so, many activists also realized that if the two issues could be joined, the movement's impact and constituency would be considerably broadened.

In 1978, an attempt was made to create an organizational link between environmental and peace groups. The impetus for this effort was the article "Doomsday Strategy," appearing in the February 1976 issue of the *Progressive*. Written by labor and antiwar activist, and editor of the *Progressive*, Sidney Lens, the article helped touch off widespread antinuclear concerns among activists. In December of 1977, Lens and a group of 1960s antiwar and religious leaders organized a national conference of groups from both the peace and antinuclear power movement, an effort that resulted in the creation of the "Mobilization For Survival" ("Mobe") in the summer of 1978. About 280 local, regional, and national peace, religious, feminist, and environmental groups joined in this federation (Davidon, 1979; Nelkin, 1981). No major national environmental group joined, but numerous local and regional antinuclear power groups affiliated with such national peace groups as the WRL, AFSC, WILPF, and Clergy and Laity Concerned (CALC) did.[4]

The new leadership included such nationally known activists as Lens, Benjamin Spock, war resister David Dellinger of the "Chicago Seven," and former Pentagon official Daniel Ellsberg. Lens (1982, p. 16) recalled that one aim in organizing the Mobe was to shift the "Left's attention back to the fundamental threat of the arms race." By the mid 1970s, Lens wrote, the arms race had been virtually forgotten. Antiwar activists were unfamiliar with the arcane jargon of nuclear strategy (counterforce, damage limitation, mutual assured destruction, and so on), and incapable "of mounting a factual challenge to the Pentagon's claims." If the struggling peace groups could join forces with the antinuclear power movement, a greater impact could be expected.

Mobilization for Survival espoused four aims: stop the arms race, eliminate nuclear weapons, eliminate nuclear power, and convert to human needs. The first action of the Mobe was to organize a mass march in New York City, timed to coincide with the First Special Session on Disarmament of the U.N. General Assembly, and aimed at stimulating mass consciousness-raising and mobilization. This June 1978 demonstration attracted a crowd of 20,000 and resulted in 400 arrests (including anti-war activist Daniel Berrigan). The Mobe also helped organize many antinuclear power protests in 1978, yet the two issues still remained relatively distinct. With its mixed agenda and diverse constituency, the Mobe experienced continued strain between the environmentalists and those who wanted to make disarmament the top priority.

Two precipitating incidents occurred in 1979 that helped fuse the two issues and capture the national limelight. In March of 1979 the Three Mile Island accident occurred at the nuclear reactor plant near Harrisburg, Pennsylvania; and in the winter of the same year, major newspapers ran numerous articles on the delayed health effects of the 1950s A-bomb testing in Utah and Nevada. Activists directly compared efforts to minimize the extent of the accident and to restore confidence at Three Mile Island to the reassurances provided during the period of atomic testing. As one physicist-activist stated:

> Nuclear power and nuclear weapons are two sides of the same coin. They are controlled by the same people, produced by the same corporations and serve the same political and financial interests. They give off the same radioactive poisons, generate the same deadly waste. . .and both threaten catastrophic

destruction. The people who brought you Hiroshima now bring us Harrisburg. (Kaku, 1979, p. 1)

The danger of radiation leaks and the disposal problem of nuclear wastes provided immediacy to the public, as the "fallout" issue had two decades earlier. Nuclear war, after all, was an abstract and remote possibility for most Americans. Indeed, many citizens had long "accepted the claim of political leaders that, by developing more advanced nuclear weaponry, the United States was more likely to avoid a nuclear holocaust" (Wittner, 1984, p. 294). Yet during this period of heightened awareness, many activists became convinced that the two issues could no longer be separated, and that the arms race was indeed the more pressing problem. As one activist put it:

> What are the dangers of nuclear power stations compared to the dangers of tens of thousands of bombs? What is the so-called worst reactor accident compared to a nuclear war? (quoted in Nelkin, 1981, p. 37)

A NEW COALITION

Several key existing organizations switched to, or revitalized around, the issue of nuclear weapons. The Union of Concerned Scientists, its prestige bolstered by its correct prediction of a nuclear power plant accident, returned its attention to the arms race in 1980. Henry Kendall, the prominent MIT physicist who had helped found the organization, pushed for the organization to return to its original goal. "The dangers of nuclear power are too small compared with nuclear war," he explained in an interview, "it seemed to me like a tangential issue" (Butterfield, 1982, p. 17). Influenced by a Yankelovich poll showing that there was both a latent concern and a widespread ignorance about nuclear weapons, and that more people would join peace groups if they understood the issues, the UCS planned to conduct teach-ins at various colleges in 1981 (Butterfield, 1982).

While Professor Kendall was trying to reorient the UCS in Cambridge, distinguished cardiologist and professor at the Harvard School of Public Health Bernard Lown was making a similar attempt with a group he helped start in 1961. At that time, a group of prominent Harvard and Boston area physicians, later known as Physicians for Social Responsibility (PSR), started to investigate the medical consequences of a nuclear war. In an article published in the prestigious *New England Journal of Medicine* in 1962, Lown, Jack Geiger, and Victor

Sidel wrote about the total inadequacy of any medical response in an American city hit by a nuclear bomb.

After the partial Test Ban Treaty was signed in 1963, PSR atrophied and was not revived until 1979, when Lown, with the help of the dynamic Australian-born Harvard physician Helen Caldicott, put new life into the moribund organization. Lown believed that doctors might accomplish what the physicist had never been able to do—arouse the public. "After all," he said,

> If you have a serious problem, where do you go? In a secular age, the doctor has become priest, rabbi, counselor. Then, too, the doctor brings all the credentials of a scientist." (quoted in Butterfield, 1982, p. 17)[5]

Concurrent with activist groups' shift in focus, interest in disarmament grew within the religious community. Religious antinuclear action had been confined to the historic peace churches of the Brethren, Mennonites and Quakers, and a fringe of "radicals" like the Berrigan brothers. Yet by the late 1970s, these militant activists had been joined by a number of traditional denominations.

In 1979, Billy Graham, perhaps the single most visible religious figure in the U.S., and long a virulent Cold-Warrior, began to preach the evils of nuclear weapons. This "new" Billy Graham was joined by the traditionally promilitary Catholic church, giving the peace movement a new and powerful base of support. A number of Catholic bishops and even organizations like the conservative National Association of Evangelicals also began to call for nuclear disarmament. More moderate churches like the Presbyterians and the Episcopalians began to establish "peace commissions" to examine American military policy and domestic and international socioeconomic problems (Leavitt, 1983, p. 10).

This gradual expansion of the peace movement, however, had little impact on national politics. In the wake of a series of foreign policy shocks such as the "loss" of Iran and Nicaragua, President Carter acquired the label of being "weak." After the Soviet invasion of Afghanistan in December, 1979, Carter withdrew the SALT II treaty from Senate consideration and promised a massive military build-up, including the controversial MX missile. This expensive and purportedly superaccurate, hard-target killing missile was widely perceived as a counterforce, first-strike weapon. In 1980, Carter issued his Presidential Directive-59 (P.D. 59), updating the doctrine of flexible response, which empowered American forces to undertake limited nuclear strikes against Soviet military facilities.[6]

Candidate Reagan, denouncing SALT II and asserting "spending gaps", "counterforce gaps", and increased Soviet expansionism, promised to "rearm America" with the aim of closing the "window of vulnerability" and attaining "nuclear superiority" over the Soviets. Not surprisingly, the great majority of political commentators predicted that a further rightward swing loomed on the electoral horizon. The great defense debate was not whether to raise the military budget and expand the nuclear arsenal, but how much to expand. SALT II was shelved, and the phrase "arms control," let alone "disarmament," rapidly went out of fashion. A 1982 opinion poll showed that for the first time in nuclear history, a large proportion of Americans, 41%, believed that the Russians had a stronger nuclear arsenal; only 7% believed the U.S. had a superior force (Kramer, 1983, p. 17). In such a climate, little heed was paid to the resurgence of a wide range of peace groups.

Forsberg's Call

The history of the "Call" has been widely told. By 1980, the infrastructures for a new social movement was in place. What was needed was a unifying concept. The issue entrepreneur to provide that key idea was a then little known, thirty-eight year old defense analyst by the name of Randall Forsberg.

With her elite educational background and experience, Randall Forsberg is clearly a member of the new class. She received a B.A. in English from Barnard College, Columbia University, and taught briefly at Bryn Mawr. Forsberg's first contact with arms control came in 1968, when she moved to Stockholm with her Swedish husband. There she took a job as a typist at the government supported Stockholm International Peace Research Institute (SIPRI). Becoming interested in what she typed, Forsberg advanced to become an editor, researcher, and then a writer in her seven years at the Institute.

In 1974, Forsberg returned to the United States to enter graduate studies in arms control at MIT. She quickly became immersed in the activist politics of Cambridge and together with the Boston Study Group (mainly analysts from MIT and Harvard), coauthored the *Price of Defense* (1979). This book claimed that a purely defensive military posture would require only about half of the then current U.S. military force strength. After returning from Sweden, she completed her doctoral coursework in Political Science at MIT. As a graduate student, she received Green, Warburg, and MIT fellowships, spending one year as a visiting fellow at the Harvard Program for Science and International Affairs. She also taught at Boston University. In 1983, she received the coveted MacArthur Award, a five-year, full-support grant, "in recognition for her accomplishments in defense studies and arms control."

Yet Forsberg is unique in the Freeze Movement. Prior to her involvement in the Nuclear Weapons Freeze Campaign, she avoided as much as possible—even disdained—staff work in social movements. She views herself as an arms control analyst, not a social movements professional, a distinction that created some tension with the peace movement. Nevertheless, Forsberg became frustrated with both the academic and peace communities. Academic research and teaching, according to her, "does not aim to provide an educated basis for efforts for constructive social change," nor does it "refute the intellectual challenges of the activists", it "simply ignore them." In the peace community Forsberg also found "little debate about conflicting assumptions and worldviews" among activists themselves.

> In none of these settings—research, educational, or activist—was there any attempt to undertake a systematic investigation of the conflicting assumptions held by scholars, educators, and activists about the causes of war and the possible route to a stable, disarmed peace. (Forsberg, 1984, p. vii)

The key to disarmament progress, Forsberg became convinced, lay in a series of clearly stated, intermediate steps around which the whole spectrum of peace groups could rally. Such steps must be realistic, significant, and attractive to the public. Forsberg stated:

> If you looked for a common denominator, a near-term future position that would be profound enough so that the pacifists would work on in, and moderate enough to interest the people concerned with institutional change. . .so that you could unite all the people in the movement, then this disarmament group would comprise an enormous movement. . . . If all these groups worked. . .on one proposal they would have enormous disseminating power. (quoted in Leavitt, 1983, p. 12)

But in order for a movement to succeed, Forsberg was convinced that the American middle class had to be mobilized. "No major disarmament effort can succeed without the support of the majority of middle class, middle-of-the-road citizens" she stressed (quoted in Leavitt, 1983, p. 13).

The peace community, with its existing organizational structure and communications network, was to be the vehicle for mobilizing the middle class. Forsberg thought that activists' politics were often tedious and unproductive, but saw no practical alternative. Her first task was to persuade the various peace groups to go along with her more moderate ideas. She contended that the activists' disarmament proposals were too broad, sweeping, or politically unworkable, especially given the conservative atmosphere of the late 1970s.

Various freeze proposals had been offered previously. In the summer of 1979, the AFSC and CALC adopted a proposal for a three year moratorium on the production and deployment of new nuclear weapons. This unilateral proposal was based on the belief that the Soviet Union would reciprocate, making it possible for both sides to then negotiate major reductions. The Mobe proposed a moratorium on both nuclear weapons and nuclear power. Senator Mark Hatfield, with the support of the Sojourners religious community and Richard Barnett's Institute for Policy Studies, introduced an amendment to SALT II, calling for a U.S.-Soviet freeze on strategic nuclear weapons deployment.[8]

Speaking at rallies, teach-ins, and arms control symposia around the country, Forsberg argued for a mutual and comprehensive U.S.-Soviet freeze of the arms race. Addressing a December 1979 meeting of the Mobe, she claimed that a complete halt to testing, production, and deployment was politically feasible because it was bilateral and because it was verifiable without relying on the Russians. She further told movement leaders that unless they all united around such a goal, they would never accomplish anything substantial.

> We will only succeed if we work together. This is a viable idea. It is no doubt the best idea. I urge you to adopt this idea and do it. (quoted in Leavitt, 1983, p. 15)

These arguments were persuasive to many leaders of the various peace, social justice, and research organizations at the convention. Forsberg's expertise and her connections with the scientific/arms control community also seemed attractive to some activists who saw such a liaison as an advantage. Forsberg was given the mandate to distill her ideas for publication.

At this time Forsberg left MIT to set up her own think tank, the Institute for Defense and Disarmament Studies.[9] She spent the winter detailing her freeze proposal, seeking advice from sympathetic MIT arms experts such as Philip Morrison, a prominent scientist from the Manhattan Project, and George Rathjens, chief Pentagon scientist during the Eisenhower administration and arms control specialist for the Carter administration. By April 1980, Forsberg had a draft of the *Call to Halt the Nuclear Arms Race*. The *Call*, a four page proposal that would become the founding document of the Nuclear Weapons Freeze Campaign, began with the preamble:

> To improve national and international security, the United States and the Soviet Union should stop the nuclear arms race. Specifically, they should adopt a mutual freeze on the testing, production and deployment of nuclear weapons and of missiles and new aircraft designed primarily to deliver nuclear weapons. This is an essential, verifiable first step toward lessening the risk of nuclear war and reducing the nuclear arsenals. (Nuclear Weapons Freeze Campaign, 1982)

This freeze proposal was different from earlier ones in that it called for a halt to production, as well as testing and deployment, of all new nuclear weapons. It also differed from activist proposals in that it was not unilateral. The *Call* went on to state that the U.S. and the Soviet Union together possessed 50,000 nuclear weapons, a vast overkill, since a tiny fraction of these weapons could destroy all cities in the northern hemisphere, and that the two superpowers planned to build an additional 20,000 over the next decade, along with a new generation of missile systems. These new weapons programs, if not stopped, would pull the "nuclear tripwire tighter." At a time when "economic difficulties, political dissension, revolution and competition for energy supplies are rising worldwide," the *Call* continued, hair-trigger readiness for a massive nuclear exchange will make the world a much more dangerous place in the 1980s and 1990s than ever before. The *Call* also put forth the claims that a "parity" or rough equivalence existed between the superpower arsenals (contrary to conservatives' claims), that a comprehensive freeze could be verified through national technical means (i.e., the vast array of satellites, radar systems, and listening posts), and that there was an urgency to freeze now, since a freeze would prevent the planned destabilizing systems which would undermine deterrence.

The *Call* was endorsed by three MIT faculty: Philip Morrison, George Rathjens, and Bernard Feld, chairman of the Pugwash conferences and editor-in-chief of the *Bulletin*. The AFSC agreed to publish an initial 5,000 copies of the *Call*, and along with FOR and CALC, formed the Ad Hoc Task Force for a Nuclear Weapons Freeze, and worked to disseminate the idea.

Growth of the Movement

FROM GRASS-ROOTS TO NATIONAL ORGANIZATION

Independent of Forsberg's work, the stirrings of a new grass-roots movement began in western Massachusetts. This new movement was led by a little-known issue entrepreneur and Quaker, Randall Kehler. From our perspective, Kehler may be seen as both a social movements professional and member of the new class. A graduate of Phillip Exeter Academy and Harvard University, where he received a B. A. in Government, Kehler also attended graduate school at Stanford University. From 1967 to 1970 he was a staff member of the War Resister's League, after which he spent 22 months in federal prison (listed in his resume) for draft noncooperation. Before assuming his position as the first National Coordinator for the Freeze Clearinghouse, he was a founder and staff member with the Traprock Peace Center, which promoted disarmament and the nonviolent resolution of conflicts. He was also an antinuclear power activist and member of the Ad Hoc Strategy/Planning Committee for the Formation of the National Campaign for a Nuclear Weapons Freeze. After leaving the Freeze, he became a staff member with the Peace Development Fund, a foundation heavily involved in financing the Freeze.

In 1979, Kehler became intrigued with Senator Hatfield's freeze amendment to SALT II. In January of 1980 he and his colleagues in Deerfield launched a nine-month campaign to put on the ballot in three Western Massachusetts state senate districts a referendum calling on the President to propose a mutual nuclear weapons freeze to the Soviets. They needed to collect 12,000 signatures in each district to place the freeze proposal on the ballot. With the help of AFSC, they developed a public outreach program stressing the consequences of a nuclear war, the economic hardships of the arms race, and the merits of a mutual freeze. The grass-roots response was gratifying: signatures came quickly, and with them, volunteers and donations. The endorsement of Republican Congressman Silvio Conte added key support before the election. On November 4, 1980, the freeze passed in the three districts with a 59% margin. Even more significantly: 30 of the 33 towns that Ronald Reagan carried also passed the freeze.

The Freeze referendum that worked so well in Western Massachusetts would be repeated many times across the country. Improbable as it seemed, this campaign was to become the model for the entire movement, and the charismatic Randall Kehler, who told us in 1986 that his personal heroes were A. J. Muste, Gandhi, and Martin Luther King, Jr., became the principal tactician for the National Freeze Campaign.

Other organizations quickly become involved: WILPF, Sojourners, William Sloane Coffin's Riverside Church, the Coalition for a New Foreign and Military Policy (CNFMP) and Pax Christi USA, all pledged their support to the budding Campaign and made the Freeze their priority.[10] A number of church groups also became active in the Freeze. Due largely to the efforts of Harvard theologian Harvey Cox, who previously had worked with Forsberg in a peace study group, the National Council of Churches adopted a Freeze resolution in May of 1980. The endorsement of these groups gave the Campaign a large and solid base of experienced local activists, many of whom had developed extensive ties within their communities.

In September, representatives of about a dozen organizations met in New York to discuss longer-term strategy for promoting the Freeze. Forsberg had written a strategy paper outlining a five-year campaign of electoral and legislative pressure politics. Most of the organizational leaders present had no objection to the five-year plan, but felt that local organizers needed to be involved from the beginning, and pushed for a national organizing and strategy conference. This conference was to have both national leaders and a wide selection of local organizers so that all could provide input into strategy.

Forsberg, more elitist and less experienced than the activists present, saw little need for such a conference, but agreed to participate. She later explained in an interview:

> I had felt from early on that this idea [of a freeze] would survive or fall on the basis of its innate attractiveness to people, not on the basis of its structure; that if it was a good enough idea it would simply spread and motivate people. . . . But I think that the little core group. . .had already decided that

we had to do it. . . . So because I was very inexperienced. . . . I was prepared
to go along. (quoted in Leavitt, 1983, p. 20)

In March of 1981, with $5,000 donated by Boston businessman Alan
Kay, the First National Strategy Conference of the Nuclear Weapons
Freeze Campaign was held at the Center for Peace Studies at Geor-
getown University in Washington, D. C. It was attended by over 300
national leaders and local organizers from 33 states (Nuclear Weapons
Freeze Campaign, 1981).

During the three-day conference an intense struggle evolved over the
organizational structure, and the tactics and strategies of the future
Campaign. Forsberg was determined to keep it a single-issue, moderate
campaign, uncomplicated by longer-term questions beyond a freeze,
and confined to established political pressure tactics. She also insisted
that it should become a populist, middle-class movement, and not be
controlled by a small cadre of leftist activists. As she explained:

> I was very concerned that the idea should not be co-opted and sort of
> diminished by the more radical peace groups with whom I was working and
> relying on, by their expressing the freeze in language that reflected all these
> other values—the sort of pacifist-vegetarian anti-corporate value system—
> and by limiting the actions made in its name to direct action/civil dis-
> obedience kinds of things. I was very anxious that the language be very
> neutral and the ultimate focus be very political, and therefore very middle
> class, within-the-system, working with the system and within the system
> rather than alienating it from the system and giving up on it. (quoted in
> Leavitt, 1983, p. 23)

Thus Forsberg defined "political" action in a very narrow sense,
equating it with established political practices. Activists who wanted to
use a variety of political actions, including direct action and civil
disobedience, would have to defer to Forsberg's wishes or drop out of
the Campaign.

To make sure that east coast activists would not gain control over the
Campaign, and to foster a heartland image, the proposed Clearinghouse
and headquarters of the Freeze would be located in St. Louis, Missouri.
Some activists had felt that the AFSC, being the largest and best
financed organization, should house the Freeze in their national offices
in Philadelphia. But Forsberg and others prevailed. According to one
participant, this decision to locate the Freeze in the mid-west meant
that it "was not going to be owned by any of these organizations" and

"its dominant characteristic was not going to be pacifism. . .it was going to be more broadly American" (quoted in Leavitt, 1983, p. 24).[11]

The most bitter debate came over the single versus multiple issue. Many activists felt the Freeze was too narrow, that it ignored the underlying forces fueling the arms race, such as the military-industrial complex and Third World interventionism. Others, concerned that it was mainly a white, middle-class campaign, thought that there should be more emphasis on economic issues to facilitate outreach and coalition with minority groups. After a long and acrimonious floor debate, the more moderate faction prevailed. As Currie Burris of CALC stated:

> A lot of us. . .felt that diluting the *Call* that way [to stress economic conversion to counter unemployment] would ruin the potential for outreach to a broader segment of the U. S. public and it might look like just another left wing radical thing. . .that had a long political agenda behind it . . . . So it was bitter. . .and some people left the campaign and never came back. (quoted in Leavitt, 1983, p. 26)

In the end, Freeze leaders decided that minorities and controversial issues were to be sacrificed for broad, middle-class appeal. At this point, several groups, such as the Mobe and WRL, all but opted out of the Campaign. These two groups did endorse the Freeze, but never made it a priority.

The organizational structure of the Campaign also was a point of contention. Most activists were suspicious of any kind of centralized control, whereas Forsberg and others saw a need for accountability to a national committee. Something of a compromise was reached. To forestall centralized control, final authority over strategy was placed with the National Conference itself, to be held annually; every Congressional district would be eligible to have one voting candidate. On the other hand, a fifty member National Committee, meeting twice a year, was empowered to develop overall policy and strategy, and make ongoing decisions for the Campaign; this National Committee would hire and supervise the national staff. A ten member Executive Committee would meet monthly to oversee interim decisions between National Committee meetings. The guiding principle of the Freeze Campaign was to be "national coordination" with "local self-determination" (Nuclear Weapons Freeze Campaign, 1981). Randall Kehler was hired as National Coordinator and Executive Director, and moved to St. Louis when the Clearinghouse opened there in January of 1982.

COLD WAR RHETORIC AND EXPANSION

After the first national meeting, the Freeze grew rapidly. It seems supremely ironic, but another example of the dialectics of history, that credit for this growth goes to Ronald Reagan.[12] His Cold War rhetoric about the evils and dangers of Soviet communism, his complete rejection of arms control, and his talk about fighting and winning a "limited" nuclear war, frightened and mobilized not just the peace community in Europe and in the U. S., but also a broad spectrum of previously uninvolved citizens. As *Newsweek* (1982b, p. 24) stated:

> The saber-rattling rhetoric of the President has prompted vast and growing numbers of mainstream Americans to look past the technicalities of arms-control procedures to a simple, symbolic first step such as the freeze.

It was not that the Reagan nuclear doctrine was that different from his predecessors'. What was different was the administration's blunt language, stripped of euphemistic and cumbersome jargon. What previous defense secretaries had vaguely called "options," Caspar Weinberger called "nuclear war fighting." When Secretary of State Haig bluntly talked about firing a nuclear warning shot over Europe to deter possible Soviet expansion, recruiting thousands of Europeans of the disarmament movement with a single phrase, he was not stating a new policy but only making an old one explicit. When under-secretary of defense T. K. Jones made the widely publicized statement that a fully effective defense against a nuclear attack could be improvised with a shovel and a door over a hole in the ground, even conservatives became alarmed (Center for Defense Information, 1983). With his own sense of timing, Weinberger chose August 9, 1981, Nagasaki Day, to announce the manufacture of the controversial neutron bomb. As Waller (1987, p.18) states:

> What Ronald Reagan did, that no other president had ever done was to rip off the psychic bandage that covers public fears and anxieties over nuclear weapons. Americans, simply put, do not like to dwell on the subject of nuclear war, and they become skittish when their leaders talk about it.

The grass-roots Freeze campaign fed on the Reagan Administration rhetoric. In May of 1981, the Massachusetts state legislature almost unanimously endorsed the Freeze; Oregon, New York, Connecticut,

Maine, Vermont, Minnesota, Wisconsin, Kansas, and Iowa soon followed. At the same time, the most sophisticated Freeze Campaign developed in California under the direction of millionaire Harold Willens. In 1972 Willens, an opponent of the Vietnam War, had helped finance the liberal think-tank, Center for Defense Information, which often challenged information released by the Pentagon. In September of 1981, inspired by the western Massachusetts example, Willens launched a state-wide Freeze Referendum campaign. The initial goal was to collect the needed 346,000 signatures, but six months later the campaign had more than 600,00 signatures, and boasted such prestigious supporters as Nobel laureate Jonas Salk, Archbishop Quinn of San Francisco, Cardinal Manning of Los Angeles, Rabbi Joseph Asher, and Norman Cousins (now on the faculty of UCLA Medical School), as well as numerous Hollywood celebrities. Friends of the Earth, with its national headquarters in San Francisco, also endorsed and worked for the Freeze, encouraging other environmental groups to follow suit.[13]

During the early 1980s, a symbiotic relationship developed between the Freeze and a number of national organizations. Several groups made vital contributions to the Freeze and in turn benefited greatly in terms of organizational growth. PSR was one of them. This group of physicians was revitalized when Helen Caldicott became president in 1980. An internationally recognized leader of the antinuclear weapons movement, Caldicott is clearly a member of the new class. She is popularly identified as a pediatrician; in fact she was a professor at the Harvard University Medical School before she resigned to devote full-time to the movement.[14] After leaving PSR, Caldicott founded Women's Action for Nuclear Disarmament (WAND).

PSR had developed the tremendously effective pedagogical tactic of showing how a megaton bomb would destroy Boston, and the utter futility of a medical response to such an occurrence. This tactic was used at the nation's leading medical schools, with an appropriate city substituted as the exemplar of annihilation. Many local chapters, affiliated with medical schools, were established. In concert with the Council for a Livable World, PSR participated in more than 150 teach-ins at American colleges and universities in November of 1981. The film "The Last Epidemic" showing the consequences of a nuclear bomb dropped on San Francisco, was widely shown and also proved to be a very effective mobilizing device.

The conservative American Medical Association (AMA) passed a resolution in December of 1981 which called on doctors to assume responsibility for informing their patients of the dangers of a nuclear war. Howard Hiatt, dean of the Harvard School of Public Health who coined the phrase "the last epidemic," called on President Reagan and described to him what would happen if a one-megaton bomb should explode over Washington. Hiatt also created a new chair at Harvard devoted to the effects of nuclear war on health (Stone, 1982; World Press Review, 1982).

PSR officially endorsed the Freeze in the Summer of 1981. Physicians conducted "bombing runs" at local gatherings, and sought support for the Freeze. As the Associate Director of PSR explained:

> People were really scared out of their pants by our presentations and saying "What can we do?" So we in turn helped build the freeze movement. The fact that we could give a message and then say here's a course of action also helped build our own organization in the sense that our members saw purpose to their educational work. (quoted in Leavitt, 1983, p. 31)

PSR experienced a phenomenal growth in membership. In 1979 the group consisted of a handful of Boston area (mainly Harvard) physicians; by 1982 membership had reached 18,000 with 300 new applications coming in each week. The organization's budget for 1982 was $1.6 million, its staff consisting of twenty-four full-time employees (Butterfield, 1982; Geiger, 1984). By 1983 PSR had 30,000 members in 180 chapters across the country. Co-founder Jack Geiger, Professor of Community Medicine at City College of the City University of New York, summed up PSR's effectiveness:

> We have cultural authority, we have known commitment to preserve life, we are a politically conservative group. . . . we contributed a level of scientific detail. (1984, p. 43)

Thus could self-described conservatives support the Freeze.

To complement PSR, Bernard Lown organized the International Physicians for the Prevention of Nuclear War. This group held its first conference in 1981, with leading physicians from the U.S., the U.S.S.R., and nine other countries participating. Subsequent annual conferences attracted participants from over 30 countries, the organization becoming quite influential in Western Europe (Wright, Rodriguez, & Wartzkin, 1985). By 1986 their membership had reached 136,000, the same year the group was given the Nobel Peace Prize (Forsberg, 1986).

The guild approach to organizing appealed to other professional groups as well. In May of 1981, a two-day conference organized by the

Chaplain's office at Harvard held a series of occupation-specific workshops. These workshops spawned, among others, the Business Alert to Nuclear War, Educators for Social Responsibility, Nurses Alliance for the Prevention of Nuclear War, High-Technology Professionals for Peace, Artists for Survival, Musicians Against Nuclear Arms, Computer Professionals for Social Responsibility, Communicators for Nuclear Disarmament, and the Lawyers Alliance for Nuclear Arms Control (LANAC). Most of these groups were set up with the Freeze as their primary goal. This "middle-class" organizing approach served to bring thousands of new recruits to the Campaign. As a spokesperson for LANAC contended, the guild approach worked extremely well, since a letter or phone call from a peer was a key factor in convincing conservative professionals to join the movement (Butterfield, 1982, p. 28).

The Union of Concerned Scientists staged an impressive series of Veterans Day teach-ins on nuclear war, starting in 1981 at 150 colleges and universities across the country. UCS established United Campuses to Prevent Nuclear War (UCAM) in 1982, with Sanford Gottlieb, formerly of SANE, as its Executive Director. UCAM's aim was to establish affiliated chapters on college and university campuses, to help establish peace studies curricula, and to assist in the convocations. That year, more than five hundred colleges had such convocations, in concert with PSR at medical schools and LANAC at law schools. The timing of the first convocation was excellent, coming in the wake of huge European demonstrations against the U.S. deployment of Pershing II and ground-launched cruise missiles. The European protest had sensitized the American news media, which started to look for domestic counterpoints. As the *New York Times* later commented:

> The Veterans Day events proved an important turning point [for the Freeze], attracting widespread attention in the press and from television, focusing still more public interest on the issue. (Butterfield, 1982, p.17)

All major newspapers and magazines carried features on the convocation. For example, *Newsweek* ran an article titled "Anti-Nukes, U.S. Style" (1981, pp. 44-49), with a picture of Notre Dame President Theodore Hesburgh addressing a crowd and quoted as saying: "The world's other problems become meaningless if we don't solve this one—and do it quickly." Other speakers charged the Reagan Administration with having lost all credibility on nuclear matters, likening the "window of vulnerability" to the bomber and missile "gaps" of the

1950s and 1960s. The real gaps, charged Joshua Cohen, an MIT political scientist, are "gaps of credibility."

MOMENTUM BUILDS

Two events early in 1982 accelerated the momentum of the Freeze Movement. One was Jonathan Schell's three-part series in *The New Yorker*, later published as the best-selling 1982 book, *The Fate of the Earth*. Schell eloquently pleaded for a halt to the seemingly inexorable march toward a nuclear holocaust. Nothing short of the fate of the planet, he claimed, was at stake. The book became popular in intellectual circles, and was widely quoted in peace literature.

In April of 1982, peace activities coalesced nationwide with Ground Zero Week, a week-long endeavor to educate the public about the dangers of nuclear war. Extensive and dramatic press reports claimed that over one million Americans, in more than 600 cities and 350 college campuses, attended seminars, watched films, and flocked to rallies (Waller, 1987). *Newsweek* reported that speakers—who spanned the ideological spectrum from "leftist activist Seymour Melman to the evangelical friend of presidents, the Rev. Billy Graham"—decried the arms race. Yet the majority of participants represented a cross-section of citizens.

> They are homemakers and businessmen, clerks and doctors, clergymen, teachers, scientists and even military men—a cross section of Americans suddenly enlisted in a loosely linked, burgeoning campaign to end the nuclear arms race. Their numbers are mushrooming now like the deadly clouds they are determined to forestall, growing faster than even their leaders ever expected. (pp. 20-25)

Though their arguments sometimes are "simplistic or emotional," the article continued, the Freeze Movement managed to move the crucial issue of nuclear weapons out of the "rarefied domain of think-tank strategists and Pentagon planners."

The events were sponsored by the Washington, D.C. based organization, Ground Zero, founded in 1980 by physicist and former National Security Council staffer Roger Molander. Author of the glibly written bestseller *Nuclear War, What's In It For You?* (1982), Molander stressed educational and nonpartisan routes to achieve arms control. Taking its name from the point on the earth directly below the center of a nuclear explosion, Ground Zero soon had chapters in over 140 cities.

Two established groups which started to work for the Freeze, and in turn benefitted organizationally, were SANE and Common Cause. In 1981, the New Jersey SANE organized the successful statewide Freeze Campaign which, in turn, spurred the National Committee to get involved. On May 23, 1982, SANE placed two full-page ads in the *New York Times* in support of the Freeze. SANE and its affiliated political action committee and Education Fund then conducted extensive lobbying efforts, educational programs, and broadcasts on 120 radio stations on behalf of the Freeze. During the early 1980s, SANE's membership, staff, and prominence skyrocketed. By 1983 its membership had reached 75,000, its Washington staff increasing to twenty, and by 1984 the word "Nuclear" reappeared in their full organizational name (Katz, 1986, p. 154).

Common Cause, a public interest group established in 1970, started its Congressional lobbying efforts on behalf of the Freeze in 1982. Membership contributions to Common Cause were solicited in the name of nuclear disarmament and the Freeze. The aim was to raise the issue of the nuclear arms race to the top of the national agenda, for which Common Cause is "uniquely qualified" (*Common Cause*, undated). Its membership had reached 250,000 in 1985 (Forsberg, 1986).

Perhaps most important in gaining momentum for the Freeze were the actions of the Catholic hierarchy. The Catholic Bishops' endorsement of the Freeze legitimized the Campaign in the mainstream religious community and brought the leadership of many other denominations into the movement. The National Conference of Catholic Bishops began discussing the Church's stand on war and peace issues in 1980. The two-year deliberation resulted in the highly publicized and controversial pastoral letter, "The Challenge of Peace: God's Promise and Our Response" (National Conference of Catholic Bishops, 1982).[15]

The document based its opposition to nuclear weapons and the arms race on the principles of the traditional just war theory formulated by St. Thomas Aquinas.[16] The Pastoral concludes that nuclear war is immoral because it would violate all the principles of a just war. The letter also expressed "profound skepticism" that any nuclear exchange would remain "limited," and urged NATO to adopt a "no first use" policy. It also urged the U.S. and the U.S.S.R. to renounce any intention of using nuclear weapons against civilian populations, even as a retaliatory strike.

The Pastoral stopped short of an outright condemnation of deterrence doctrine, but noted that deterrence is justified only if accompanied by serious efforts toward disarmament; deterrence is not justified "as a long-term basis for peace" (National Conference of Catholic Bishops, 1982, pp. 14-18). The Bishops recommended support for an immediate, bilateral, verifiable halt to the testing, production, and deployment of new nuclear weapons systems (particularly war fighting systems), as well as "deep cuts" in the arsenals of both superpowers.

The Pastoral was a compromise between the more liberal and conservative bishops; nevertheless it allowed clergy to oppose nuclear weapons on moral rather than political grounds. The Pastoral addressed the appropriate role of the church in the political world by claiming that the church has a necessary and distinctive part to play.

> Questions of war and peace have a profoundly moral dimension which responsible Christians cannot ignore. They are questions of life and death.... We reject, therefore, criticism of the Church's concern with these issues on the ground that it "should not become involved in politics." We are called to move from discussion to witness and action. (National Conference of Catholic Bishops, 1981, p. 26)

Some bishops, on their own, took more radical action. Archbishop Raymond Hunthausen of Seattle denounced the arms race and told his congregation that he had visions of thousands of citizens refusing to pay part of their taxes in protest of nuclear weapons. Bishop Leroy Mathiessen of Amarillo urged Catholic workers at nuclear weapons plants to examine the morality of their jobs (Newsweek, 1982a; World Press Review, 1982).

Other mainline denominations also began calling for a halt to the arms race. The Freeze was endorsed by the American Baptists, the Lutheran Church of America, the Episcopalian House of Bishops, the United Presbyterian Church, the Reformed Church, American Hebrew Congregations, the United Methodists, the United Church of Christ, and the Unitarians, among others (Bently, 1984; Dwyer, 1983).

PEAK AND DECLINE

Nineteen eighty-two was the biggest year for the Freeze Campaign. Its growth and popular appeal surpassed even the leadership's wildest expectations. The Clearinghouse in St. Louis was deluged with requests for information. Public opinion polls showed that over 70% of Americans supported a bilateral freeze (Milburn, Watanaba, and Kramer, 1986). By spring of 1982, the Freeze Campaign had reached into such "unlikely precincts" as conservative, rural Loudon County,

Virginia, where county supervisors unanimously approved a Freeze resolution. "And in Kalamazoo, Michigan, 300 residents raised $10,000" to rent seventeen billboards in the Washington, D.C. area with the message: "Hear Us. . .Nuclear War Hurts Too Much" (Lens, 1982).

On June 12 came the demonstration described in the opening of this book. A steering committee of 13 organizations including the Freeze Campaign planned the rally and march, but much of the groundwork had been done by the Mobe. Performance by rock and folk music stars such as Bruce Springsteen, Linda Ronstadt, and Joan Baez were interspersed with speeches by movement leaders. The *New York Times* reported Randall Forsberg looking out over the crowd and exulting:

> We've done it. The nuclear freeze campaign has mobilized the biggest peacetime movement in the United States history. (Herman, 1982, p. A-43)

Three months earlier, in March, a joint House resolution for a freeze was introduced in Congress. This action took Freeze leaders by surprise; many felt the Campaign was not yet ready to have the Freeze subjected to a national political debate. In the House of Representatives, the Freeze resolution gained support so quickly that a vote was taken in August. The resolution lost by only two votes, a 204-202 margin.

This narrow defeat encouraged Freeze workers to double their efforts for the November elections. When the 1982 election returns were in, the Freeze emerged a clear winner. Sixty percent of those who had a chance to vote on the Freeze (about 30% of the American electorate), approved it. The Freeze passed in nine of the ten states where it was on the ballot, and in the District of Columbia. Only in Arizona did it go down to defeat. By the end of 1982, more than 150 national and international organizations supported the Freeze, and the Campaign was active in all 50 states, with about 650 local Freeze organizations. The peak of the Freeze had come in less than two years.

This groundswell of support for the Freeze turned out to be shallow. The years 1983 and 1984 were frustrating for the Freeze. In 1983, the House passed an almost meaningless Freeze resolution, which the Senate did not even bother to bring to a vote. In November of 1984, Ronald Reagan was returned to the White House by an even bigger landslide than in 1980, dashing the hopes of the Campaign to influence the election and frustrating months of hard work. In 1985 the Freeze began to fall apart. Both Forsberg and Kehler resigned, and the organization sank into dire financial straits.[17] In 1986 the Freeze organization spent the year negotiating a merger with SANE; this was finalized in 1987.

Our task is to understand and assess the Freeze, both existentially and historically. Thus, in the chapter which follows we turn away from a chronological approach in order to emphasize some underlying force which shaped the rise and fall, the successes and failures, of the Freeze.

Notes

1. See, for example, Lord and Hurley, 1985; Price and Pfost, 1983; and Wernette, 1985.

2. Analyses of the Freeze by political scientists have been less theoretical, but not less ideological: for a neoconservative perspective, see Garfinkle, 1984.

3. Harrington had long attempted to draw together elements of the old left and the liberal center, and to eschew the more radical left. This strategy had caused a mutual and intense enmity between Harrington and the student "new left" of the 1960s (see Gitlin, 1987, p. 117 ff).

4. CALC was founded in 1965 as Clergy and Laymen Concerned about Vietnam, an interfaith group opposing that war. At the close of the war, the group turned to more general peace and justice issues, changing its name to reflect this retrenchment.

5. This "medicalization" of nuclear war is an excellent illustration of Peter Conrad and Joseph Schneider's (1980) concept of the "medicalization of deviance."

6. Nuclear war fighting plans did not originate with the Reagan or Carter administrations. In 1974 President Nixon's Defense Secretary, James Schlesinger, announced a new targeting doctrine that emphasized "selectivity and flexibility." This announcement in fact reflected only further refining of previous nuclear war fighting plans, allowing for a greater number of "limited" nuclear options. Schlesinger's announcement was the first public rejection of Mutual Assured Destruction (MAD), which had made nuclear war fighting unthinkable. MAD had called for "countervalue" (civilian centers) targeting, whereas the new plan emphasized "counterforce" (military installations) targeting. Actual U.S. nuclear war fighting plans date to 1960, with the installation of the Single Integrated Operational Plan (SIOP). Refined by Robert McNamara in 1962, SIOP-63 was a nuclear war fighting plan targeting both military complexes and major population centers, thus making nuclear war thinkable, at least from the Pentagon's point of view.

7. See, for example, Bently (1984), Cole and Taylor (1983), Garfinkle (1984), Kennedy and Hatfield (1982), Kojm (1983), and Waller (1987).

8. Senator Hatfield was on the board of *Sojourners*, an evangelical magazine founded in 1970. The Sojourners Peace Ministry, founded in 1979, was involved in a broad nuclear moratorium campaign. Richard Barnett, senior fellow and cofounder of the Institute for Policy Studies (and contributor to *Sojourners*) had outlined a bilateral moratorium in the Spring 1979 issue of *Foreign Affairs*. He called for a similar freeze in testimony to the Senate Foreign Relations Committee and repeated his proposal on September 9, 1979 in a *Washington Post* article entitled "A Way to End the Arms Race."

Several freezes have been proposed by both the U.S. and the Soviet Union. The Soviets proposed a prohibition on the development and manufacture of nuclear weapons and new types of systems, and a test ban, in 1976 and 1977. Variations of this proposal were issued from 1978 through 1980 to the U.N. General Assembly.

Lyndon Johnson and Secretary McNamara proposed a freeze in 1964. Arms Control and Disarmament Agency Director Gerard Smith urged a general freeze in 1969. The Senate actually passed a freeze resolution in 1970; and President Carter offered a freeze to Leonid Brezhnev in 1979 (Miller, 1984; Stone, 1984).

The Forsberg Freeze was different from previous proposals in two significant ways. First, it intended to prevent further modernization of nuclear forces, stopping the qualitative arms race. Second, and more narrowly, it included a ban on production of warheads, going to the very heart of the arms race. This was the most controversial aspect of the comprehensive freeze, since critics contended that such a ban could not be verified except by highly intrusive means of inspection.

9. Originally a shoestring operation funded by businessman and Harvard Ph.D. Alan Kay, Forsberg quickly managed to secure foundation grants to expand her operation by hiring several full- and part-time staffers, including a researcher, librarian, and computer programmer. By 1984, she had a professional staff of ten and an office staff of four (Institute for Defense and Disarmament Studies, 1984-1985). The Institute, modelled after SIPRI, conducts research on worldwide military forces, which is published in the monthly *Arms Control Reporter* and the bi-monthly *Defense and Disarmament News*. The Institute also has published two comprehensive peace directories.

10. CNFMP is a coalition of 55 groups founded in 1976 to work for disarmament, nonintervention, and military conversion. Pax Christi USA, the Roman Catholic peace group headed by Detroit Bishop Thomas Gumbleton, was founded in 1977 (an offshoot of the European Pax Christi) to bring the Church's teaching on war and peace to the Catholic people. The Riverside Church Disarmament Program was started in 1978. A full-time staff was hired to develop a 15-week college and seminary course on disarmament; the course is taught across the country (*Nuclear Times*, 1983, p. 16).

11. The clear implication here, and an important one for the Freeze, was that pacifism was somehow inconsistent with broad American values.

12. Most movement insiders, analysts, and reporters support this view (see, for example, Leavitt, 1983; Waller, 1987). Most significantly, both the neoconservative Garfinkle (1984) and leftists Cockburn and Ridgeway (1983) agree on this point.

13. Willens had brought in a Washington based direct-mail specialist to help with solicitations. As a general rule, a direct-mail solicitation needs to draw a 1.25% response rate to pay for itself. The Freeze mailings in California averaged 3.5%, with some lists yielding up to 8%. These returns suggested a "gold-mine virtually unparalleled in the history of modern political fund-raising" (*Village Voice*, 1982).

14. Although the impression is often given that PSR is a grass-roots organization, it was begun by Harvard and MIT professors of medicine including five Nobel laureates.

15. The pastoral letter went through three drafts. The final version was approved by a 238-9 vote at a special meeting held in Chicago, May 3-4, 1983 (Briggs, 1983). Much of the staff work for this effort was done by theologians who, from our perspective, are members of the new class. They not only hold advanced degrees, many from prestigeous universities, but many are employed in academe.

16. This theory holds that a nation must have a just cause for going to war, as well as a reasonable hope for a successful outcome. A war is justifiable only if the conflict produces more good than evil, and if large populations are protected from indiscriminate

injury. Numerous works have appeared on the just war theory. For some American texts, see Johnson (1968, 1975) and Ramsey (1968).

17. The two individuals to succeed Kehler were both members of the new class and had extensive social movement experience. Jane Gruenebaum, Kehler's immediate successor, received her B.A. from Earlham College, her M.S. in Politics from the London School of Economics, and her Ph.D. in Political Science from Columbia University. Her dissertation topic was "The Women's Movement: A study in Protest Politics." From 1980 through 1982, Gruenebaum was a faculty member at Sarah Lawrence University. Gruenebaum has extensive experience outside academe as a staff researcher and writer for Governor John D. Rockefeller IV, a legislative assistant for Congressman John D. Culver (D-Iowa), and a research consultant for NBC. Before joining the Freeze, Gruenebaum was Director of Public Affairs for the National Abortion Federation. Carolyn Cottom, who succeeded Gruenebaum and was Executive Director of the Freeze when it merged with SANE, holds a Ph.D. in Educational Policy from the George Peabody College of Vanderbilt University. Prior to occupying her position with the Freeze, she was chairperson of the Nashville Peace Alliance, Chair of the Minority Outreach Task Force for the National Common Cause, and Executive Director of Common Cause in Tennessee.

Chapter 6

The Freeze:
Strategy, Tactics and Social Control

Freeze leaders usually blame Ronald Reagan and the media for the failure of the Freeze. Randall Forsberg (1986) wrote that the "great wave of the freeze movement" dashed against the "bulwark of resistance among the national media, the professional experts, and the nation's political leadership" (p. 33). Similarly Randall Kehler (1984d) stated that the Freeze broke the "psychic numbing on the greatest issue of our times," but

> President Reagan simply manipulated the feeling once it surfaced, using his greatest weapon: the media. By distorting the facts and the meaning of the arms race and his own arms control proposals, he has confused and obfuscated the urgent requirement of the day: real disarmament. (p. 3)

These explanations may partially account for the failure of the Freeze in meeting its goals. Yet we seek explanations not only for the failures of the Freeze, but for its very real successes. Moreover, we believe that the same factors accounted for the early victories as created the later problems of the Freeze. We begin this chapter by analyzing the role of foundations in shaping and directing Freeze actions. This is followed by a detailed assessment of official Freeze decisions on tactics and strategies. We then show how the Freeze was coopted by the government, particularly by the movement's nominal friends in the Democratic Party. Finally, we argue that the greatest success of the Freeze, and one that it never explicitly attempted to accomplish, was to help define the nuclear arms race as the paramount social problem of the 1980s.

Philanthropic Foundations

One way to account for both the phenomenal growth of the Freeze, and some of its later problems, is to examine the support it received from philanthropic foundations. U.S. philanthropies, which in the past had concentrated on domestic social and educational programs, began in the early 1980s to devote significant resources to slowing the arms race and reducing the threat of nuclear war. "The prevention of nuclear war is going to be for the 1980s what civil rights was to the 60s," according to William Dietel, President of the Rockefeller Brothers Fund, "and foundations are increasingly concerned about the whole question of how we get at peace and what role they can play" (quoted in Teltsch, 1984, p. 1).

The specific influence of foundations on the peace movement is difficult to assess. The only systematic data set on this issue was collected by the Forum Institute and published in 1985 as the report, *Search for Security*. In November of 1984 and January of 1985, the Institute conducted a survey of all national foundations that fund "international security and the prevention of nuclear war." Seventy-four foundations were identified and included in the study.[1]

Several major findings emerged from the survey. First, most of the foundations had only since 1980 begun to support international security and the prevention of nuclear war.[2] Seven new funds had been created exclusively for the purpose of generating and distributing money to international security groups. Second, foundation support for international security and the prevention of nuclear war rose dramatically in the early 1980s. In 1982 total funding for such projects was $16.5 million; in 1983 it was 24 million, and by 1984 more than $52 million—a three year increase of more than 200%—was spent on such projects. This sum constituted approximately 5% of all grants from these foundations in 1982, 6.5% in 1983, and about 12% of their total for 1984.

Third, of the 74 foundations in the Forum study, eight of those organizations provided 75% of the 1984 funding. The MacArthur Foundation alone provided $18 million in 1984, about 30% of the total of all grants reported, followed by Carnegie, Ford, and Rockefeller. Of all large foundations, Carnegie concentrated the greatest proportion of its funding in this area, committing 27% of its 1984 total to international security and prevention of nuclear war, followed by Rockefeller (26%) and Pew Foundation (19%). Mid-size foundations tended to commit a greater proportion of their total funds for such purposes. For example, Ploughshares gave its entire 1984 total ($482,000), as did the Peace Development Fund ($343,000) for peace-related activities.

Fourth, foundations tended to support certain activities more than others. In particular, support for research analysis and policy activities rose sharply—up over 300% from 1982 to 1984. In 1984 some 73% of all foundation money reported for international security went to "research and policy analysis" activities, 23% supported "public education, information and action," 2% supported "citizen diplomacy and international exchange," and 2% supported "visual and performing arts programs."

The amount of foundation money committed to elite universities for policy analysis was staggering. In 1984 alone, according to the Forum Institute, Carnegie gave Harvard a two-year, $1.1 million grant "to support a program of research and education designed to define an agenda of action that could be taken to reduce the likelihood of a major nuclear war and to engage the policy-making community in serious deliberation about this agenda" (p. 65). MIT received an identical amount for the same period. The MacArthur Foundation gave three-year institutional grants to Columbia, Harvard, MIT, Stanford, and the University of California, Berkeley "to support talented and productive young scholars capable of cross-disciplinary work that broadens the scope of security studies" (p. 128).

Fifth, foundation money promoted selected issues. Funds for the study of "U.S.-Soviet relations and the balance of power" increased significantly. From 1982 to 1984, funding for these issues increased by some 600%, compromising in 1984 some 56% of total foundation support. For example, in 1984 Columbia was given a 39-month, $1.5 million grant "for support of research and training on Soviet aspects of international security and arms control" (p. 66). The Ford Foundation gave Columbia two grants totaling $530,000 for research and training on "psychological dimensions of U.S.-Soviet relations" and other security issues (p. 84). An additional 25% of foundation money went for "arms control and awareness of the nuclear dilemma," 9% to "third world relations and regional security," and 4% to "weapons development and deployment." Only about 1% of the reported grant total for 1984 supported "alternative approaches to security."

The Forum Institute also conducted a survey of recipient organizations working in the area of international security and the prevention of nuclear war. Of the 81 national organizations identified, each of which had an annual budget for these activities of at least $150,000, 68 organizations (84%) returned the Forum questionnaire. Over 70% of these organizations reported that "arms control and awareness of the nuclear dilemma" was their primary focus in 1984; two other issues listed as foci were "U.S.-Soviet and international relations" (54%) and "weapons development and deployment" (47%).

These findings seem to correlate with data from the Peace Resource Book, a listing and summary of activities of all extant peace-related groups in 1985 (Forsberg, 1986). Our analysis shows that of the 318 extant groups supplying founding information, 42% were formed between 1980 and 1984, compared with 16% in the previous five-year period, 1975-1979, and only 9% formed between 1970 and 1974. Our presumption is that foundation support was crucial for many of these startups, and accounts for the sharp increase in the number of groups being formed.

In 1984 some 30% of all organizational income was derived from foundations, and 29% from large donations by individuals. Almost one-quarter of these groups obtained at least 50% of their income from foundations. In 1984 SANE received grants from twenty different foundations, the largest coming from the Field Foundation, which gave $500,000 to various antinuclear weapons groups that year (Teltsch, 1984). Also in 1984, Forsberg received $95,000 in grants from the Rockefeller and Mott families, only one year after she had received a five-year, full-support grant from the MacArthur Foundation. In 1983, Sanford Gottlieb told us in an interview that in its first two years of existence, United Campuses to Prevent Nuclear War (UCAM) received 90% of its income from foundations.

Particularly important for the Freeze had been the Peace Development Fund (Forum Institute, 1985), where Randall Kehler obtained employment after he left the Nuclear Weapons Freeze Campaign, and the Mott Peace Fund (Cockburn and Ridgeway, 1983). Stewart Mott's role, in particular, seems crucial in Freeze history. During the Congressional debate over the Freeze resolution, the Freeze opened an office in Washington D.C. to coordinate various interest groups working for the resolution. Each Monday, representatives of these organizations met at Mott's home for sandwiches and strategy. This so-called "Monday group" drew up a list of 50 undecided members of Congress, and matched each with the most effective lobby group in their coalition. Later in the 1982 elections campaign, the Monday Group identified key Congressional races where the Freeze was likely to be a pivotal issue (Freighan, 1983).

Finally, *Nuclear Times*, the magazine of the antinuclear movement, received considerable and diverse foundation support. In 1984 alone, the magazine received $5,000 from the Boehm Foundation, $2,300 from the CarEth Foundation, $30,000 from the Field Foundation, $10,000 from the Funding Exchange/National Community Funds, $10,000 from the Max and Anna Levinson Foundation, $10,000 from the Ruth Mott Fund, $3,000 from the Stewart R. Mott Fund, and $4,000 from the Topsfield Foundation (Forum Institute, 1985, pp. 55, 62, 86, 94, 123, 135, 138, 229), a one-year total of $74,300. Indeed, it is likely that *Nuclear Times*, on which the movement had come to rely for its news and communications, had itself come to rely on the availability of foundation support for the maintenance of its operation.

Despite their success in obtaining foundation money and forming links with philanthropists, the Forum survey indicates that organizational leaders are concerned, or even distressed, by their heavy reliance on foundations. Because most grants were short-term, several leaders worried about the lack of a stable funding base, and expressed frustration over "constantly having to 'market' new ideas and promises to meet every new issue." Another aspect of the same concern is "issue-hopping"—"The issue which received support last year is not as interesting to foundations as the new one emerging this year" (p. 250).

Even beyond these fears, it seems to us that foundations exercise considerable social control over peace groups. In controlling the purse, foundations create dependency; they also exercise a not-so-subtle influence on movement tactics and strategy. One effective means of exercising such control is to promote, support, and thus influence education on arms control. As sociologists understand, education is never devoid of political content; rather, institutions and teachers exert significant programmatic control (both manifest and latent) over curriculum and content. With so much money at stake, it is obvious that certain kinds of education will become most valued. Middle-of-the-road programs and theories, and professors who select their problems and methods for study with sensitivity to foundation interests, will have an advantage competing for funds.

Selective funding for elite schools may have a tremendous influence on the entire educational apparatus. For example, the MIT/Harvard

Summer Program on Nuclear Weapons and Arms Control trains scholars to develop and teach courses at their home institutions. The program was begun in 1982 with a grant from the Alfred P. Sloan Foundation; its 1984 funding was $280,000 (Forum Institute, 1985, p. 220).

In 1983 we participated in that program. All of the faculty were internationally known arms control experts; many of the Harvard faculty were from the Harvard Study Group which, later that year, published *Living With Nuclear Weapons*. A major conclusion of that book, which was reviewed widely in the mass media, was that disarmament was impossible; rather, the task was to control nuclear armaments and learn to live with them. Indeed, this was the message of the course. Though the faculty opposed many new weapons systems as destabilizing, particularly "Star Wars," they did not view disarmament as a viable option and never questioned the doctrine of deterrence.

These arms control experts had a history of ambivalence toward the Freeze. At a 1982 conference at the Harvard Center for Science and International Affairs, made possible by grants from the Rockefeller Brothers Fund and the Rockefeller Family Fund, the Freeze was characterized as simplistic and lacking the sophistication of other arms control proposals (Miller, 1984). During the Summer Institute, most faculty took the position that the Freeze had symbolic and public relations value, but could not on its merits substitute for legitimate arms control efforts.

Just as educational projects will likely appeal to foundations, direct action programs, let alone civil disobedience, will likely not. Such a context constantly pressures social movement organizations away from the radical, and toward the middle of the political spectrum. An analysis of the role of foundations in interest groups dating as far back as the 1950s, notes such social control:

> Foundation officials believed that the long run stability of the representative policy making system could be assured only if legitimate organizational channels could be provided for the frustration and anger being expressed in protests and outbreaks of political violence. (Walker, 1983, p. 401)

In a wide-ranging critique of the relation between philanthropy and the peace movement, Wright, Rodriguez, and Wartzkin (1985), charge that corporate interests in preventing nuclear war stem from at least two sources. The first is a global stability in which multinational markets can best expand. This position leads to advocating a reduction of nuclear weapons, a no-first-use policy in case of war, but at the same time a conventional arms buildup—in short, nuclear peace in a military-industrial complex. The second corporate concern involves framing peace issues in a way that will not challenge basic structures of power and finance. Foundation largess supports groups that do not engage in a systematic critique of the arms race, and that do not call for fundamental changes in the political economy. Support for such groups is good public relations: "It conveys a symbolic impression of concern for peace without the need to encourage actual political work that might contribute to peace more directly" (Wright et al., 1985, p. 20).

Funded peace groups inevitably advocate liberal reforms, rather than promoting fundamental changes in the political economy. "Incrementalism, " they write, "is the hallmark of respectable peace activism" (Wright et al. 1985, p. 21). Another essential feature of respectable peace activism is a single issue focus. No matter how much other issues—imperialism, racism, and so on—may relate to the dangers of nuclear war, they must be ignored. Though single issue focus may obscure the political and economic underpinnings of militarism, it is rewarded with foundation money.

According to Wright et al. (1985), the epitome of a respectable peace group is one with a medical focus, most particularly PSR. This group emphasizes a single issue, eschewing any critique of the military-industrial complex. Indeed, PSR avoids any explicit critique of U.S. foreign policy. For example, it has never taken any position on chemical or biological warfare, nor has it addressed the ethics or politics of regional conflicts (e.g., Nicaragua). Yet PSR has been a favorite of foundations. From 1979 to 1981 it received $121,000 in grants from the Rockefeller Family Fund, in addition to grants from the Stern Fund, the J.M. Kaplan Fund, and the Ruth Mott Fund. Even with a successful direct mail campaign in 1983, philanthropic money still accounted for 28% of the PSR budget in that year.

Strategies and Tactics

Freeze strategy and tactics cannot be understood *de novo*, as a process by which historical agents make year-by-year existential choices. Rather, tactics and strategies grow out of a movement's underlying assumptions or ideology, be they implicit or explicit. It is our contention that the Freeze leaderships' failure, or deliberate refusal, to develop a distinct movement ideology and long-range vision eventually led to internal confusion and factionalism. Such short-term focus has exacerbated the strategic, tactical, and organizational dilemmas faced by all social movements. More specifically, because the Freeze lacked a coherent, well-articulated ideology, it fell back on status-quo, pluralist assumptions to guide its strategy and tactics.

The pluralist model of power has widespread, middle-class appeal, but unfortunately it also vastly misperceives social and political power in America. This model assumes that the American political system is structurally open and responsive to all organized groups with grievances. Change is conceived as reform, to be accomplished within an already given political context. Thus change begins with education and proceeds through the electoral process. Freeze advocates, never explicitly challenging the dominant political economy, thus had to assume that: (a) education is neutral: facts speak for themselves; and (b) ordinary people in sufficient numbers have real power. Conventional political tactics and strategies should suffice. Individuals, through their grass-roots organizations, lobby their locally elected leaders, who in turn change national and international policy.

As we have shown in Chapter 2, recent scholarship in the field of social movements has contested the pluralist model of power, and much of the traditional social movement literature which is based on pluralist assumptions. Resource mobilization contends that power is *not* distributed equally among a multitude of competing groups, but rather concentrated among a small group of elites. The political structure is thus not easily permeable or responsive to all groups with grievances. A mass base of aggrieved publics is not seen as a prerequisite for effective social change efforts, since the masses do not control key resources. Significant change, in this view, occurs only when elites are coopted, or otherwise influenced, by the movement. Education, though hardly neutral, is needed to define a new social problem, but is seen as ineffective in changing elite behavior. Similarly, electoral politics is deemed a poor strategy in changing an elite-controlled political system.

Given the similarities and organizational ties between the antinuclear power and weapons movements, Barkan's (1979) analysis of the former is most relevant to the problems faced by the Freeze Movement. Barkan pointed out that social movements face strategic, tactical, and organizational dilemmas in their attempts to mobilize elusive resources. A particular course of action may achieve some goals but make it more difficult to achieve others. Specifically, the antinuclear power movement faced the single versus multiple issue dilemma. So as not to alienate the public and government officials, antinuclear power groups mostly shied away from extending the movement's focus beyond atomic plants. Yet this approach alienated more radical and committed activists who wanted to broaden the movement by attacking capitalism and including issues that would appeal to minorities, workers, and peace groups. Similarly, the movement's decentralized structure and emphasis on democratic decision making maximized personal satisfaction and effectively mobilized grass-roots support, but significantly hindered its strategic effectiveness in bringing about institutional change.

Additionally, movement leaders face the dilemma of having to appeal simultaneously to at least four different constituencies: (1) their own membership and core activist base; (2) the news media; (3) the public; and (4) target groups or antagonists, including government officials (Lipsky, 1968). In the case of the Freeze, there were actually five constituencies, core activists being well to the left of the broad-based, middle-class supporters at large.

STRATEGIC AND TACTICAL STRENGTHS

The strategic, tactical, and organizational choices made by the Freeze Movement account for many of its successes. From the start, the Freeze Campaign attempted to remain essentially a non-ideological, nonpartisan, and single-issue movement. Though its strategic focus changed from trying to influence local and state leaders to the President and the Congress, tactics always remained within the realm of "legitimate" political action.

To accomplish its goal of a bilateral Freeze on the testing, production, and deployment of nuclear weapons, the Freeze articulated its strategy at its first National Conference in 1981. The strategy paper stated: "In a democracy, a proposal becomes politically viable when it has sufficient public support" (Nuclear Weapons Freeze Campaign, 1981, p. 5). Thus the overall campaign strategy was to develop, over a 5-year span, widespread public support for the Freeze, and then make the Freeze a national policy objective. To achieve this goal, four steps were outlined: (1) demonstrate the positive potential of the Freeze to stop the arms race; (2) build broad and visible public support for the Freeze; (3) focus public support on policy-makers; and (4) adopt the Freeze as national policy.

With this liberal agenda the Freeze derived great strength. First, its goal was easily understood within a normal political context. No jargon or abstract theory was needed to explicate its main idea: the intricacies of Marx, the difficulties of praxis, were avoided. Moreover, bewildering scientific and technical terminology was abandoned: even the most committed social analyst has difficulty with "build-down," dependent as it is on the mathematics of "throw-weight."[3] The Freeze is a simple idea which, unlike the various SALTs, can be appreciated by the untrained, average citizen—an idea with which to build a social movement.

Second, by deliberately keeping the steps beyond a Freeze vague, and by never explicitly challenging the doctorine of deterrence, the Freeze, in the short-term, was able to assemble an extremely broad coalition. The modest proposal of a bilateral freeze as a first step to halt the arms race was attractive to middle-class centrists and liberals, and also offered a carrot to more radical factions in the peace movement. Claims about nuclear parity, the economic costs of continuing the arms race, huge nuclear stockpiles, and the tremendous "overkill" potential of nuclear weapons also made sense to more conservative factions, who saw a stockpile beyond the capacity of assured destruction of the Soviets as superfluous and a waste of tax dollars. These claims countered those advanced by the ruling apparatus and gained wide acceptance, in part because of widespread distrust of government and business (legitimation crisis), and also because of an economic recession in which bread and butter issues became more salient.

Though the Freeze challenged certain government and Pentagon claims, it never took a pro-Soviet stance. It took great pains to remain impeccably respectable. In order to avoid ideological debates, the Freeze offered no blame or praise in designating responsibility for the arms race, and avoided inflammatory phrases such as "military-industrial complex." Thus it is not surprising that the Freeze idea not only attracted a constituency from existing peace groups and from the antinuclear power movement, but also ameliorated the "free-rider" problem and attracted followers who had never been social movement participants. Because of this widespread appeal, at least among the white middle-class, the Campaign's fundraising efforts proved extremely successful. Not only was the response to direct mail solicitations good, foundation support was extremely generous. One insider contends that foundation monies by December of 1982 had reached $20 million (Cockburn and Ridgeway, 1983, p. 17). The 1985 operating budget for the National Campaign alone was about $1,200,000 (Nuclear Weapons Freeze Campaign, 1985a).

Third, Freeze tactics were the ones learned in civic classes: work for candidates who believe as you do. As a grass-roots organization, the Freeze differed from its allies in the peace movement. Whereas most of them operated out of New York or Washington D.C. in an attempt to influence national policy, the Freeze being headquartered in St. Louis had many of its resources invested in, and controlled by, its local groups. Community involvement, and the involvement of community leaders, was a central strategy. As the third annual strategy paper, written in 1983, maintained: "Getting the political and civic leadership of our communities. . .publicly on record in support of the Freeze is critical to achieving our political goals at the national level. This is the work that most local Freeze Campaigns have thus far done best and, again, it is the foundation, the bedrock, of all further efforts" (Nuclear Weapons Freeze Campaign, 1983a).

It is in this area, grass-roots organizing, where the Freeze succeeded brilliantly. In a very short time the Freeze was endorsed by 370 city councils, 71 county councils, and 446 town meetings. Twenty-three state legislatures passed Freeze resolutions, and in the Fall of 1982, more than 30% of American voters had a chance to vote on the Freeze in 10 State referenda, the District of Columbia, and 38 cities and counties: 60% of those voting affirmed the Freeze. Finally, in May of 1984, the U.S. House of Representatives passed a Freeze Resolution (admittedly watered down) by an almost two-to-one margin. And later that year, the Democratic presidential candidate, Walter Mondale, promised an immediate Freeze if elected (Nuclear Weapons Freeze Campaign, 1984a).

STRATEGIC AND TACTICAL WEAKNESSES

The great problems of the Freeze, as its strengths, also derived from its cautious and liberal traditions. So as not to alienate its middle-of-the-road constituents, Freeze leaders sacrificed deep analysis and long-range vision beyond the basic Freeze call. For the most part, Freeze leaders failed to confront the political and economic infrastructure which fuels the arms race. Also, a long-term program, envisioning a more secure world and plausible ways of getting there was never developed. Trying to avoid potentially divisive ideological discussions, Freeze leaders glossed over their differences. But by not facing hard questions of ideology and long-term goals, they were not solved—only delayed. When the Freeze was frustrated in meeting its short-term goal, not having developed a coherent movement ideology, these differences came to the surface and fractured the movement.

Although the need for a long-range task force was voiced at both the Fifth and Sixth National Conferences, the Campaign ultimately refused to fund such an effort (Nuclear Weapons Freeze Campaign, 1984b, 1985b). As Pam Solo, former Freeze Strategy Task Force Chair, admitted, "It is a cultural problem of the American peace movement to emphasize process over substance" (quoted in Magraw, 1986). The failure to engage in deep analysis and the lack of long-range vision had strategic consequences. Incremental change through electoral politics became the main strategy of the Freeze. If the basic structure of society needed no change, the Freeze would seem to be a logical first step. But how many steps does it take to achieve disarmament, the ultimate stated goal of the Freeze Movement? It is difficult to believe that the military-industrial complex, and the elite leadership beholden to it, would favor such a series of steps. Rather it seems more likely that the arms race, which has become institutionalized, will continue until elites find it in their interests to disarm, or self-destruct.

As its Third National Conference, February 4-6, 1983 (Nuclear Weapons Freeze Campaign, 1983a), when it had become obvious that President Reagan could not be pressured into initiating a freeze, leaders changed their strategy to pressure Congress to cut off funds for nuclear weapons. This strategic switch was partially based on a misperception of the President's popularity. In giving its rationale, the strategy paper reads: "While the President is thus far unalterably opposed to a freeze, *he is becoming increasingly less popular and more isolated*" (p. 4, emphasis added).

This strategy may also have been based on a misperception of the Freeze's own power, not surprising after all the heady victories just experienced. But asking Congress to cut off funds for certain weapon systems went far beyond asking it to endorse a nonbinding, relatively politically safe, resolution. Any attempts to defeat weapon systems by legislation are, by definition, unilateral. Congress can effectively address only one side, the United States'. This left the Freeze leaders in a political bind. Defeating major weapon systems like the MX would maintain the movement's momentum and make real progress towards a comprehensive freeze, but it also risked the broad-based support for a "mutual and verifiable" freeze.

Critics were quick to pick up these inconsistencies. At hearings held by the Foreign Affairs Committee, Assistant Secretary of Defense Richard Perle called the Freeze Movement a "dangerous and destabilizing" movement for "unilateral disarmament" that pulled "the rug out from under the administration in its negotiations with the Soviet Union" (quoted in Feighan, 1983, p. 42). Freeze supporters in Congress denied these charges but were also careful not to endorse the request for a cut-off of funds made by the National Conference. The lack of coherent ideology created strategic and tactical inconsistencies that weakened the movement's ability to attain even modest and partial goals.

At the Fourth National Conference in December of 1983, responding to cristicisms that the production of warheads was not verifiable, the Campaign decided to pull back from a comprehensive freeze. This change in strategy became known as the much criticized "quick freeze." Whereas the original Freeze had called for a mutual halt on the testing, production, and deployment of nuclear weapons and their delivery systems, the quick freeze was restricted to the testing of nuclear warheads and the testing and deployment of ballistic missiles (but not the production). Excluded from the quick freeze were also Pershing and cruise missiles, previously described as the most destabilizing new systems. To implement the quick freeze, the strategy was to call on Congress to cut off funding for testing and deployment—independent of the President.

In our view, as observers of these proceedings, the quick freeze strategy proposed by Forsberg drew heavy criticism from conference participants. It was seen as both too much and too little. Those with Capitol Hill connections thought asking Congress for a direct foreign policy initiative in an election year was self-defeating. Many other activists thought that backing away from a comprehensive freeze was undermining the integrity of the Campaign. Forsberg defended her position by calling it a tactical response to political realities, not an indication of giving up on the original goal of the Freeze (Forsberg, 1984).

Another strategic decision made by the conference, and advanced by Forsberg, was to enter fully national electoral politics. To that end, Freeze Voter '84 was established as a political action committee designed to raise money and work for Congressional and presidential candidates supportive of the Freeze. Forsberg served as president of the PAC during 1983 and 1984. Freeze Voter raised almost $1.5 million for the 1984 elections; but the impact was minimal.

In restrospect, most peace activists see this total investment of time and resources into a national election as an enormous mistake (Taylor, 1985). The Mondale political director suggested the movement might accomplish more if it concentrated on grass-roots activities and remembered that it could not compete as a power broker in Washington. The overall shortcomings of this ill-fated strategy were seen as three-fold:

(1) resources spent on elections had little impact and could have been used more effectively on movement building; (2) electoral work took focus away from disarmament; and (3) the partisan image of the movement was reinforced.

The Campaign's almost exclusive commitment to electoral politics was not only marginally effective but also produced descensus, and ultimately factionalism. An increasing number of activists began to call for some type of direct action, including civil disobedience (CD), and a broadening of movement goals.

Disturbed by the factionalization of the movement, Randy Kehler issued a "call for unity," printed in the June, 1984 issue of *Nuclear Times*. He proposed a federation-type organizational structure uniting the groups in the movement, with the Freeze serving as their umbrella organization (Kehler, 1984a, pp. 9-10). The response of the peace groups, published in *Nuclear Times* in a five-part series was, except for SANE, overwhelmingly negative. Though many groups favored some type of federation, by this time they firmly rejected the Freeze as an umbrella organization. The main objections voiced were that the Freeze's focus was too narrow, that it ignored the fundamental structure of society that produces war, and that participation in electoral politics was counterproductive (Ehrlich, 1984). Sidney Lens summed up the feelings of many activists when he suggested that "relying on citizens protest and nonviolent direct action" (instead of electoral process) would represent "a major step toward achieving our common goals" of peace and disarmament (quoted in Mitchell, 1984, p. 13).

Kehler tried to broaden the tactics and strategies, as well as the focus, of the Freeze Campaign a few months before he resigned. He reminded Freeze supporters that the nuclear arms race is "inextricably related to poverty and hunger, at home and abroad," and that these social ills constituted a "growing cancer of the human spirit." He urged the Freeze to try to gain the "active support and participation" of "non-white sisters and brothers" and to join and take on the causes of a rainbow coalition (Kehler, 1984b, p. 3). He also urged the Freeze to incorporate nonviolent direct action in its overall strategy, citing that ending the war in Vietnam, advances in civil rights, formation of trade unions, abolition of slavery, women's suffrage and the "American independence movement of 200 years ago, were all rooted in various forms of direct action" (Kehler, 1984c, p. 3).

At the National Conference in 1984, Randall Kehler announced his resignation as Executive Director and stated that he was personally in sympathy with civil disobedience and planned to be arrested at an anti-Apartheid rally. Randall Forsberg remained opposed to CD: "People are really afraid the movement will become radicalized. And the fact is, we haven't exhausted all other routes yet. In a way CD is a cop-out—you're giving up on the legislative and electoral channels" (quoted in *Nuclear Times*, 1985, p. 8).

At the sixth national strategy meeting in November of 1985, the CD simmer came to a boil when the convention voted 118 to 99 not to endorse that tactic (Nuclear Weapons Freeze Campaign, 1985b). Most couched their opposition to CD in the claim that it would not work. As one organizer stated: "While I'm not against CD personally, campaign endorsement of it will alienate the millions of reachable people out there who are" (quoted in *Nuclear Times*, 1985, p. 8). After the negative vote, the cochair of the convention resigned from the podium in order to launch a new national organization. The new group, called American Peace Test (APT), planned to disrupt the Nevada Test Site for nuclear weapons. "My hope is," the cochair stated, "that our efforts will be so attractive that we will be re-embraced [by the Freeze]" (quoted in *Nuclear Times*, 1986, p. 14).

The broad middle-class constituency of the movement, generally seen as a strength, ultimately proved to be problematic. First, the breadth was not matched by depth. Many who supported the Freeze did so superficially—"a mile wide and an inch deep" (Solo, 1988, p. 24)— and not as a part of a well developed ideology. Second, any attempt to broaden the focus of the Freeze—to include positions on issues such as Nicaragua, South Africa or even biological warfare—was always rejected for fear of losing white, middle-class support. Attempts at the 1983 and 1984 conventions to attract minority and union support were total failures. As the Freeze campaign was unwilling to aid minority causes—apart from passing symbolic resolutions, so in the world of hardball politics were minority organizations and activists unwilling to support the Freeze.

In a problem related to outreach, the Freeze never developed an effective strategy to capture prolonged media attention. One analysis of media coverage of the Freeze showed that since May 1983, there had been a virtual blackout in network TV news coverage. This news blackout did not result from a media conspiracy or any deliberate media effort to subvert the Freeze (although that charge has been made; see Spiegelman, 1982), but after a full year of coverage the national press corps "was sick of the freeze and had decided it had peaked" (Hertsgaard, 1985, p. 44). Particularly after President Reagan became interested (or gave the appearance of becoming interested) in arms control, the Freeze became old hat.

Yet the Freeze is not blameless. As one insider charged, "at no time did national groups sit down and plan an overall media strategy" (quoted in Taylor, 1985, p. 18). Not until November of 1985 did the National Conference decide to establish a media campaign and "a public relations plan for the Freeze Campaign" (Nuclear Weapons Freeze Campaign, 1985, p. 4). Yet the "respectable" activities that the Freeze engaged in seldom attracted media coverage. The organization repeatedly denounced direct action protest, an activity that attracts media attention. For example, when nine Catholic activists spray-painted a Trident submarine with the words "USS Auschwitz" and poured blood down the hatches in symbolic protest, Freeze leaders denounced them as vandals (Cockburn and Ridgeway, 1983, p. 20). The Sixth National Conference voted again not to include direct action/civil disobedience in their national strategy (Nuclear Weapons Freeze Campaign, 1985, p. 6).

Another constituency problem of the Freeze was its inability to garner the support of the scientific community. According to physicist von Hippel (1986, p. 19), most disarmament proposals have failed, in part, "because activists and analysts have not succeeded in working together." One reason for the analysts' lukewarm response to the Freeze was because of the purported difficulties in verifying production of warheads; but through dialogue, von Hippel argued, these problems could have been worked out. Liberal arms control experts, such as Herbert Scoville of the Arms Control Association, Jeremy Stone of the FAS, and Admiral Eugene LaRoque, all later supporters of the Freeze, declined to support the Freeze during its initial stages (Solo, 1988, p. 46). A few prominent scientific analysts did endorse the Freeze, but never worked effectively on its behalf. For example, Bernard Feld personally supported the Freeze; but as editor of the *Bulletin* he never endorsed or even editorially supported it.

There are myriad reasons for this failure. Randall Forsberg, who was to be the liaison between the two communities, was unable to procure the scientists' support. Perhaps her credentials, impressive to activists but lacking a Ph.D. and publications in scholarly journals, were judged insufficient by academic elites. Arms controllers may have also been quick to dismiss an idea that did not originate with them. Most damaging to the Freeze was the Harvard Study Group's 1983 book *Living With Nuclear Weapons*, and Harvard and the American Academy of Arts and Sciences' conference published in book form, *The Nuclear Weapons*

Freeze and Arms Control (Miller, 1984). Here nationally known academics and arms controllers mostly denounced the Freeze as simplistic and unworkable as an arms control measure.

At the bottom of this difficulty is that arms controllers and peace advocates have vastly different orientations. Generally reformist in outlook and primarily engaged in technical discourse, arms control scientists have problems relating to the more radical and "expressive views of the peace activists" who "focus more on moral and political issues than on technical goals" (Nelkin, 1981, p. 37).

Yet Freeze leaders always attempted to frame their discourse in a way that would appeal to arms controllers. At the first National Conference, Sidney Lens argued against the word "verifiable" in the *Call*, maintaining that this prerequisite would divert the Freeze debate into a technical argument. Pam Solo (1988), founding member of the Freeze and former chair of its Strategy Committee agreed: Focusing on the technical discourse worked to the detriment of the Freeze, and led it to a "cul-de-sac," by transforming it from from a peace movement to an arms control movement. Thus did the Freeze abdicate "the very moral and political ground on which its appeal to the American public had been based" (1988, pp. 25, 59, 132).

The Campaign's decentralized, grass-roots structure also created a problem: although it maximized democratic participation, it diminished efficiency and strategic effectiveness. In Solo's judgement, Kehler's leadership style—with its emphasis on mediation, participation, and consensus—may have suited the early Freeze campaign; but it created a "significant leadership vacuum" later on. Moreover, the ideology of Freeze leaders included ambivalence about power, mistrust of their own leaders, a "projection of the alienation that some members feel about society onto the movement itself," a "negativity about the dominant culture" and "no identification with the United States as 'our country.'" These behaviors, according to Solo, became "pathological" for many Freeze activists (1988, p. 143).

Months of hard work by the national staff to draw up strategy proposals were often ignored or routinely overturned by the grass-roots. This problem was recognized by Freeze leadership. At the Fifth National Conference, in 1984, leaders proposed an extensive restructuring to strengthen the organization. The proposal included changing to a paid membership organization and transferring decision-making power from the National Conference to a newly structured National Committee. Randall Kehler argued that the Campaign had outgrown its loosely federated structure. Becoming a membership organization "will help build an enduring organization, and is a vehicle for people to make a committment" (quoted in *Nuclear Times*, 1985, p. 8). The delegates, opposed to the loss of local control, defeated this proposal and, moreover, asserted the primacy of the convention delegates over the leadership (Nuclear Weapons Freeze Campaign, 1984c).

Immediately following the 1984 convention, the leadership did make one decision contrary to the decentralized model; but this probably was dictated as much by emerging financial problems as strategy. In 1985, headquarters were moved from St. Louis to Washington D.C. "When we started," Kehler said,

> we had no grass-roots. Symbolically we had to tell people this was a heartland movement. Now we have three-and-a-half years of grass-roots tradition and the national staff is split in too many places. Washington is a horrible place in many ways, but it's efficient, and we need that. (*Nuclear Times*, 1985, p. 8)

By the end of 1985, in dire financial straits, the Freeze voted to become a membership organization even though this was perceived as undermining its grass-roots orientation. The Campaign also started to explore mergers with other organizations. At the Sixth National Conference, in November of 1985, the Campaign retreated further from a comprehensive freeze and instead set strategy for achieving a ban on testing of warheads (the Soviets had unilaterally stopped testing), the same goal that provided the impetus for SANE thirty years earlier (Nuclear Weapons Freeze Campaign, 1985).

By 1986, beset by increasing financial and managerial problems, the Freeze was in complete disarray. In July of 1986 we contacted the national staff, which had been reduced to 6 from 20 the previous year. They could not find, nor were they aware of, any past "strategy papers," though the Campaign had produced them annually since 1981. The newsletter sent out to announce the Seventh National Conference incorrectly identified it as the "sixth" and gave the wrong date for the meeting (*Freeze Focus*, 1986).

During 1986, the Campaign began negotiating a merger with SANE, which Randall Kehler told us was "strongly encouraged" by the foundations. But Carl Connetta told us that the "Freeze would be subsumed into SANE", and would lose its identity. SANE had become an organization with a much broader focus, and was also less democratically organized, most of SANE's decisions being made by its National Committee. The merger was officially approved in December of 1986, with details finalized in November of 1987. The Reverend William Sloane

Coffin, Jr., senior minister of Riverside Church, was hired in July, 1987, as president of SANE/Freeze with David Cortright and Carolyn Cottom as co-directors of the merged organization.

Social Control

Freeze leaders knew Ronald Reagan was no friend of the Freeze; but they thought they could win the sympathies of Congress, particularly the majority of the Democrats. Forsberg was worried that her idea would be coopted by her more leftist supporters, but was not equally wary of the Democratic establishment. Yet it was not leftists or even conservatives who ultimately proved most problematic for the Freeze. What happened to the Freeze in Congress, under the liberal wing of the Democratic party, was an instructive lesson in cooptation and social control.

In 1982, the Freeze was gathering momentum, a phenomenon noted by a few politicians. On February 10, Representative Edward Markey introduced a Freeze Resolution into Congress. Markey, a four-term Democratic Representative from the Boston area, was an outspoken foe of nuclear power and very concerned about nuclear proliferation. In writing a book about nuclear power and proliferation, he became interested in arms control and how it related to nonproliferation. Markey's administrative assistant, Peter Franchot, had come across Forsberg's *Call* and brought it to Markey's attention. A former antinuclear activist and lobbyist for the Union of Concerned Scientists, Franchot recognized the potential of the grass-roots movement and urged Markey to ride its crest:

> The freeze is going to sweep the country. I can feel it in my bones. And there's no reason why we shouldn't be in the middle of it. (quoted in Waller, 1987, p. 47)

Markey agreed that the Freeze was an excellent political issue. His resolution was intended to be symbolic, a nonbinding statement by the Congress that the nuclear arms race should be frozen. Markey's main concern was "only with making a statement"; thus it was politically quite safe (Waller, 1987, p. 52). Yet Markey's resolution got only a lukewarm response from his colleagues; only 42 of his colleagues, mostly Democrats, cosponsored the resolution.

What was needed was a member of Congress with more stature. Few national leaders had yet paid much attention to the potential of this new movement; one who had was Senator Edward Kennedy. By the end of 1981, he was already campaigning for President. During a trip back to Massachusetts over Christmas, he was struck by the range of support for the Freeze. Everywhere he went, people wanted to know about the Freeze; it seemed as if a "sleeping giant of public opinion had suddenly awakened" (Kennedy and Hatfield, 1982, p. 123). Suddenly there was an issue around which to build a presidential campaign. After returning to Washington, Kennedy consulted with top arms control and defense analysts about the feasibility of a freeze and also sought to get dovish Republican Senator Mark Hatfield to join him in a bipartisan team.

On March 10, 1982 Senators Kennedy and Hatfield introduced a joint Freeze Resolution. A companion bill was introduced in the House by Democrats Markey and Jonathan Bingham of New York, and Republican Silvio Conte of western Massachusetts. The resolution had 24 cosponsors in the Senate, and 150 in the House. Kennedy held a press conference at American University in Washington D.C., announcing the introduction of the resolution. The location of the press conference was no accident, but a planned public relations ploy. Nineteen years earlier, the late President Kennedy had there made his historic detente speech announcing the Test Ban Treaty. Senator Kennedy reminisced about his brother's speech and announced that it was "time to break the deadlock that defeats efforts of arms control. It is time to take the first decisive step back from the brink" (Freeze Newsletter, 1982, p. 1).

A carefully chosen roster of speakers endorsed the Freeze: former Arms Control and Disarmament Agency Director Paul Warnke, Bishop John Armstrong of the National Council of Churches, Rabbi Alexander Schindler of the Union of American Hebrew Congregations, Jack Geiger of PSR, and Randall Forsberg of the Freeze. An array of political dignitaries including Averell Harriman, J. William Fulbright, and former CIA director William Colby were also present, along with Ethel Kennedy and Eunice Shriver. Shortly thereafter, the Kennedy-Hatfield book *Freeze! How You Can Help Prevent Nuclear War* (1982), written by Kennedy's staff, was published urging people to support a freeze, but also clearly designed to help Kennedy's presidential campaign.

Douglas Waller, former legislative aide to Markey, later aide to Senator Proxmire, claims that sponsoring the Freeze was a "political masterstroke for the Massachusetts senator and his presidential candidacy." Kennedy was a force to be reckoned with on economic and domestic issues, but on arms control he had "no portfolio to speak of." But now

> Kennedy in one fell swoop, captured the freeze resolution with its growing constituency and became custodian of the Democratic party's litmus test on arms control. (Waller, 1987, pp. 71-72)

Waller also claims that Kennedy's sponsorship was a political windfall for the Freeze Movement. It instantly thrust the movement into the national limelight and gave it political legitimacy. Yet the movement also was well on its way to being lost to its originators.

Some of the movement leaders expressed unease at this instant "success." "It's hard to know how to respond to recent support," said Boston Freeze organizer Melinda Fine. "I'm thrilled about it, but I distrust it" (quoted in *Newsweek*, 1982b, p. 24). Others, like Campaign Director Randy Kehler, worried that the Freeze was moving too fast, advancing ahead of its schedule to build the adequate foundation they believed was so necessary to sustaining the movement over the long haul (Freeze Newsletter, 1982). "I feel like I'm on a comet," Kehler told the *New York Times*, "but I don't know whether I'm leading it or on its tail" (Miller, 1982, pp. B-12).

Freeze leaders had reason to worry. Once in Congress, the Freeze quickly came to be seen as a partisan political issue, and worse, an adjunct of Kennedy's candidacy.[4] The Democratic Party endorsed the Freeze at their 1982 mid-term conference, believing that a large Freeze constituency could be mobilized to support Democratic candidates. During 1982 and 1983, the Freeze became thoroughly enmeshed with Congressional politics over a broad range of issues. The Kennedy-Hatfield resolution, as a nonbinding piece of legislation, was seen as largely symbolic. As the political cost of openly opposing the Freeze grew, many amendments were added to the resolution, making it even easier to support. A tactical argument developed in Congress for its support: it was good politics for Democratic Congressmen; and it was seen as forcing the Reagan administration to become serious about arms control.

By the time the House resolution came to a second vote in 1983, reintroduced by Markey and Clement Zablocki (D-Wis.), more than 30 amendments had been added; the resolution was so watered down that it became almost meaningless. Voting for the Freeze resolution did not preclude voting for any of Reagan's weapons systems. Zablocki explained to his colleagues that nothing would be frozen until a freeze was negotiated, signed, and ratified. Any weapons system that both sides did not agree to would not be frozen. He stated:

> my resolution calls for a negotiated mutual and verifiable freeze. . . .. No element of the Reagan defense program is stopped by the Freeze. (quoted in Freighan, 1983, p. 43)

This was a far cry from Forsberg's proposal, which called for an immediate halt to the production, testing, and deployment all nuclear weapons. The main idea of the *Call* was to reverse the usual arms control process—to stop first and then negotiate reductions. Another Congressman, Leon Panetta (D-Calif.), expressing his astonishment that anyone would still oppose the resolution, pleaded with his colleagues:

> Whether you are a hawk or dove. . .you can interpret anything you want in this resolution. When you go back home you can say anything about this resolution. (quoted in Garfinkle, 1985, p. 118)

Finally, even many who disapproved of the Freeze seized tactical advantages: voting for the resolution was a way of staying on the right side of public opinion, gaining political favors from colleagues, and still avoiding the issues of national security and arms control. As one analyst concluded, the Democrats managed to parry the political seriousness of the Freeze movement with the "substantive unseriousness of the Freeze proposal" (Garfinkle, 1985, p. 119).

Ironically, the legislative aide to Representative Markey recalls:

> From the day we first introduced the nuclear freeze resolution, we all realized that Mr. Reagan could take away the momentum of the movement in an instant. All he had to do was embrace the proposal, welcome with open arms the millions of people who worried about nuclear war, smother their concerns with platitudes and generalities, coopt the freeze with vague language and public relations. (Waller, 1987, p. 76)

Yet that is exactly what Congress did. On May 4, 1983, The Freeze Resolution passed the House with a 287-149 vote. Three weeks later the House voted in favor of the MX missile by about the same margin, and the largest defense budget in U.S. history was also approved that same year.

In contrast, Reagan and the far right's clumsy attack on the Freeze Movement only helped it. When Reagan accused the Freeze of being communist-led or a KGB plot to weaken U.S. security (apparently taking his information from *Readers Digest*), he later had to retract his statement and the FBI eventually cleared the Freeze Movement (*New York Times*, 1983, p. 1).[5] These attacks were widely interpreted as red-baiting and brought more people into the movement. With its tactics backfiring, the administration softened its criticisms, maintaining that the movement was well-meaning but misguided. The administration then began to proclaim the same goals as the movement, a more effective strategy for social control. Administration proposals such as build-down, the Jackson-Warner freeze, the "peacekeeper missile," START, and zero-options all sounded like peace initiatives.[6]

In the final analysis, it seems to us that the Freeze—to use William Gamson's (1975) idea—was coopted. To apply this concept developed in Chapter 2, the Freeze's ideas were "accepted", but in terms of movement goals no "benefits" were derived. By introducing and passing a Freeze Resolution, Congress accepted and legitimized the concept of the freeze; but by rendering it a meaningless resolution, nothing tangible (such as a halt to, or even a diminution of, the arms race) happened.

We would also concur with Barkan that "perhaps no social movement can escape completely the dilemmas of protest activity" (1979, p. 33). Had the Freeze Movement adopted different strategies, it is possible that it would have fared even worse. A broader, more ideological focus might have prevented the factionalism of committed activists, given coherence to tactics and strategies, and allowed for long-term coalition building with other peace and justice groups. But it also may have isolated the Freeze even more from the corridors of power, and most certainly would have inhibited its middle-class appeal.

Yet resource mobilization tells us that mass public constituencies are unnecessary for movement effectiveness. Once a new social problem is defined, to continue spending resources to convert bystander publics produces diminishing returns, because it is elites who control the most important resources. Resource mobilization also tells us that bureaucratic centralized organizations using "unruly" tactics are more successful; but centralization comes at the expense of participatory democracy.

The larger politico-economic context, over which the Freeze had little control, also worked to its detriment. Progressive movements usually experience more success when a center-left governing coalition is in power. The Freeze came into being during a center-right coalition and bore the brunt of this swing. By the 1984 elections, the economy had sufficiently recovered so that guns versus butter issues became less salient; and Reagan could take credit for the recovery. Also, the Democratic Party co-opted the Freeze idea for its own political ends. In mainline political discussion the Freeze Movement was regarded as a wholly owned subsidiary of the Kennedy presidential campaign (Cockburn and Ridgeway, 1983, p. 14). Its later inclusion into the Democratic platform ended all pretense of the Freeze being nonpartisan.

In conclusion, though the Freeze Movement must be given partial credit for Reagan's apparent reversal on arms control, the actions of both Congress and the administration can be interpreted as social control. As Waller has noted:

> Americans have come to accept a "symbiotic" relationship between nuclear arms control and nuclear arms. As long as there is progress in arms control, or at least a commitment by a president to pursue arms control, Americans have generally allowed nuclear weapons programs to proceed as rapidly as the technology would take them. (1987, p. 19)

Those who sympathize with the movement, ourselves among them, need to offer more than sympathy. Good sociology informs us that a movement such as the Freeze may have limited success, but that in all probability it will ultimately fail. To reject this conclusion is to reject resource mobilization and the power elite model in favor of the pluralist model.

The Creation of a Social Problem

The American public has always been concerned about war. Public opinion polls taken from 1935 through 1975 consistently identified "war and peace" as an important social problem. In 29 Gallup polls taken during that period, the problem of "war and peace" was mentioned more often (27 times) than any other. When rank-ordered by frequency, those issues emerged as the greatest public concern, ranking above such commonly identified social problems as inflation, unemployment, civil rights and racial issues, and crime and delinquency (Lauer, 1976).

Yet public opinion data show that the period from 1963 to 1970, a time of considerable international tension, was particularly quiescent on issues relating to nuclear weapons and the arms race. Boyer (1984) lists five reasons for this diminished concern—perception of diminished risk, loss of immediacy, the neutralizing effect of the "peaceful atom," the complexity and reassurance of nuclear strategy, and the preoccupation with the Vietnam war.

Public opinion data from 1945, 1971, and 1982 show little change in approval of the nuclear bombings of Japan: at all three points in time, approximately two-thirds of the American public approved of the bomb as it was actually used. Nor was there a linear increase in apprehension over a nuclear war: in 1956 some 39% reported the belief that they would perish in a nuclear war, a figure which increased to 52% in 1963 but then stayed virtually unchanged through 1982. Thus we find a modest increase in apprehension, which peaked and stabilized some 18 years before the Freeze. Nor was there an increase in the perception of the likelihood of a conventional war turning nuclear: in 1946 three-quarters believed nuclear weapons would be used in the next war, a proportion which dropped to 63% in 1954, and increased slightly to 68% in 1973. In 1982, some 60% felt that war with the Soviet Union would lead to an all-out nuclear exchange; an additional 19% felt that such a conflict would remain a "limited" nuclear war.

These data show that the public has long been concerned about issues of war and peace, but not in any way that might promote disarmament or even a freeze. Moreover, public concern about war and antinuclear weapons protest are not necessarily correlated. It was the Freeze that brought together concern about nuclear war, concern about the arms race, and social movement activity.

There has been a significant change in public opinion on halting the nuclear arms race. In 1946 only 34% of the population favored a halt to the building of nuclear weapons. By 1982 fully three-quarters endorsed a freeze (Kramer, Kalick, & Milburn, 1983). Moreover, in nine separate polls taken between April, 1982 and April, 1984, support for the Freeze stayed consistently above 70%; and in 1984—after the Freeze movement had passed its peak—more than 80% of all Americans still favored a freeze (Milburn, Watanaba, and Kramer, 1986).

Moreover, polls show broad and consistent support for the Freeze across various demographic categories. Analysis of a CBS/New York Times poll taken in May of 1982 found no significant differences in Freeze approval between Democrats and Republicans, nor among groups classified according to education, income, race, religion or age.[7] "This lack of division between various groups in their support for the nuclear freeze," concluded Milburn et al. (1986), "contrasts significantly with the historical pattern of cleavages between different groups on nuclear-related issues" (p. 667).

We would not only be remiss, but sociologically naive, in emphasizing the negative legacy of the Freeze. For in the final analysis, the Freeze changed, or at least was in part responsible for changing, the way Americans think about nuclear weapons. By the time the organizational apparatus of the Freeze had virtually disappeared, the nuclear arms race was for the first time defined as one of the most significant and dangerous of all American social problems.

Because of their extensive formal education, and their activist experience, movement leaders were able to put forth a series of powerful claims. As intellectuals they were able to master the esoteric and highly complex nature of nuclear issues, and were thus able to challenge government experts. In this sense, their credentials allowed them, as Alan Mazur (1981) has facetiously defined expert, "to authoritatively disagree with one another," and engage in critical discourse with Pentagon analysts.

As movement professionals, they were able to coopt a pre-existing organizational structure and communications network. By making a strong claim for the connection between nuclear power and nuclear weapons, they were able to take over some of the resources of the antinuclear power and environmental movements. Freeze leaders, by claiming that nuclear war would annihilate the human species, and thus redefining it as a moral rather than a political problem, prompted church leaders—traditionally reluctant to speak out on defense issues—to support the movement.

They also had a critical mass. What is unique about these leaders is the appearance of Boston and Cambridge in so many of their biographies. As the seat of government, Washington, D.C. is, of course, an important center for social movements; New York, as cultural capitol, is similarly important. But it is Boston that seems to serve as the locus of new class social movement activity. Forsberg and Kehler were educated there. Three MIT arms experts, one of whom was editor of the *Bulletin*, were the first to endorse the Freeze proposal. Helen Caldicott taught at Harvard. And several key social movement organizations, including the Council for a Livable World, Union for Concerned Scientists, and Physicians for Social Responsibility, are located in Boston, with Harvard and MIT professors in key roles. In explaining this concentration of activity, Bernard Feld of MIT wrote—ironically—of a "critical mass effect." "We have so many universities around here that people don't feel isolated and can talk to each other without feeling strange" (quoted in Butterfield, 1982). They have, in Gouldner's words, formed a speech community.

In short, in an excellent example of the process that Spector and Kitsuse describe, Freeze leaders succeeded in defining nuclear weapons as the preeminent social problem of the 1980s. They accomplished this feat not only by making claims, but by mobilizing resources to put these claims—copiously and constantly—in the public eye.

Aside from public opinion, another way to argue this thesis is to examine the content of popular magazines. In an analysis of the *Reader's Guide to Periodical Literature*, Paarlberg (1973) has shown that magazine attention to "nuclear-related issues" was quite volatile from 1945 to 1971.[8] A brief peak in published articles after the Hiroshima and Nagasaki bombings was followed by considerable variance; the data peaked with some 450 publications in 1963, the year of the test-ban ratification, followed by a long decline. By the early 1970s, Paarlberg counted only 50 relevant articles per annum.

To assess the extent to which Freeze claims reached the public, we conducted a similar analysis, shown in Table 6.1, for the years 1978 through 1986. We counted all *Reader's Guide* articles in three subject areas: "atomic warfare," "atomic weapons," and "disarmament."[9] The data show little attention to any nuclear-related issues prior to 1980. Indeed, *Reader's Guide* did not even have a separate heading for "disarmanent" until 1981. By the early 1980s, however, magazine coverage of nuclear weapons related issues had increased dramatically: attention to atomic weapons, atomic warfare, and disarmament all peaked in 1983 for a total of 723 articles that year. In other words, approximately 60 articles per month on nuclear weapons and related issues were appearing in national, mass-circulation publications. Thereafter, magazine attention declined precipitously, though 1986 levels for all categories remained higher than those from the early 1980s.

A final way to demonstrate the power and range of Freeze claims is to examine their impact on academe. We have conducted no systematic analysis on this point. Yet it is obvious that the recent proliferation of peace studies programs in academe is a response to the momentum generated by the Freeze. In her 1984 *American Peace Directory*, Forsberg lists 69 programs of study in "peace, conflict resolution, arms control and related topics" (p. 2); in the *Peace Resource Book* (1986), she lists 107 comparable programs. Indeed, our own training at the

Table 6.1. Articles on Atomic Warfare, Atomic Weapons and Disarmament in *The Readers Guide to Periodical Literature*, 1978-1986

Year	Atomic Warfare	Atomic Weapons	Disarmament	Total
1978[a]	25	23[b]	—	48
1979	18	25	22[c]	65
1980	39	46	44	129
1981	60	91	163[d]	314
1982	119	149	272	540
1983	148	223	352	723
1984	98	112	182	392
1985	91	137	321	549
1986	45[e]	106[e]	224	375

NOTE: [a]From 1978-1985, each year begins with March and concludes with February of the following year
[b]Includes articles on disarmament
[c]Disarmament is a sub-heading under atomic weapons
[d]Disarmament is a separate heading
[e]Atomic is changed to nuclear

MIT/Harvard program, funded by the Alfred P. Sloan Fund, is one such response to the antinuclear weapons movement.

Our own field, sociology, may serve as an exemplar to examine the influence of the Freeze on academe. More than a quarter of a century ago, Peter Rose and Jerome Laulicht (1963) charged that despite its overwhelming importance as "the number one social problem in the world today" (p. 4), sociologists had ignored war and peace research, leaving the subject "to physical scientists and economists as well as some psychologists and political scientists" (p. 3). McCrea and Kelley (1983) documented the historical dearth of sociological research and re-issued a call for scholarship on nuclear related issues. In a special issue of *Sociological Quarterly*, Kramer and Marullo (1985) repeated the McCrea and Kelley call, and emphasized in particular the theoretical contributions that sociologists might make in understanding nuclear weapons protest: "a sociological understanding of the process of social construction of social problems may in the end be the most important contribution sociologists can make to the world peace movement" (p. 228).

Most significant in this area is the 1988 book, *The Nuclear Cage*, by sociologist Lester Kurtz. Written as an undergraduate college text, the purpose of the book is "not only to report some of the knowledge we have about nuclear weapons. . .but also to analyze that knowledge from a critical perspective" (p.xiv). That a large commercial firm would publish such a book indicates the perceived popularity of the subject. Moreover, as Thomas Kuhn has shown, the college text, by the very fact of its existence, plays a major role in objectifying and legitimizing disputable knowledge claims.

Many new editions of social problems texts (e.g., Eitzen; Currie and Skolnick) now contain, for the first time, a chapter on militarism or the arms race. Such treatments are a far cry from an older, best-selling social problems text which claimed

> An adequate national defense is, needless to say, necessary in a world where an international revolutionary movement is joined to an aggressive major power. This is a military problem, not a sociological problem, and is not discussed here. (Horton and Leslie, 1955, p. 6)

Finally, Ian Robertson's 1988 third edition of *Sociology*, a best-selling introductory textbook, contains a new final chapter on "War and Peace." Mostly devoted to the issue of nuclear war, the chapter is filled with dramatic rhetoric, graphics, and photographs that are entirely consistent with the claims of the Freeze. The point is not that Robertson believes such issues to be an integral part of sociological knowledge, but that such a treatment is entirely new to the book. In academe the claims of the Freeze have made great headway.

In conclusion, although Freeze victories are largely symbolic and in substantive terms have not altered the arms race, the Freeze Movement has achieved important goals. Technocratic consciousness has been challenged. Nuclear weapons issues are no longer seen as the exclusive domain of military and political experts, but have become a topic of public discussion. Most importantly, the movement has defined a new social problem and has deepened the legitimation crisis faced by the ruling elites. Various texts have begun to include chapters on militarism and the nuclear threat, and more and more people perceive the arms race and stable peace as demanding moral and political solutions rather than technical and military ones.

Notes

1. Thirteen foundations did not respond to the Forum questionnaire; so it became necessary, in those cases, to rely on Internal Revenue Service Form 990 for a supplemental data collection.

2. For years the Ford Foundation, and to a lesser degree the Rockefeller Foundation, were virtually alone among the big philanthropies in awarding grants to the peace and security field. Their substantial grants in this area went primarily into research, for which Ford spent $33 million in the quarter-century preceding 1984 (Teltsch, 1984).

3. Senators Sam Nunn (D-Ga.) and William Cohen (R-Maine) offered their "mutual, guaranteed strategic build-down" as a substitute for the Kennedy-Hatfield Freeze. It required both nations to dismantle two nuclear warheads before deploying a new more modern one, but equivalent in throw-weight. Critics claimed that this was a thinly disguised modernization program that would only escalate the technological arms race. Throw-weight refers to the total weight that a ballistic missile booster can carry into orbit, divided into explosive devices, penetration aids, and in the case of MIRVed missiles, the postboost vehicle (PBV) or "bus." The actual damage a warhead can do is calculated by circular error probables (the estimated distance of impact from actual target) divided by the square root of throw-weights. This is what instrumental rationality can do!

4. Again it is worth noting that analysts from the left (Cockburn and Ridgeway, 1983) and the right (Garfinkle, 1984) agree on this point. Garfinkle, an opponent of the Freeze, asserts that the attempt by a "host of liberal politicians to harness and co-opt the burgeoning freeze movement for both partisan and personal benefit" was profoundly detrimental to the Freeze and contributed greatly to its demise (1985, p. 10).

5. For the right-wing attack on the Freeze Movement see Donner (1982) and Garfinkle (1984). On June 12, 1982, the eve of the huge New York disarmament rally, an article in the *Wall Street Journal* by Dorothy Rabinowitz entitled "The Building Blocks of the Freeze Movement" and a piece in *The American Spectator*, "The Counterfeit Peacemakers: Atomic Freeze" by Rael and Erich Isaac, charged that the groups who organized the rally were either Communist fronts or Soviet dupes. On September 20, 1982, *Reader's Digest* claimed that it had documentation linking the Freeze Movement to the KGB. On October 4, Reagan, speaking to a veterans group in Ohio, alluded to these charges, stating that the Freeze Movement was "inspired by not the sincere, honest people who want peace, but by some who want the weakening of America and so are manipulating honest people and sincere people" (quoted in Donner, 1982, p. 457). A few days after the Reagan remarks, Senator Jeremia Denton from Alabama, speaking on the floor of the Senate, charged that a coalition peace group supporting the Freeze, Peace Links (chaired by Betty Bumpers, wife of Senator Dale Bumpers) was tainted with subversion and exploited by the Soviet Union. To bolster his charges, he placed forty-five pages of literature, prepared by right-wing groups like the John Birch Society, into the Congressional Record. These charges caused an uproar in the Senate, with profuse apologies to Bumpers from other Senators. A few days later, on October 7, The *Washington Post* published an editorial deploring the Reagan-Denton slurs, but charged that two peace groups—Women's International League for Peace Freedom, and Women Strike for Peace (a group established during the test ban project)—were Soviet dupes. After widespread protest, the *Post* retracted its editorial. All these attacks were widely perceived as red-baiting, and unlike the charges of communism against SANE after the Madison Square Garden rally, the Freeze was not damaged by these claims, but rather benefited in increased support.

6. The ultimate coup occurred when on March 25, 1983, Reagan announced his Strategic Defense Initiative (SDI), quickly dubbed "Star Wars." This space defense system was to make nuclear weapons "obsolete"—a promise of technological deliverance which appealed to many Americans (New York Times 1983, p. 1). Spending $20 to $30

billion for research and development toward SDI during the 1983-1989 period would most likely create its own military-industrial-scientific complex with a powerful lobbying force to make arms control that much more difficult.

7. There were only two statistically significant differences in this survey of 1,470 people: women, more than men, favored the Freeze ($p < .004$); and liberals, more than conservatives, favored the Freeze ($p < .02$).

8. Paarlberg's imprecision makes his data difficult to interpret. Though he reports counting "nuclear-related issues," he never specifies what categories or headings were actually counted. Indeed, even *Reader's Guide* did not categorize relevant articles under the heading "nuclear" until 1986; prior to that the *Guide* had used the heading "atomic."

9. These headings are mutually exclusive; that is, articles do not appear under more than one heading. We counted all articles under these three headings even if they were not directly reporting the Freeze. Our contention is that the Freeze stimulated articles on all aspects of nuclear weapons, warfare, and disarmament. Because of the limited coverage of the *Reader's Guide*, our counts obviously underestimate the dispersal of Freeze claims. The data are best seen not as a point estimate of an absolute count, but as a way of assessing trends in popular literature.

Chapter 7

Beyond the Freeze

For more than forty years, various individuals and organizations have struggled to end the nuclear arms race and promote disarmament. In the preceding six chapters, we have presented a theoretical and empirical analysis of the Atomic Scientists Movement, the Ban the Bomb Movement, and the Freeze. In this chapter we compare and contrast these three movements and consider what sociologists, social analysts, and social activists might learn from this struggle. To accomplish this, we first present a summary of our findings and evaluate the utility of our theory. We then attempt to go beyond our case study and use our research as a way of commenting on a series of broad social themes. We conclude with suggestions for future research and a reflective note about the antinuclear weapons social movement.

Summary of Findings

First, we have shown that strain theory, particularly the functional model developed by Neil Smelser, inadequately explained the origins of social movements. In Chapter III, we pointed out that the *Bulletin*'s clock, conceptualized as a measure of strain, did not correlate—as Smelser's theory would suggest—with antinuclear weapons movement activity. For example, from 1953 to 1960, the height of the Cold War, the clock was set at two minutes, its closest setting ever to midnight. Yet this period was the nadir of protest activity. It was not until 1980, with the *Bulletin* clock set back to seven minutes, and perceived strain thus reduced, that the Freeze movement emerged on the American scene.

The presence of strain, according to Smelser's theory, is necessary—but not sufficient—to produce a social movement. According to him, strain must increase to bring about a public response. Yet a close examination of public opinion polls, presented in Chapter 6, showed no correlation between attitudes toward the nuclear threat and social movement activity, and in particular no heightened concern immediately preceding the Freeze.

Indeed, in the 1950s, heightened concern led not to antinuclear weapons protest, but rather to building fall-out shelters, and to "duck and cover" air raid drills for school children. At the close of the fifties, John F. Kennedy exploited these fears by claiming that the U.S. trailed the Soviet Union in missile production—the so-called missile gap; and the near-war caused by the Cuban missile crisis led not to calls for disarmament, but to patriotic self-congratulations in forcing the Russians to back down. Finally the Reagan victory of 1980, coincident with the rise of the Freeze, was premised not on the reduction of international tension, but on a massive military build-up to erase a purported "window of vulnerability."

Thus it is obvious that the public is concerned about war and peace issues. But it is also apparent that such "strain" does not in any way automatically lead to protest. Social movement activity does not just happen; it must be created through effective claims making and the skillful mobilization of resources.

Second, we have found that the origins of the major antinuclear weapons movements have a common component. Intellectuals played a key role in the founding of the Atomic Scientists Movement, the Test Ban Movement, and the Freeze Movement. Their claims making, their role as issue entrepreneurs, and their activities as social movement professionals cannot be underestimated in understanding the effectiveness of antinuclear weapons protest. Were it not for such intellectuals as Eugene Rabinowitch, Leo Szilard, Norman Cousins, Benjamin Spock, Randall Kehler, and Randall Forsberg, antinuclear weapons protest would have certainly followed a different history. These leaders aside, the entire infrastructure of the movement was composed of members of the new class. Whenever new social movements organizations were created, or older ones directed toward disarmament issues, intellectuals were not merely present, but their roles in shaping organizational activity were most often decisive.

More generally, social movement activity represents not just strain or discontent. At a much deeper level it seems to be an expression of class-conflict. However, the protesters at the barricades are not soldiers or proletarians, but—most interestingly and importantly—are dominated and led by intellectuals. As the United States has moved toward a postindustrial society, antitechnocratic protest led by members of the new class has come to characterize, rather than be the exception, of social movement activity.

Third, using a comparative historical design, we have shown that the major manifestations of the antinuclear weapons protest—the Atomic Scientists Movement, the Test Ban Movement, and the Freeze Movement—all had similar strengths and weaknesses. This conformity grew out of common world views, and the resultant strategies and tactics of each movement. Each was based on a liberal political model of power and social change. Thus each movement eschewed radical political change, and rather promoted education along with traditional electoral and pressure politics. The role of education was seen as neutral—to lift the veil of ignorance, which was viewed as the primary cause of the nuclear arms race. Electoral politics was the handmaid of education—honest disagreements over policy ought to be resolved by the electorate.

The problem with this view is that it works only in an open and permeable political system. Yet the U.S. political structure falls short of this ideal. Each movement failed to challenge the powerful vested interests that support the arms race; indeed each failed to challenge the ideology of deterrence. In accepting a liberal view of the world, each movement traded short-term success for long-term failure. Smaller social movement organizations, such as the War Resister's League, never ascribed to the liberal analysis or invoked liberal strategies and tactics. Their direct action and civil disobedience created a small cadre of devoted followers, but at the same time isolated them from the mainstream of political influence and power.

Fourth, across various contexts and times, we found that nuclear weapons protest and social control exist in a dialectical relationship. Each tends to create and promote the other. Most analysts, particularly those influenced by resource mobilization theory, focus on the social movement organization as their unit of analysis, and explain outcomes in terms of movement structure and tactics. Yet to ignore historical context, particularly as manifested by official reactions, is to misunderstand the story. The subtle relationship between resource mobilization and social control promoted a common outcome—cooptation—for each of the major antinuclear weapons movements.

Though SANE's goal was disarmament, the organization was a product of both middle class society and the Cold War. This intersection of class and history meant that protesters had to walk a fine line. While objecting to the conditions of society, protesters had to maintain respectability, and even more importantly, had to object virulently to anything that might be labelled communism. Cousins and some SANE leaders accepted these restrictions willingly, even enthusiastically. But to other protesters on the left, some of whom were SANE activists, the Communist issue was seen as a McCarthyist witch hunt. Thus it was easy for Senator Dodd to use the "red scare" to exacerbate internal tensions within SANE and seriously diminish its effectiveness.

Social control may be more subtle. In the early 1960s, SANE found its issue: atmospheric testing of nuclear weapons was spreading radioactivity over the face of the earth and into the food chain. SANE protested brilliantly, but in so doing, the issue was transmogrified from disarmament to environment. The immediate goal was no longer disarmament, or even a comprehensive test ban, but to stop the pollution of the atmosphere with radioactivity. When the partial Test Ban Treaty was negotiated, environmental concerns were mitigated. More, and more sophisticated, weapons could be produced by testing underground; but the atmosphere, at least for the time being, was not to be denigrated by either superpower. After the partial Test Ban Treaty was ratified, SANE's influence diminished rapidly. It had traded environmental victory for disarmament defeat.

Official reactions also shaped the Freeze, Many analysts believe that it was the Reagan victory in 1980, and particularly his subsequent speeches about "winning" a nuclear war, that created a favorable atmosphere for the launching of the Freeze. Ronald Reagan and his Cold War rhetoric provided a perfect foil for the Freeze. Yet the Reagan foil was a two-edged sword. When the Freeze made his electoral defeat their top priority for 1984, the ensuing landslide marked the Freeze as a marginal, not a major, factor in American political life. Thus as Reagan helped to create the Freeze, his political endurance and popularity also delimited its success.

Even before the 1984 elections, the Freeze had lost its impetus. By allying itself with the Democratic party, particularly under the aegis of Edward Kennedy, the Freeze was coopted into the larger issues of party politics. Though many Freeze advocates saw the House of Representatives resolution as a victory, it was nothing of the sort. The non-binding resolution, full of loopholes, allowed Congressmembers to go on record for the idea of a freeze, yet still support the military-industrial complex. In sum, the Freeze tried to influence electoral and congressional processes, but instead became controlled by the very forces it was trying to shape.

Finally, we showed that the Freeze was able to accomplish what its predecessors had been unable to do—to define nuclear weapons as a major social problem of our time. Prior to the Freeze, Cold War politics had overwhelmed the antinuclear weapons movement. Logical, scientific articles in the *Bulletin* and brilliant ads in the *New York Times* fell short of their goal. Government officials were able to translate fear of nuclear war not into disarmament, but into militant anticommunism.

The Freeze succeeded where other antinuclear weapons movements had failed in that it was able to define not war, but the nuclear arms race as a paramount social problem of the 1980s. This great success cannot be explained easily, certainly not by a single cause. In retrospect, the combination of several factors—a strong antinuclear power movement, a post-Vietnam peace movement looking for an issue with which to renew itself, an inexperienced and clumsy Reagan administration— contributed to the creation of a new social problem. Perhaps most importantly, a brilliant public relations campaign was responsible for broadening the Freeze constituency beyond what any peace and disarmament movement had ever achieved. By casting disarmament as a moral issue, traditional church leaders—and their followers—were brought into the movement. By defining war as a medical problem, physicians were for the first time brought into the movement, which in turn led the way for many other professional groups to participate in the Freeze.

Evaluation of Theory

Our sociohistorical analysis is consistent with, and supports, the theoretical synthesis presented in Chapter 2. At the micro level, social constructionism sensitized us to the importance of claims making and individual enterprise. The whole idea that social problems are created, rather than perceived, is central to this research. From Leo Szilard's "Crusade" to Norman Cousins' "New Age" to Randall Forsberg's "Call," claims were put forth to define nuclear weapons as a social problem.

Yet we also found that claims making must be viewed and assessed in political and historical terms. Not all claims are equal. Claims by the more powerful have a greater chance of being accepted as truthful. In a postindustrial society, where the production of knowledge is so crucial to the national interest, claims by scientists are given particular attention. It is not surprising that scientists' claims about fallout of SDI are taken seriously. What is noteworthy is that even moral claims made by scientists are given wide attention. This attention is a form of power, but not one with which scientists have been comfortable or successful. By choice, most scientists conducted their dialogues with one another, eschewed practical reasoning, and therefore failed in most cases to reach the public. A notable exception to this thesis would be the physicians, who were able to "medicalize" the problem of nuclear war and receive wide attention for their efforts.

For various reasons, many claims by social movement activists never reach the public. From a contemporary perspective, the AFSC (1955) document, *Speak Truth to Power,* and Lewis Mumford's "Gentlemen: You are Mad!" (1946) read as brilliant political tracts. Yet in their time—during the height of the Cold War—these documents were generally ignored. Their authors attempted—but failed—to reach a larger audience. The lesson here is that historical contingencies are extremely important in shaping the evaluation of a claim. Randall Forsberg may have been brilliant, but she was also in the right place at the right time.

The other component of our theoretical synthesis, resource mobilization, helped us understand the formation and dynamics of social movement organizations involved in the antinuclear weapons movement. Empirical studies of organizational strategy and tactics were particularly helpful in our assessment of the Freeze. In turn, our historical data offer partial support for resource mobilization theory, particularly the entrepreneurial model. Here we consider how our study sheds light on three issues—the role of professionals, the import of external support, and the free-rider problem—in this literature.

In its four decade history, the movement has certainly become, as predicted by the entrepreneurial model, more professionalized and bureaucratic. Part of the problem of the Atomic Scientists Movement, and the *Bulletin,* was the initial absence of professional staff. The postwar organization was staffed entirely by working scientists; and Eugene Rabinowitch, a university professor, did much of the work and writing for the *Bulletin* until Ruth Adams joined the organization in 1961. SANE and Freeze, on the other hand, had full-time and experienced staffs at the time of their inceptions.

Consistent with the ascendency of professionals is the decreased import of the public. We found that mass support, though consistant with the democratic ideal, was not crucial to movement success. The Atomic Scientists Movement and SANE had little public support. Though the Freeze had massive support, its grass-roots were ephemeral to organizational life and played little role in movement direction. Rather, issue entrepreneurs manipulate resources and, through claims making, create issues for mobilization.

Consistent with the entrepreneurial model, external support, particularly from foundations, has become increasingly important for movement formation and continuance. Yet as Craig Jenkins (1983) has noted, the role of such support may be problematic for the movement. The Atomic Scientists Movement began before the foundations started to fund peace issues: the gift of $10,000 from University of Chicago President Robert Hutchins probably was not crucial to movement continuance (though later the *Bulletin* was able to attract considerable funding). However, as we argued in Chapter 6, foundation support was crucial in two ways for SANE and Freeze: external funds allowed the organizations to grow and flourish, but at the same time exercised a conservative influence over movement strategy and tactics.

The case of *Nuclear Times*, the "official" magazine of the peace movement, illustrates the problematic nature of external funding. The magazine has become dependent for its very existence on substantial philanthropy, a fact which has changed the character of protest in the 1980s. If the movements of the 1960s relied on the mimeograph, at least those low-technology machines were widely available, and more importantly, available at little or no cost to anyone in a university community. We think that the mimeograph was responsible, in part, for the decentralization of protest writing in the 1960s. By contrast, the slick, glossy protest periodicals of the 1980s, typified by *Nuclear Times*, rely on high technology and its attendant centralization. And, of course, centralization means less diversity of opinion—a situation which almost always decreases input of radical views; it also suggests different fiscal arrangements and increases opportunities for social control. It is ironic, and dangerous to the cause, that the major vehicle for communication in the peace movement is dependent on corporate funding decisions.

The social movements that we studied were vexed by the free-rider issue. In theory, the Atomic Scientists Movement should not have had a free-rider problem: it defined its constituency narrowly, as (to use Mancur Olsen's (1965) terms) "privileged" actors who could gain "selective benefits" from movement action. Yet movement participation by these direct beneficiaries was low, never amounting to more than a few percent of the population of atomic scientists. We presume that the ideology of these scientists mitigated strongly against participation in any protest action. SANE and Freeze, on the other hand, assumed a mass following and always acted in their name. SANE did little to court this group; *New York Times* ads were written to them, but little feedback was sought or expected from them. The Freeze not only acted in their name, but organized and communicated with them at the grass-roots. Yet in the final analysis, support from this "conscience constituency" (to use McCarthy and Zald's term) proved to be shallow.

In addition to these debates, our research reveals other problems of resource mobilization. The theory generally ignores or underestimates the importance of three concepts from traditional social movements literature: ideology, relative deprivation and status inconsistency. These ideas may not be important in explaining mass following, as the traditional literature suggests. But they may be important in explaining and understanding why members of the new class become movement leaders, and particularly how they assume the key role of issue entrepreneur.

The final component of our theoretical synthesis, new class, helps us place the antinuclear weapons movement in historical perspective. If resource mobilization tells us what happened, it does not always shed light on why it happened. Our case study supports Touraine's contention that postindustrial societies are characterized by progressive social movements which are antitechnocratic in nature. Moreover, new class theory offers a novel interpretation of the antinuclear weapons movement. It explains why highly educated and privileged actors take antiestablishment positions. Viewing such protest as a form of class conflict, critical discourse allows new class members to vie for the control of cultural capital.

As stated in Chapter 2, we use new class as a sensitizing device, much in the way that social scientists have long used the concepts of middle class, working class, and so on. We relied on Alvin Gouldner's ideas, and this helps us explain why members of the new class were on "both sides of the barricades"[1] in antinuclear weapons protest. According to Gouldner, intellectuals and intelligentsia engage in intra-class conflict within the new class. Whereas the former took the side of protest, and have been the focus of this study, the latter most often sided with the establishment, even serving the role of "defense intellectuals" (Kaplan, 1983).

Yet our analysis pointed out certain limitations in the development of new class theory. Gouldner claimed that intellectuals and intelligentsia form a single speech community that engages in critical discourse. He did not view critical discourse as a source of intra-class conflict. From our analysis, we now believe that the new class consists of two somewhat distinctive and identifiable speech communities: the intelligentsia, who rely mostly on instrumental reasoning, and the intellectuals, who most likely engage in moral/practical reasoning.

Moreover, in viewing new class activities, Gouldner emphasized the role of individual actors. Perhaps, consistent with resource mobilization theory, we should have emphasized the role of new class organizations and institutions in promoting class conflict.[2] In this sense the university, foundation, or SMO serves the new class in the same way as the labor union serves the working class or the corporation empowers the upper class.

Overall, we probably overestimated the importance of the new class, and concomitantly underestimated the importance of religious pacifists, in the antinuclear weapons movement. We are impressed with the tenacity and perseverance of the religious pacifists who protested not only when such activity was chic and popular, but also during times when protest was defined as unpatriotic and un-American. During the darkest of times it was religious pacifists who kept practical reasoning alive. Though many of these pacifists are also intellectuals, their activist orientation is rooted in religious tradition and conviction. If their role is sometimes difficult to discern, it is because by choice they stayed in the background, away from the glare of publicity. But an examination of every major antinuclear weapons protest movement finds religious pacifists present in the making, involved in the acting, and persevering in the interregnum.

THE DIALECTICS OF CHANGE

As Karl Marx (1969) wrote in "The Eighteenth Brumaire of Louis Napoleon", "men make their own history, but they do not make it just as they please." Following this dictum, we have tried to avoid both historicism and psychological reductionism—the views, respectively, that individuals are passive reflections of their history, and that history is the sum total of individual motives, actions, and stories. Rather, we invoked a dialectical model and account for change as the product of actors working in—and struggling against—historically constrained circumstances.

We have examined in detail a particular social movement over four decades, and have attempted to view this phenomenon within the context of creative social science theory. Now we use our case study to comment on three issues—the dialectics of science, the problem of praxis, and the dilemmas of protest—which are likely to face, and vex, future social movements.

THE DIALECTICS OF SCIENCE

Of all modern social movements, scientists have played a major role in only one—the protest against nuclear weapons. Their role has been marked by the difficulties, ironies, and contradictions of being caught between two worlds. Albert Einstein's biography may serve as an exemplar. His theoretical discoveries made the atomic bomb possible. Yet the Nazis forced him to leave Germany and come to America, where—along with Leo Szilard—he petitioned President Roosevelt to build an atomic bomb before the Germans could. Because of his outspoken politics—his pacifism and probably his Zionism—Einstein was entirely excluded from the Manhattan Project.[3] Einstein devoted his later life to the cause of disarmament.

A similar life of contradictions existed for Robert Oppenheimer. As chief scientist for the Manhattan Project, he played a crucial role in building the bomb. Though he was morally outraged by the destructive power of the bomb, his ethical position remained ambiguous. In 1945 he listed as reasons for building the bomb the fear of Nazi Germany, the wish to shorten the war, and, most interestingly, "a sense of adventure." "When you come right down to it," he continued

> the reason that we did this job is because it was an organic necessity. If you are a scientist you cannot stop such a thing. . . .. It is not possible to be a scientist unless you believe that the knowledge of the world, and the power which this gives, is a thing which is of intrinsic value, and that you are using it to help the spread of knowledge, and are willing to take the consequences. (quoted in Rhodes, 1986, p. 761)

Plagued by doubts, Oppenheimer later opposed building the more powerful hydrogen bomb; his patriotism was attacked and he lost his security clearance for secret research.

Neils Bohr himself was a profound dialectician. In the late 1920s he had developed a dialectical, non-Aristotelian system of physics in which classical and quantum physics stood side-by-side, seemingly paradoxical, in contradiction. He called this view "complementarity," and used this system to understand not only the physical world, but the social world as well. It follows, then, that he saw the bomb through complementarity—as paradoxical and contradictory. As a man of peace, he was appalled by the destructive power of the bomb. Yet, as he wrote Einstein in 1950, "the very effort to forestall such ominous threats to civilization would offer quite unique opportunities to bridge international divergences" (quoted in Rhodes, 1968, p. 534). Thus the final contradiction: scientists, in the employ of the state, produced the bomb, the antidote to which is international control. Yet the preeminent transnational community of our time is science; that which produced the bomb might save us from it.

Einstein, Oppenheimer, Bohr and hundreds of other scientists on both sides of the Atlantic shaped the post-World War II world. They, in turn, were shaped by events not of their own making or control. The war interrupted and changed their careers. Yet the war also provided heretofore unlimited research opportunities. Money and material were available in abundance, and exciting theoretical and technical paradigm problems were solved in rapid succession. Just as World War I was known as the chemists' war for the crucial role that profession played in the development of poison gas and munitions, World War II became known—in dubious honor of atomic and other accomplishments—as the physicists' war (Kevles, 1978).

By the close of the war, elite atomic scientists had become leading world figures. No longer considered anachronisms and curiosities of the laboratory, Niels Bohr, Enrico Fermi and scores of others became celebrities, the focus of media attention as well as the councils of government. As C.P. Snow wrote: "Physicists became, almost overnight, the most important military resource a nation-state could call upon" (quoted in Rhodes, 1986, p. 751).

Yet there was a backlash to this fame. National security was now seen to depend on atomic research, and this research was thus too important to leave to the whim of scientists, particularly a group that spoke with so many foreign accents. Information, once discovered, could not be published freely or even submitted to peer review. Rather, secrecy was imposed as science came under the control of the military. Atomic scientists certainly had moral qualms about their research. Yet the chief goal of the atomic scientists movement was to retain—or regain—autonomy over their own research; and the movement was defeated when scientists were coopted by the establishment of the AEC and the emerging military-industrial complex. Now they had power— real power—and this quieted many discordant voices.

More than four decades have passed since atomic scientists began protesting. During that time other scientists have sought to end the arms race. In the next several decades scientists will become increasingly involved in other antitechnocratic protest movements (environment, genetic engineering, etc.). The success of these efforts will depend, in part, on the ability of scientists and others to reach praxis.

THE PROBLEM OF PRAXIS

Praxis, the nexus of thought and action to produce meaningful social change, is particularly difficult to achieve. An examination of the historical record indicates times during which good theory flourishes, and times when it wanes; similarly, history seems to show an ebb and flow of intense action. What seems particularly relevant about the antinuclear weapons movement is that the two components of praxis, rather then appearing simultaneously, seem to be inversely related.

It seems to us that protest activity is more prevalent during periods of relative openness (during progressive, liberal administrations), and thus more dependent on what Smelser (1962) calls "structural conduciveness." Repressive, conservative periods, on the other hand, are characterized by a retreat in protest activity but an intellectual flowering—a period of regrouping and reflexive, theoretical development. Examples of the latter would be the writings of intellectuals in the *Bulletin* following the atomic scientists movement, pacifist writings during the early Cold War, and the theoretical development of the new left following the turbulent times of the sixties. A notable exception may be the Freeze Movement, which developed during the conservative Reagan era, a context which also might help explain its rapid decline.

The absence of praxis in the antinuclear weapons movement may be explained, in part, by key differences in education and outlook between its two major groups of supporters. Nuclear scientists, even in protest, have emphasized instrumental reasoning and technical discourse: the way to solve a technical problem is through the invocation of better science. Leading scientists, such as Rabinowitch, consistently eschewed "emotional" appeals such as the SANE *New York Times* ads; and he and other key scientific analysts withheld support from the Freeze because they viewed it as simplistic.

The way in which the Freeze was conceptualized made support by scientists problematic. Freeze leaders claimed that halting the arms race was a matter of moral and political will that did not require technical skill or solutions. Thus the special skills of scientific analysts and arms controllers were deemed irrelevant.

As C.P. Snow pointed out in his book, *Two Cultures*, scientists and other intellectuals live in different worlds. Professors of social science and humanities have made little effort to understand scientific and technical issues. Though some scientists (e.g., Einstein and Pauling) have engaged in practical reasoning, that mode of argument was primarily left in the hands of various social scientists and humanitarians within university settings. Yet as Russell Jacoby has argued in his 1987 book, *The Last Intellectuals*, these academicians turned not outward to reach a broad lay audience, but inward to communicate with ever smaller groups of technical specialists. Thus social movement professionals, in determining future courses of action, received little help from university scholars. The success or failure of future social movements depends, in part, on reversing this trend—on decreasing the insularity of the modern university and increasing the links between intellectuals inside and outside the academy.

Dilemmas of Protest

Behind any social movement lies a vision of the future. Though activists may understand their own limitations to change the course of history, they also understand the imperative of planning for such a change. Any attempt to implement social change is inevitably reduced, to a large degree, to a debate over strategy and tactics. Within a given social movement, goals may differ, so it is to be expected that different strategies and tactics will characterize organizational behavior.

The antinuclear weapons movement was composed of many individuals and organizations of differing vision and style. To analyze and appreciate these differences, we have conceptualized three factions of the antinuclear weapons movement: their goals, their analysis of the causes of war, their change targets, and finally, their strategy and tactics.

The first of the factions is the anti-imperialists, typified by the "new left" Students for a Democratic Society (SDS). Though we did not focus on SDS in this research, their consideration here helps us appreciate the strategic and tactical options available to antinuclear weapons movements. Founded in 1960, SDS was an amalgam of student radicals, civil rights workers, and action-oriented intellectuals. SDS opposed corporate power, and advocated democratic socialism. They argued that status-quo liberalism was a regressive, not a progressive, force in American society. As the causes of war, they identified imperialism, global inequality, and instrumental rationality. Their strategy was revolutionary change, and their tactics were direct action and civil disobedience. Unlike the other two factions, they did not always disavow violence.

Unlike the "old left" of the 1930s, new left militants valued action over theory, inclusiveness over sectarianism, and institutional

Table 7.1. Factions of the Antinuclear Weapons Movement

Faction/Prototype Organization	Goals	Causes of War	Change Target	Tactics & Strategy
Anti-Imperialists SDS	Democratic Socialism Global Justice	Imperialism Global Inequality Instrumental Rationality	Corporate Ruling Class Status-Quo Liberals Civil Disobedience	Non-Violent or Violent Resistance Direct Action
Radical Pacifists WRL	Democratic Socialism Global Justice	Imperialism Global Inequality Instrumental Rationality	Injustice Institutional Violence "Inner-Self"	Non-violent Resistance Direct Action Civil Disobedience
Peace Liberals SANE	Nuclear Disarmament World Government	Nationalism Arms Race Political Error	Cold War Zealots	Political Pressure Electoral Politics

decentralization over bureaucratic structure. New left leaders argued prophetically that the partial Test Ban Treaty of 1963 was a trap in that it distracted movement attention away from both exploitation of the Third World and inequalities existing in the United States. Yet the new left, and particularly SDS, became so preoccupied with Vietnam that it was unable to transfer its potential resources in any significant way to the nuclear arms race.

The second faction is the "radical pacifists," typified by the War Resisters League, founded in 1924, and the Committee for Non-Violent Action, founded in 1957. Their ultimate goal was democratic socialism, peaceful coexistence, and justice. As radicals, they identified the causes of war in the same way as the anti-imperialists. Their change target was not just capitalism as much as it was general injustice and institutionalized violence. They were revolutionaries who despised, as Chatfield (1978, p. 37) has written, "the traditional revolutionary tendency to think of people as mere instruments for bringing about a future revolution." Rather, radical pacifists sought first "to work for an 'inner-transformation' within peace-minded individuals as a way of organizing a popular revolution against war and institutionalized violence" (DeBenedetti, 1980, p. 152).

Radical pacifists practiced non-violent resistance, including both legal direct action and civil disobedience. The CNVA, which De-Benedetti (1980) has characterized as "activist in orientation, Quaker in coloration, and democratic socialist in its politics" (p. 161) engaged in tax resistance, trespassing on atomic test sites, and international walks for peace and disarmament. In the process they won jail terms and publicity, but their emphasis on civil disobedience distressed and split the Quaker community.

The third faction is the peace liberals. In addition to SANE, the prototypic organization of peace liberals, we have included in this faction the Freeze and traditional pacifist groups such as FOR and AFSC. The goal of this faction was not revolution, but rather an end to the arms race, nuclear disarmament, and for some, world government. Peace liberals believed that war was caused by nationalism, the arms race, and "political errors" such as the U.S. policy of Soviet containment. Their target for change was cold-war zealots who, peace liberals believed, were responsible for the nuclear arms race.

The strategy of peace liberals was to exert as much political pressure as possible, principally through electoral politics. Though SANE and Freeze participated in demonstrations, the organizations never advocated or endorsed any civil disobedience. SANE defended its exclusion of Communists on tactical grounds: their presence would lose votes. By contrast the radical pacifists favored the inclusion of Communists, and the anti-imperialists insisted on it.

Despite these differences, the three factions were able to operate as a loose coalition—mostly remaining at odds, but at times coming together on certain issues. All three factions spent much of their time engaged in education; and all engaged in critical discourse and a critique of the ruling class. In terms of our own theoretical analysis, all factions were led by members of the new class. Indeed, the data show that in their origins and dynamics, the role of intellectuals in these various organizations and factions is difficult to overestimate.

For the activist, these tactical differences form the basis of an extremely important and exceptionally difficult dilemma. In order to attract mass support, social movement leaders must employ tactics, such as education and participation in electoral politics, that are acceptable to a middle class constituency. Such an organization may achieve broad support, yet that support is likely to be only skin deep. Typical middle class constituents will lend support to movement organizations to the extent that they are convenient, chic, or non career-threatening. Such support is likely to be withdrawn during hard times—the times that such support is most needed.

Some organizations, on the other hand, use tactics such as direct action, civil disobedience, or even violence, which would never appeal to most middle class constituents. These groups have fewer members, but they tend to be highly committed. Popular or not, in or out of style, threatening or not to their careers, these activists do not abandon their causes. Yet such organizations are, and have always been, on the fringes of American politics; and their ability to influence public policy has always been minimal.

Future Research

This research, for us, has raised more questions than it has answered. We would hope that our readers will address these and more questions and issues. Of the various future directions for our own research, two will merit immediate attention: the role of philanthropic foundations in social change and social control, and the conflict between intellectuals and intelligentsia within the new class.

In this study we addressed the role of philanthropy in the antinuclear weapons movement, particularly the Freeze. Time and space limitations prevented a more detailed analysis. Yet it is obvious, as Wright, Rodriguez, and Wartzkin (1985) have written, that corporate interests in the Peace movement stem from two related concerns: to protect and expand world markets, and to use the power of the purse to encourage movement tactics which do not challenge basic structures of power and finance.

From our glimpses into this subject, we are convinced that a full-scale treatment of the role of foundations in American social and political life would prove illuminating. Recent scholarship has shown that major foundations, particularly Carnegie, Ford, and Rockefeller, have exercised tremendous influence on the direction of U.S. foreign policy. For example, these foundations virtually created the Harvard Center for International Affairs, the MIT Center for International Studies, and the Georgetown Center for Strategic Studies, and then promoted selected theoretical approaches and scholarship at these locations (Arnove, 1980; Berman, 1983). From our theoretical perspective, it seems as though philanthropy might be a way in which the old class attempts to exert social control over the new class.

Another topic which needs further analysis is the internal composition of the new class. We have accepted Gouldner's distinction between the intellectuals and the intelligentsia, and yet we have not pursued vigorously how that distinction has influenced antinuclear weapons protest. It seems probable that most intellectuals, particularly those in tenured university positions, have lent some degree of support to the movement; intelligentsia, particularly those in the employ of military-related business, have presumably withheld support or opposed the movement.

In the larger sense, however, we should like to investigate the intra-class conflict between these two groups and how this might affect the future of the new class. One interesting site for such research would be the university itself, where large numbers of intellectuals and intelligentsia are employed side-by-side. These groups are in constant struggle over resources and curriculum. Such battles might properly be viewed as having significance far beyond academe, and rather be indicative of the future pose, direction, and power of the new class.

A Reflexive Note

This study has left us pessimistic. As we read about the various antinuclear weapons protest organizations, we saw history constantly repeating itself. A movement would form, briefly flourish and then either splinter into competing ideological factions, be coopted by policy makers and illusions of political power, or fall victim to historical forces well beyond its control.

Nor are we sanguine about the possibilities of meaningful change coming from the margins of American politics. With few exceptions, the peace movement has never been a public movement, and certainly never for any significant length of time. Its leaders have labored in obscurity. A name, for example, such as A.J. Muste—certainly one of the key leaders of the pacifist movement—is virtually unknown to the American public.

As we conclude this manuscript (in the autumn of 1988) we note with pleasure the INF treaty negotiated between the United States and the Soviet Union. This agreement is certainly a step, albeit a small one, in the right direction. But if we are skeptical of changes from the margins, we are even more pessimistic about changes coming from the mainstream. Michael Dukakis views his previous support of the Freeze as a political liability, and George Bush derrogates the Freeze as naive at best, unpatriotic at worst. For expediency or myriad other reasons, the leaders of the United States and the Soviet Union may wish to reduce nuclear stockpiles. But they will not alter in any fundamental way the national security states which they lead. "Nationalism conquered both the American thesis and the Russian antithesis of the universalist faith," wrote Barbara Ward (1966). "The two great federated experiments, based upon a revolutionary concept of the destiny of all mankind, have ended, in counterpoint, as the two most powerful nation-states in history" (p. 99).

And so, in conclusion, we are left with a series of dilemmas. In his 1946 book, *Neither Victims Nor Executioners*, Albert Camus wrote that in the battle between violence and friendly persuasion, the former has "a thousand times the chances of success over the latter." Yet, he continued, "If he who bases his hopes on human nature is a fool, he who gives up in the face of circumstances is a coward. . .. The only honorable course [is] to stake everything on a formidable gamble: that words are more powerful than munitions" (1972, p. 55). To do something—anything—for peace may prove ineffective; but to do nothing is unforgivable. We exercise our free will and therefore have no choice.

Notes

1. This is Louis Kriesberg's observation, in a private communication to us. Of course most new class members were on neither side of the barricade, preferring instead to free ride.

2. We thank John McCarthy for pointing this out to us.

3. As Vannevar Bush stated:

I'm not at all sure that if I place Einstein in entire contact with his subject he would not discuss it in a way that it should not be discussed. . . . I wish very much that I could place the whole thing before him. . .but this is utterly impossible in view of the attitude of people here in Washington who have studied into his whole history. (quoted in Rhodes, 1986, p. 635)

Appendix A:
Theory and Method

According to recent scholarship in the sociology of science, all knowledge is strongly shaped by culture and context. Physicists, chemists, and biologists may claim an objective scientific method as their guide. Yet the actual processes of their research—the meanings, interpretations, and conclusions drawn from their data—are always grounded in both micro-laboratory practices (Latour and Woolgar, 1979) and macro-cultural beliefs (Bloor, 1976). Thus, to use Kuhn's (1962) term, all science is in part derived from, and practiced within, constellations of beliefs called paradigms.

In the social sciences, knowledge—and ways of thinking about knowledge—is similarly influenced by time and place. Choices about theory and method are paradigm-bound. In other words, they are not as much choices as ways of proceeding that remain consistent with one's world view. And there are many competing world views.

Across these different world views, social scientists use the terms "theory" and "method" in many different ways. The former may refer to a highly systematized way signifying social structure and culture, or a general way of thinking about the human condition; the latter may outline a step-by-step procedure for collecting and analyzing data, and for testing hypotheses, or suggest at a much more general level a strategy for approaching data.

In this Appendix we outline our views—and suggest what we hope to have accomplished in this book—with theory and method. A discussion of what some call metatheory and metamethods will, we hope, allow our readers to more fully evaluate and assess—and hopefully appreciate—our effort.

Perspectives on Theory

Scott McNall (1979) has outlined six aims for functions of theory. First, theory may be considered as science. Here the sociologist believes that formal laws underlie human behavior, and that these laws may be discovered, codified, and put into propositional form. A theory, then, becomes a system in which explanations consist of deducing lower order propositions from higher order ones. These systems may range in scope, as Merton (1957) has pointed out, from very broad, such as Parson's systems theory, to middle range, to axiomatic theories about one particular subject—e.g., suicide.

Second, theory can also function as method. Rejecting the positivism of theory as science, some sociologists assume a phenomenological world in which society is the result of people, individually or collectively, interpreting and constructing their realities. Since all action is presumed to be context bound, general laws of human behavior become impossible to formulate. Rather, phenomenological sociologists, exemplified by ethnomethodologists, view theory as statements about the way research is to be conducted and human behavior is to be understood.

In the third view of theory, as a technique of illumination, sociologists attempt to understand a particular concept at a particular place and time. Concepts such as melting pot, authoritarian personality, Protestant ethic, and new class are not trans-historical, but were constructed—with some success—to illuminate a certain period of history. With such a goal, the sociologist is, to use Hannah Arendt's metaphor:

> Like a pearl diver who descends to the bottom of the sea, not to excavate the bottom and bring it to light, but to pry loose the rich and the strange, the pearls and the corals of the depths, and to carry them to the surface. (quoted in McNall, 1979, p. 3)

A fourth way of conceptualizing theory is as a belief system or ideology. In this sociology of knowledge approach, exemplified by Marx and Mannheim, ideas are seen as rooted in the material world— for example, within a dominant social class during a particular time period. The purpose of this type of theory is to challenge official ideology and substitute for it a new way of viewing the world. As Gouldner (1974, p. 17) has written: "theory thus becomes a sub- or counter-culture, a basis for community solidarity among those theorists" to encourage a particular set of not yet accepted ideas. Kuhn's (1962) concept of "paradigms" and underlying assumptions as metatheories fits nicely in this tradition.

Closely related to theory as illumination and ideology is theory as critique, which refers to a theory that serves simultaneously as ideology, critique, and illumination. Here, theory addresses itself to the facts of the human condition and the ways in which the social world has created unnecessary suffering. The aim of critical theory, in the tradition of the Frankfurt School, is to demystify the world, to show people what constrains them, and to illuminate their routes to emancipation. The aim of good social theory has always been to create understanding and explain human suffering. A number of sociological concepts, such as racism, sexism, class, and bourgeoisie, clearly have demystifying and emancipatory potential. This is the role for theory that Peter Berger (1963) identified in *Invitation to Sociology* when he wrote about the emancipatory possibilities available through sociological understanding.

The final view of theory, closely related to the previous two, is praxis. Here theory not only demystifies and clarifies, but also demands action. Though normally associated with Marxism, McNall (1979) argues that part of any theoretical framework might be the marriage of thought and action. Any theory, he concludes, "generated from an analysis of a specific historic situation, might be an argument for intervention" (p. 4).

One could argue that good theory should encompass all six aims, though it is unusual to find such efforts. What McNall (1979) calls for, and what we aim for, is a social theory that gives us "some practical handle on the world" (p. 5). Positivist sociology, and particularly its associated method, is helpful to all research, including this study. Yet positivist theory and method, if used exclusively, have certain limitations. It is difficult to understand the social world if it is treated as a nonreactive object; rather all views, findings, and conclusions about the social world are derived, in part, from a cultural context of which the analyst is an inescapable part. Moreover, as Derek Phillips (1971) has pointed out, the formal logico-deductive theory of positivists— with its emphasis on models, schemata, and classifications—does not seem to be about the world in which real actors live.

As Chapter 2 shows, we have been strongly influenced by phenomenological theory, and find social constructionism particularly useful. Yet this approach also has its limitations. Our principal problem with phenomenology is that in emphasizing the individual actor, it is prone to slip into solipsism. Thus the dialectic is ignored. Individuals may interpret and construct their world—but only in part. Individuals are also historically located actors and reflect, also in part, their social and cultural heritage and milieux, and are constrained and shaped by material conditions. To state an obvious, but important, point: residents of Hiroshima at the beginning of August, 1945, had little control over events that would soon shape their lives—and deaths.

Most useful of all to us are McNall's latter three aims of theory. Theory ought to illuminate the dark corners of the world; as a set of ideas, it ought to guide one's work; as critique, theory ought to look beneath the respectable veneer and expose those forces that limit human freedom. Finally, action and theory need to inform one another. Just as theory should not be developed exclusively in the "ivory tower," action ought not be divorced from thought. Each developed in isolation of the other will be inadequate and bound to fail.

In the final analysis, perhaps C. Wright Mills said it best: Theory is a form of imagination, or a way of making sense of things. Our own goal is not to reify theory, but to use it as a guide to imagination—to help make sense of a tremendously complicated, difficult, and in a very real sense, ultimately important subject.

From Theory to Method

In *The Sociological Imagination*, Mills (1959) (translated into nonsexist language) said: "Let every [Person] be [his or her] own methodologist." By that he meant that method ought never be an end in itself, but rather should be used for the sole purpose of addressing questions raised by theory. Thus must the sociologist design a method for each study.

This study is an historical, comparative case study: historical not only in the sense that it covers several decades in time, but that the events to be analyzed cannot be separated from historical context. Thus, the protest activity of atomic scientists must be viewed as a reaction to the political and military control of science; problems of the antinuclear weapons protest of the 1950s and 1960s cannot be separated from the Cold War; and the Freeze, both in its origin and decline, must be seen as part of the Reagan era. The prominent role of intellectuals in social movement activity cannot be understood apart from the new contradictions of advanced capitalism. Yet the study is also comparative, not across culture, but across time. It seeks similarities and differences, progression and regression, lessons learned and ignored, in the various actors and organizations examined over a four decade period.

The promise and problems of this type of research have been summarized by Edwin Schur. According to him, there are two levels on which sociohistorical research should proceed simultaneously: one is the broad historical development and overall function; the other is the sequences of more specific events, and the efforts of various individuals or groups to influence these events. Yet Schur notes that the long-term and the short-term stories are related dialectically: "the concrete developments at any given time must reflect the broader forces; yet it is also true that the broader history is 'made up of' many such more specific events" (1979, pp. 420-421).

The historical aims of this study have important methodological implications. According to Skocpol (1984, p. 1) historical sociological studies have four basic characteristics: (1) they ask questions about social structures or processes concretely situated in time and space; (2) they address processes over time and take temporal sequences seriously in accounting for outcomes; (3) they focus on the interplay of meaningful actions and structural contexts in order to make sense of the unintended as well as the intended outcomes of individual lives and social transformations; and (4) they highlight both the particular and the varying features of specific kinds of social structures and patterns of change. For the sociologist studying history:

> The world's past is not seen as a unified developmental story or a set of standardized sequences. Instead it is understood that groups or organizations have chosen, or stumbled into, varying patterns in the past. Earlier "choices" in turn both limit and open up alternative possibilities for further change, leading toward no predetermined end. (Skocpol, 1984, p 2)

Skocpol identifies three basic approaches for the sociologist who wishes to study history. First, sociologists may apply a general model to explain historical instances. One example of this approach is Neil Smelser's (1959) *Social Change in the Industrial Revolution*, a major structural functionalist work which applies theory to an analysis of the British cotton industry. Kai Erikson's (1966) *Wayward Puritans*, an examination of deviance in colonial America, is another example in this genre. As Erikson wrote, "The data gathered here have *not* been gathered in order to throw new light on the Puritan community. . .but to add something to the understanding of deviant behavior" (p. viii).

Other sociologists attempt to find causal regularities in history with the goal of building sociological theory. Unlike the previous deductive approach, this method stresses induction. To Stinchcombe (1978), "people do much better theory when interpreting the historical sequence than they do when they set out to do theory" (p. 17). To construct such theories of history, the sociologist's task is to seek "causally significant analogies between instances" (p. 7).

Scholarly works from these two approaches give great insight into our culture and lives. Yet the problem with the deductive approach, particularly exemplified by Smelser, is that it relies too much on preconceived notions and formalism. To Skocpol (1984), "the exercise can seem like a highly unaesthetic imposition of sociological jargon onto arbitrarily selected and arranged historical facts" (p. 336). The problem with the inductive approach is that it tends to be atheoretical. How does one know the significance or irrelevance of particular instance? Such investigations, though purporting to be eclectic, either contain hidden theory or may generate theory built on contradictory assumptions.

The approach endorsed by Skocpol (1984), intepretative historical sociology, is skeptical of both deductive general model testing and inductive theory building. It seeks a middle ground in which interpretative scholars attempt to use concepts to develop meaningful interpretations of broad historical patterns. These pay careful attention to the "culturally embedded intentions of individual or group actors in the given historical settings under investigation" (p. 368). Moreover, the topic chosen for study and the kinds of arguments developed about it should be "culturally or politically significant in the present, that is, significant to the audiences, always larger than the specialized academic audiences" (p. 368).

Our research, both in the collection and treatment of data, follows the interpretative approach. To conduct this type of research, the analyst must use both primary and secondary sources. "A dogmatic insistence on redoing primary research for every investigation," according to Skocpol (1984) "would be disastrous; it would rule out most comparative historical research" (p. 382). If excellent studies by specialists are already available, secondary sources should be the basic source of evidence for a given study. In so doing, the sociologist must pay careful attention to varying historiographical interpretations based on different views of political economy. Finally, secondary research can also be "strategically supplemented by carefully selected primary investigation or reinvestigation" (p. 382).

The methods used in this study are consistent with the interpretative approach. To address our research questions, we employ a broad range of techniques to analyze qualitative and some quantitative data. We conducted extensive content analyses of media and movement documents, critically analyzed a wide variety of primary and secondary

data, engaged in field research and participant observation, and conducted semi-structured and unstructured interviews with key actors in
the movement. In using historical documents our aim was not to retell
history, but to interpret it in light of our theoretical synthesis.

Appendix B:
Historical Exegesis

American history has been shaped more by war and organized violence than by peace and harmony. Yet beneath the surface, away from the corridors of power, men and women have worked for—and sacrificed for—the cause of peace. Protest against war has a long and venerable sub-history of its own, characterized not only by periods of great protest and activity, but also by periods of disorganization and inactivity. In assessing this history we must take care not to confuse good intentions and motives with effectiveness. As historian Charles De-Benedetti 1980, whose scholarship forms the basis for this Appendix, states: "there is no reform that Americans have talked about more and done less about than that of world peace" (p. xi).

As a reform cause, peace activity has been shaped by, and developed concomitantly with, major American institutions. During the colonial period, advocacy of peace was the intellectual derivative of evangelical Protestantism and Enlightenment rationalism, and was pursued practically by Anabaptists and Quakers. Such protest began as early as 1620, when

> religious sectarians dedicated to the reconstruction of primitive Christianity
> and distinguished by their estrangement from governing authority founded in
> British North America a social commitment to the primacy of organized
> peace. (DeBenedetti, 1980, p. 3)

This "Sectarian Reform," was composed of members who opposed all war because, as one Quaker wrote in 1778, "war. . .is the premeditated and determined destruction of human beings, of creatures originally formed after the image of God" (quoted in Chatfield, 1973, p. x). The Anabaptists lived in isolated settlements; but the Quakers, or Friends as they called themselves, migrated all over the colonies. The determination to accept only Christ's authority often brought these sectarians into conflict with established churches and the developing nation-state. In addition to their opposition to war, they also opposed

173

for reasons of conscience militia drills, oath taking, jury service, and religious taxes. They sought to achieve peace with the American Indians and by 1760 became the first group of white Americans to oppose slavery. Members of the so-called Historic Peace Churches—Anabaptist and Quaker—dedicated their lives to achieve Christ's ideal of peace without violence. They (particularly the Quakers) built in the process a tradition that has strongly influenced every subsequent peace movement in American history.

From 1763 until 1815, the period of "Revolutionary Reform," American patriots resisted their English sovereign, waged and won a revolution, and created a constitutional republic. Such writers as Benjamin Rush (who, in 1798, proposed the position of Secretary of Peace in the Presidential cabinet), Thomas Jefferson and Thomas Paine sought global peace through the example of American democracy, a revolutionary alternative to the European cycle of war and monarchial excesses. The new government was at the center of peace efforts. "No other government permitted as many men of conscience to avoid military service [and] erected so many constraints against a peacetime standing army." No other nation defined "their collective identity so firmly with the work of redeeming the world for peace" (DeBenedetti, 1980, p.17). From its very beginnings, American history contained a central contradiction: as the new country developed, its power to wage war grew dramatically; yet its origins stressed not militarism, but anti-militarism, not imperialism, but free trade and democracy.

The next half century, until 1865, is characterized by DeBenedetti (1980) as the "Humanitarian Reform." War-weary Christians dramatically and fundamentally shaped all subsequent peace organizations when they "invented the modern nonsectarian peace movement by means of a new reform instrument—the private volunteer society" (p. 32). Encouraged by the spreading spirit of evangelical Christianity and endowed with a romantic faith in human perfectibility, these reformers—so unlike their evangelical descendants of the 1980s—advocated the rationality of peace. They identified war as a moral evil that the Gospel and progress would prevent through the free will of enlightenment.

In 1828 the various peace societies joined to form the national American Peace Society (APS). Within ten years, the APS established its own peace journal, mushroomed into national prominence and then, plagued by internal conflict, broke into contending factions. These humanitarian peace reformers grappled with the very questions that confounded all latter-day peace activists. What should be the first goal of peace seeking: conversion of the individual, or the restructuring of society? What was the target of change: international war, collective violence, or all forms of domination? What organizational and membership strategy would make the peace movement most effective: a broad coalition of reformers, or a purified party of believers for radical peace action? The APS proved no more capable of resolving these vexing dilemmas than did subsequent peace groups. Yet within the context of its time, the most painful and perplexing issue for APS, and the one that proved to be its undoing, was the issue of slavery: how could peace activists end slavery without the violent overthrow of a constitutionally sanctioned system of property and power? With the outbreak of the Civil War, the APS lost its influence, as social activists subordinated their peace commitment to the Union's struggle for survival and abolitionism (DeBenedetti, 1980, Chapter 3).

From the Civil War to the turn of the century, as the United States developed into an industrial and imperial power, peace reform became a cosmopolitan endeavor. Linked to a growing international peace movement abroad and dominated at home by a world-minded metropolitan elite of lawyers, businessmen, and politicians, this "Cosmopolitan Reform" (DeBenedetti, 1980) embraced Social Darwinism and valued Anglo-American cooperation and "mechanistic means of organizing an industrial world of Great Power interdependence" (p. xiii).

During the "Practical Reform," from 1900 to the outbreak of World War I, some forty-five new peace organizations appeared in the U.S. Their leadership passed to political and financial elites: Presidents Taft and Wilson, five Secretaries of State, and philanthropists like Andrew Carnegie were all members of peace societies. Under their direction, peace reform in Progressive America became concerned with practical matters such as legal settlement of disputes and the "scientific" study of war and its alternatives. Essentially, these practical peace reformers represented extensions of the "domestic and professional priorities" of those economic elites who presided over American industrialization (Chatfield, 1978, p. 116).

During this period, philanthropic foundations, whose importance to the professionalization of social movements was discussed in Chapter 2, were established as tax write-offs; they immediately began to influence the agenda and tactics of the peace movement:

> Convinced that in foreign policy as in domestic matters the dangers of violence and turmoil came largely from the 'turbulent masses,' the conservatively inclined leaders of the peace movement sought to educate the populace

in a respect for law and treaties, in qualities of self-restraint that would make them less restless and warlike. (Marchand, 1972, p. xiv)

Peace reform had become a respectable and proper calling, and such prestigious organizations as the Carnegie Endowment for International Peace, the American Society of International Law, the World Peace Foundation, and the inter-denominational Federal Council of Churches were founded.

These organizations were unable to prevent the great carnage that started in Europe in 1914. Part of the problem was elitism. Even though public opposition to war was great, peace leaders had lost touch with their followers.

[t]he strong elitism of the pre-war leadership which frustrated efforts to cultivate a mass following before the war facilitated the dissolution of the superficial support of the peace leaders after 1914. (Patterson, 1972, p. 21)

Nor were peace leaders themselves sure of how to react to the war. The American Peace society (what remained of it) and the Carnegie Endowment supported the European War, working on the assumption "that the collapse of the German Imperial government was requisite for peace" (Chatfield, 1973, p. xvi). In 1915 the Secretary of the APS, Arthur Deerin Call, had written that "the supreme fact of Christian ethic was. . .that Jesus Christ was a pacifist." After the U.S. declared war on Germany he wrote:

We must help in bayoneting the normally decent German soldier in order to free him from tyranny which he at present accepts as his chosen form of government. We must aid in the starvation and emaciation of a German baby in order that he, or at least his more sturdy little playmate, may grow up to inherit a different sort of government from that for which his father died." (quoted in Chatfield, 1971, p.10)

The outbreak of World War I stands as the watershed of the modern peace movement. As the war ground on, its totality demanded the mobilization of whole societies for the sake of producing more effective means of mass killing. A host of military innovations—machine guns, tanks, poison gases, and air and submarine warfare—meant indiscriminate death for combatants and civilians alike. The most disturbing paradox of the century, the very processes of modernization (the "dialectics of Enlightenment," in the words of the Frankfurt School)—including advancing science and technology, bureaucratization, industrial interdependence, and economic concentration—had intensified nationalism and militarization, which placed a high value on state security. This process of modernization also spawned a new class of intellectuals. Patterson (1972) has calculated that of 39 of the most active prewar peace advocates, some 33 had college degrees and 26 of these had higher degrees in law, religion, and/or education. Global peace after 1919 paradoxically seemed more "necessary" than ever to these intellectuals, but more elusive as well.

The modern peace movement, the "Necessary Reform," arose after 1915 to try to resolve this paradox. Buoyed by the Bolshevik Revolution of 1917, American new class intellectuals found an outlet in the peace movement. Through critical discourse, they aimed to expose the irrationality and contradictions of existing political and economic relationships, and actively worked towards a transformation of society. Politically, the peace movement swung to the left, and emotionally it vibrated with an unprecedented sense of urgency. Industrial nations would either learn to live together peacefully, or they would perish. Peace activists struggled to realize their cause through the League of Nations, the World Court, disarmament agreements, and more equitable economic arrangements.

A number of new peace groups created during and immediately after the war, many of which were pacifist or socialist, "roughly characterized peace forces until the mid-1950s" (Chatfield, 1973, p.xvii). Citizen reformers of 1914 to 1920, writes DeBenedetti (1986, p. 8), "laid down the three main lines of organizational action that have come to distinguish the modern American peace movement": liberal religious pacifists, feminists and internationalists, and socialists and anarchists. This coalition was radically different from its prewar counterparts "in its methods of understanding and analysis, its transnational humanism, its left wing political orientation, and its explicit lines of alternative action" (1986, p. 9).

In 1915, appalled by the ongoing, unending, and unprecedented slaughter in Europe, a group of Social Gospel clergymen and Quakers met in Garden City to consider ways of applying pacific Christian solutions to end suffering and injustice. Inspired by a newly formed British organization, the Fellowship of Reconciliation (FOR) was founded and quickly became the leading voice for liberal and even radical Protestantism. Norman Thomas, A.J. Muste, and Reinhold Niebuhr, all originally trained as ministers, were its most prominent spokespersons.

Also founded in 1915, by Jane Addams and other feminist Progressive reformers, was the Women's International League for Peace and

Freedom (WILPF). This organization, dedicated to social justice and
world peace, promoted leftist social and economic doctrines that were,
in effect, a new class critique of the old ruling class. For example, a
1934 WILPF convention proclaimed that "a real and lasting peace and
true freedom cannot exist under the present system of exploitation,
privilege and profit." In 1939 it again stated that "there can be neither
peace nor freedom without justice. The existing economic system. . .is
a challenge to our whole position." Consequently WILPF pledged to
seek "a new system under which would be realized social, economic
and political equality for all without distinction of sex, race, or
opinion" (quoted in Wittner, 1984, pp. 25-26). WILPF grew rapidly; by
1937 it had a paid staff of eleven, 120 branches "cross the country, and
over thirteen thousand members" (Wittner, 1984, p. 11). Under
Dorothy Detzer's dynamic leadership, the organization began to challenge the developing military-industrial complex, sparking the sensa-
tional Congressional investigation of the munitions industry (Wiltz,
1963).

Another group that emerged during the war years was the American
Friends Service Committee (AFSC). It was founded in 1917 by
Philadelphia-area Friends for the purpose of engaging young pacifist
Quakers in war relief and reconstruction work. AFSC quickly become
the Quakers' action organization. AFSC provided—as it still does
today—crucial resources, such as training activists in non-violent
Ghandian tactics, for new peace groups. During World War II, along
with the Historic Peace Churches, AFSC subsidized the civilian work
camps for conscientious objectors.

The War Resisters League (WRL) was founded in 1923 as the secular
and more radical counterpart to the FOR. It was designed by its
founder, Jessie Wallace Hughan, a veteran feminist and antimilitarist,
to unite political, humanitarian, and philosophical objectors to war.
Dedicated to radical pacifism and democratic socialism, the
organization's membership topped 19,000 in 1942 (Wittner, 1984,
p. 12). During World War II and after, many young men who had signed
the War Resisters pledge, mainly socialists and anarchists, served
lengthy prison sentences.

During the 1930s, the peace movement fragmented as feminists,
antimilitarists, anti-imperialists, socialists, and internationalists pursued overlapping but often contradictory agendas. Such groups clashed
over the League of Nations, Communist membership in peace organizations, and the appropriate response to Stalinism and German and
Japanese military expansion. With the onset of World War II, many

disarmament and even pacifist groups rallied around the flag. Typifying this change was Reinhold Niebuhr, theologian and chairman of FOR in 1932 and 1933. In 1929 he had written, "History has so vividly proven the worthlessness of war that it can hardly be justified on any grounds" (quoted in Wittner, 1984, p. 15). Yet by 1937 Niebuhr had renounced his pacifism, and advocated American entry into World War II even before Pearl Harbor.

Mainstream churches, which after World War I had soundly endorsed the peace movement, now lent their support to the war effort. For example, in December of 1941, the Methodist church, the largest Protestant denomination in the U.S., voted to support the war. Nineteen months earlier, it had proclaimed that it would never "officially support, endorse or participate in war" (Wittner, 1984, p. 37). Thus did the outbreak of World War II bring about the collapse of the peace movement.

References

Adams, R. 1983, October 19. Personal interview.

American Friends Services Committee. 1951. *Steps to peace: A Quaker view of U. S. foreign policy*. Philadelphia: Author.

American Friends Services Committee. 1955. *Speak truth to power: A Quaker search for alternatives to violence*. Philadelphia: Author.

Arnove, R. F. 1980. *Philanthropy and cultural imperialism: The foundations at home and abroad*. Boston: G. K. Hall.

Barkan, S. 1979. Strategic, tactical and organizational dilemmas of the protest movement against nuclear power. *Social Problems, 27*, 19-37.

Becker, H. 1963. *Outsiders*. New York: Free Press.

Bentley, J. 1984. *The nuclear freeze movement*. New York: Franklin Watts.

Berger, P. 1963. *Invitation to sociology*. New York: Doubleday.

Berman, E. H. 1983. *The influence of Carnegie, Ford and Rockefeller foundations on American foreign policy: The ideology of philanthropy*. Albany: State University of New York Press.

Berry, J. M. 1977. *Lobbying for the people*. Princeton, NJ: Princeton University Press.

Bloor, D. 1976. *Knowledge and social imagery*. London: Routledge & Kegan Paul.

Blumer, H. 1971. Social problems as collective behavior. *Social Problems, 18*, 298-306.

Boston Study Group. 1979. *The price of defense*. San Francisco: W. H. Freeman.

Boyer, P. 1984. From activism to apathy. The American people and nuclear weapons, 1963-1980. *Journal of American History, 70*, 821-844.

Briggs, K. A. 1983, May 4. Bishops endorse stand opposed to nuclear war. *New York Times*, pp. A1-B7.

Brint, S. 1984. "New-class" and cumulative trend explanations of the liberal political attitude of professionals. *American Journal of Sociology, 90*, 30-71.

Brown, H. 1946. *Must destruction be our destiny*. New York: Simon & Schuster.

Brown, H. 1954. *The challenge of man's future*. New York: Viking.

Brown, H. 1985. Numbers game won't work. *Bulletin of the Atomic Scientists, 30*, 3-4.

Bulletin of the Atomic Scientists. 1946. Editor's note. *Bulletin of the Atomic Scientists, 2*, 19.

Bulletin of the Atomic Scientists. 1974. A statement of purpose. *Bulletin of the Atomic Scientists, 30*, 2.

Bulletin of the Atomic Scientists. 1985. Annual Report. *Bulletin of the Atomic Scientists*.

Butterfield, F. 1982, May 11. Anatomy of the nuclear protest. *New York Times Magazine*, pp. 16-17, 33-35.

Caldwell, D. 1982. Educating the public about nuclear war: Ground zero week. Paper presented at the annual meeting of the International Studies Association, Cincinnati, March 24-27.

Cameron, I., and Edge, D. 1979. *Scientific images and their social uses.* London: Butterworth.

Camus, A. 1972. *Neither victims nor executioners.* Chicago: World Without War Publications.

Center for Defense Information. 1983. *Nuclear war fighting: Quotations by Reagan administration officials.* Washington, DC: Author

Chatfield, C. ed. 1971. *For peace and justice: Pacifism in America, 1914-1941.* Knoxville: The University of Tennessee Press.

Chatfield, C. 1973. *Peace movements in America.* New York: Shocken Books.

Chatfield, C. 1978. More than dovish: Movements and ideals of peace in the United States. In K. Booth and M. Wright (Eds.), *American thinking about peace and war.* New York: Barnes & Noble.

Cockburn, A., and Ridgeway, J. 1983. The freeze movement versus Reagan. *New Left Review, 137,* 5-21.

Cockburn, A., and Ridgeway, J. 1984, April 20. How the freeze is political big business. *Village Voice,* p. 11.

Coffin, T. 1964. *The passion of the hawks: Militarism in modern America.* New York: Macmillan.

Cole, P., and Taylor, W. 1983. *The nuclear freeze debate.* Boulder, CO: Westview Press.

Common Cause. n.d. Direct mail literature.

Cook, F. J. 1961. Juggernaut: The warfare state. *Nation, 193,* 285.

Cousins, N. 1945. *Modern man is obsolete.* New York: Viking.

Cousins, N. 1979. *Anatomy of an illness.* New York: Norton.

Current Biography. 1977. Cousins, Norman. pp. 118-121. New York: Wilson.

Currie, E., and Skolnick, J. 1984. *America's problem.* Boston: Little, Brown.

Curti, M. E. 1964. *The growth of American thought.* New York: Harper & Row.

Daubert, V., and Moran, E. 1985. Origins, goals and tactics of the U. S. anti-nuclear protest movement. *Rand Publications,* N-2192-SL. Santa Monica, CA: Rand Corporation.

Davidon, A. 1979. The U. S. anti-nuclear movement. *Bulletin of the Atomic Scientists, 35,* 45-48.

Davis, J. C. 1962. Toward a theory of revolution. *American Sociological Review, 27,* 5-19.

DeBenedetti, C. 1980. *The peace reform in American history.* Bloomington: Indiana University Press.

DeBenedetti, C. 1986. *Peace heroes in twentieth-century America.* Bloomington: Indiana University Press.

Domhoff, G. W. 1967. *Who rules America?* Englewood Cliffs, NJ: Prentice Hall.

Donner, F. 1982, November 6. But will they come? *The Nation,* pp. 456-458.

Dwyer, J. D. 1983. The role of American churches in the nuclear weapons debate. In P. Cole and J. Taylor (eds.) *The nuclear freeze debate.* pp. 77-89. Boulder, CO: Westview Press.

Ehrenreich, J., and Ehrenreich, B. 1977. The professional-managerial class. *Radical America, 11,* 7-31.

Ehrlich, H. 1984. The Kehler paradox. *Nuclear Times, 4,* 12.

Eitzen, D. S. 1986. *Social problems.* Newton, MA: Allyn & Bacon.

Elliot, G. 1972. *Twentieth century book of the dead.* New York: Scribner.

Erickson, K. 1966. *Wayward puritans.* New York: John Wiley.

Eyerman, R. 1984. Social movements and social theory. *Sociology, 18,* 71-82.

Feighan, E. 1983. The freeze in congress. In P. Cole & J. Taylor (eds.), *The nuclear freeze debate.* pp. 29-53. Boulder, CO: Westview Press.

Feld, B. 1976. Leo Szilard. In C. C. Gillespie (ed.), *Dictionary of scientific biography* vol XIII, pp. 226-228. New York: Scribner.

Feld, B. 1984. Valedictory. *Bulletin of the Atomic Scientists, 29,* 3-4

Forsberg, R. 1984. *American peace directory, 1984.* Cambridge, MA: Ballinger.

Forsberg, R. 1986. *Peace resource book, 1986.* Cambridge, MA: Ballinger.

Forum Institute. 1985. *Search for security.* Washington, DC: Author.

Freeman, J. 1973. The origins of the womens liberation movement. *American Journal of Sociology, 78,* 792-881.

Freeze Focus. 1986. Freeze National Conference, 1986. *Freeze Focus, 1,* 1.

Freeze Newsletter. 1982. Freeze introduced in Congress. *Freeze Newsletter, 2,* 1-23.

Friedrichs, D. 1980. The legitimacy crisis in the United States: A conceptual analysis. *Social Problems, 27,* 540-555.

Gallup, G. H. 1972. *The Gallup poll: Public opinion, 1935-1971.* New York: Random House.

Gamson, W. A. 1975. *The strategy of social protest.* Homewood, IL: Dorsey Press.

Gamson, W. 1983. Review of the *Voice and the Eye. American Journal of Sociology, 88,* 812-814.

Garfinkle, A. 1984. *The politics of the nuclear freeze.* Philadelphia: Foreign Policy Research Institute.

Garfinkle, A. 1985. The unmaking of the nuclear freeze. *Washington Quarterly, 8,* 109-120.

Geiger, H. J. 1984. Learning from the P.S.R.: Successful methods for major impact. In S.E. Muller (Ed.), *The nuclear weapons freeze and arms control.* pp. 41-43. Cambridge, MA: Ballinger.

Gella, A. 1976. An introduction to the sociology of the intelligentsia. In A. Gella (ed.), *The intelligentsia and the intellectuals.* pp. 9-34. London: Sage.

Gerlach, L., and Hine, V. 1970. *People, power, change.* New York: Bobbs Merrill.

Giddens, A. 1977. Review essay: Habermas' social and political theory. *American Journal of Sociology, 83,* 198-212.

Gilpin, R. 1962. *American scientists and nuclear weapons policy.* Princeton, NJ: Princeton University Press.

Gitlin, T. 1987. *The sixties: Years of hope, days of rage.* New York: Bantam.

Glazer, N. 1961. The peace movement in America-1961. *Commentary, 31,* 288-296.

Gottlieb, S. 1968. SANE's road: Another assessment. *War/Peace Reports, 6,* 18.

Gottlieb, S. 1983, December 3. Personal interview.

Gouldner, A. 1974. Marxism and social theory. *Theory and Society, 1,* 17-35.

Gouldner, A. 1975-76. Prologue to a theory of revolutionary intellectuals. *Telos, 45,* 3-36.

Gouldner, A. 1979. *The future of intellectuals and the rise of the new class.* New York: Oxford University Press.

Gouldner, A. 1985. *Against fragmentation.* New York: Oxford University Press.

Grayson, J. P. 1984. Review of the *Voice and the Eye. Canadian Review of Sociology and Anthropology, 21,* 359-361.

Gurr, T. 1970. *Why men rebel.* Princeton, NJ: Princeton University Press.

Gusfield, J. 1963. *Symbolic crusade.* Urbana: University of Illinois Press.

Gusfield, J. 1983, December. The current state of social problems theory. *Social Problems Theory Division Newsletter.*

Habermas, J. 1971. *Toward a rational society. Student protest, science and politics.* Boston: Beacon.

Habermas, J. 1975a. *Legitimation crisis.* Boston: Beacon.

Habermas, J. 1975b. Toward a reconstruction of historical materialism. *Theory and Society, 2,* 79-91.

Habermas, J. 1981. *Theorie des kommunikativen handels.* Frankfurt: Suhrkamp.

Habermas, J. 1984. *The theory of communicative action.* vol. I. Boston: Beacon.

Harvard Study Group. 1983. *Living with nuclear weapons.* Cambridge, MA: Harvard University Press.

Held, D. 1978. Extended review. *Sociological Review-New Series, 26,* 183-194.

Herman, R. 1982, June 12. Rally, speakers decry cost of nuclear arms race. *New York Times,* p. A43.

Hertsgard, M. 1985, June. What became of the freeze? *Mother Jones,* pp. 44-47.

Hodgson, G. 1976. *America in our time: From World War II to Nixon, what happened and why.* New York: Random House.

Horkheimer, M., and Adorno, T. 1972. *Dialectic of enlightenment.* New York: Seabury.

Horton, P., and Leslie, G. 1955. *The sociology of social problems.* New York: Appleton, Century & Crofts.

Institute for Defense and Disarmament Studies. 1984-1985. Brochure.

Jackson, L. R., and Johnson, W. A. 1974. *Protest by the poor.* Lexington, MA: D.C. Heath.

Jacoby, R. 1987. *The last intellectuals.* New York: Basic Books.

Jenkins, C. 1983. Resource mobilization theory and the study of social movements. *Annual Review of Sociology, 9,* 527-553.

Jenkins, C., and Perrow, C. 1977. Insurgency of the powerless. *American Sociological Review, 42,* 249-268.

Johnson, J. T. 1975. *Ideology, reason, and the limitation of war: Religious and secular concepts, 1200-1740.* Princeton, NJ: Princeton University Press.

Kaku, M. 1979, May 9. Ban nuke power, ban nuke weapons. *The Guardian*, p. 1.

Kaplan, F. 1983. *The wizards of Armageddon*. New York: Simon & Schuster.

Katz, M. S. 1986. *Ban the bomb: A history of SANE, The Committee for a Sane Nuclear Policy, 1957-1985*. New York: Greenwood Press.

Kehler, R. 1984a. We need a common voice. *Nuclear Times*, 2, 9-10.

Kehler, R. 1984b. Message from the national coordinator. *Freeze Focus*, August, 4, 3.

Kehler, R. 1984c. Message from the national coordinator. *Freeze Focus*, September, 4, 3.

Kehler, R. 1984d. Message from the national coordinator. *Freeze Focus*, December, 4, 3.

Kennedy, E., and Hatfield, M. 1982. *Freeze: How you can help prevent nuclear war*. New York: Bantam Books.

Kevles, D. 1978. *The physicists: The history of a scientific community in America*. New York: Random House.

Kitsuse, J., and Spector, M. 1973. Social problems: A reformulation. *Social Problems*, 20, 145-159.

Kivisto, P. 1982. Review of the *Voice and the Eye*. *Contemporary Sociology*, 11, 181-183.

Kivisto, P. 1984. Contemporary social movements in advanced industrial societies and social intervention. An appraisal of Alain Touraine's pratique. *Acta Sociologica*, 27, 355-366.

Kojm, C. 1983. *The nuclear freeze debate*. New York: Wilson.

Kopp, C. 1979. The origin of the American scientific debate over fallout hazards. *Social Studies of Science*, 9, 403-422.

Kornhauser, W. 1959. *The politics of mass society*. London: Routledge.

Kramer, B., Kalick, S., and Milburn, M. 1983. Attitudes toward nuclear weapons and nuclear war: 1945-1982. *Journal of Social Issues*, 39, 7-24.

Kramer, R., and Marullo, S. 1985. Toward a sociology of nuclear weapons. *Sociological Quarterly*, 26, 277-292.

Kriesberg, L. 1986. Consequences of efforts at deescalating the American-Soviet conflict. *Journal of Political and Military Sociology*, 14, 215-234.

Kristol, I. 1978. *Two cheers for capitalism*. New York: Basic Books.

Kuhn, T. 1962. *The structure of scientific revolutions*. Chicago: University of Chicago Press.

Kurtz, L. 1988. *The nuclear age: A society of the arms race*. Englewood Cliffs, NJ: Prentice-Hall.

Ladd, E.C. 1978. The new lines are drawn: Class and ideology in America. Part I. *Public Opinion*, 3, 48-53.

Latour, B., and Woolgar, S. (1979). *Laboratory life*. Beverly Hills, CA: Sage.

Lauer, R. 1976. Defining social problems: Public and professional perspectives. *Social Problems*, 24, 122-130.

Leavitt, R. 1983. *Freezing the arms race: The genesis of a mass movement*. Cambridge, MA: Kennedy School of Government.

Lens, S. 1976, February. Doomsday strategy. *Progressive*, pp. 12-35.

Lens, S. 1982, May. How deep a freeze? *Progressive*, pp. 16-17.

Lifton, R. J., and Falk, R. 1982. *Indefensible weapons: The political and psychological case against nuclearism.* New York: Basic Books.

Lippman, W. 1945. *U.S. foreign policy: Shield of the republic.* Boston: Little, Brown.

Lipsky, M. 1968. Protest as a political resource. *American Political Science Review, 62,* 1144-1158.

Lord, G., and Hurley, S. 1985. Using civil disobedience in the peace movement: A case study. Paper presented at the annual meeting of the Society for the Study of Social Problems. Washington, D.C.

MacLeod, R., and MacLeod, K. 1976. The relation of science and technology. In C.M. Cipolla (ed.), *The Fontana economic history of Europe.* London: Fontana. ·

Magraw, K. 1986. Short-term plans, long-term visions. *Nuclear Times, 4,* 27-29.

Manis, J. 1984. *Serious social problems.* Boston: Allyn & Bacon.

Mannheim, K. 1960. *Ideology and utopia.* New York: Harvest Books.

Marchand, C.R. 1972. *The peace movement and social reform.* Princeton, NJ: Princeton University Press.

Markle, G., and McCrea, F. In press. Forgetting and remembering: Bitburg and the social construction of history. *Perspectives on Social Problems.*

Marx, K. 1969 [1852]. The eighteenth brumaire of Louis Napoleon. In K. Marx, *Selected Works.* vol. I. Moscow: Progress Press.

Mauss, A. 1975. *Social problems as social movement.* Philadelphia: J. P. Lippincott.

Mazur, A. 1981. *The dynamics of technical controversies.* New York: Communications Press.

McAllister, P. 1982. *Reweaving the web of life: Feminism and non-violence.* Philadelphia: New Society Publishers.

McCarthy, J., and Zald, M. 1973. *The trend in social movements in America: Professionalization and resource mobilization.* Morristown, NJ: General Learning Press.

McCarthy, J., and Zald, M. 1977. Resource mobilization and social movements: A partial theory. *American Journal of Sociology, 82,* 1213-1241.

McCrea, F., and Kelley, D. 1983. *Thinking the unthinkable: Toward a sociology of nuclear weapons.* Paper presented at the annual meeting of the Society for the Study of Social Problems, Detroit.

McCrea, F., and Markle, G. 1989. Atomic scientists and protest: The Bulletin as a social movements organization. In L. Kriesberg (ed.), *Research in social movements, conflict and change.* pp.219-233. Greenwich, CT: JAI.

McNall, S. (1979). *Theoretical perspectives in sociology.* New York: St. Martins.

Merton, R. K. (1957). *Social theory and social structure.* Glencoe, IL: Free Press.

Michels, R. 1968. Intellectuals. In *Encyclopedia of the social sciences,* vol. VIII, p. 121. New York: Macmillan.

Milburn, M., Watanaba, P., and Kramer, B. 1986. The nature and sources of attitudes toward a nuclear freeze. *Political Psychology, 7,* 661-674.

Miller, J. 1982, March 15. Effort to freeze nuclear arsenals spreads in U.S. *New York Times.* p. B-12.

Miller, S. 1984. *The nuclear weapons freeze and arms control*. Cambridge, MA: Ballinger.

Mills, C.W. 1956. *The power elite*. New York: Oxford University Press.

Mills, C.W. 1959. *The sociological imagination*. New York: Oxford University Press.

Mitchell, G. 1984. Returning an important call. *Nuclear Times*, 2, 9, 13.

Mitchell, R. 1981. From elite quarrel to mass movement. *Society*, *18*, 76-84.

Molander, R. 1982. *Nuclear war: What's in it for you?* New York: Pocket Books.

Mulkay, M. 1976. The moderating role of the scientific elite. *Social Studies of Science*, *6*, 445-470.

Mumford, L. 1946. Gentlemen: You are mad! *Saturday Review of Literature*, *29*, 5-6.

Mumford, L. 1954. *In the name of sanity*. New York: Harcourt, Brace.

Muste, A. J. 1954. *The camp of liberation*. London: Peace News.

Myers, F. 1978. The failure of protest against postwar British defense policy. In S. Wand (ed.), *Doves and diplomats: Foreign offices and peace movements in Europe and America in the twentieth century.* pp.240-264. Westport, CT: Greenwood.

Myrdal, A. 1981. *The dynamics of European nuclear disarmament*. London: Spokesman.

Nagel, J. 1983. Review of the *Voice and the Eye*. *Social Forces*, *61*, 923-924.

Nation. 1960. The other summit conference. *Nation*, *190*, 482.

National Conference of Catholic Bishops. 1982, May 19. The challenge of peace: God's promise and our response, *Origins*, pp.1-32.

Nelkin, D. 1981. Anti-nuclear connection: Power and weapons. *Bulletin of the Atomic Scientists*, *37*, 36-40.

Nelson, D. M. 1946. *Arsenal of democracy: The story of American war production*. New York: Harcourt, Brace.

Nettl, J. P. 1969. Ideas, intellectuals and structures of dissent. In P. Rieff (ed.), *On intellectuals*. pp. 53-122. Garden City, NJ: Doubleday.

Newsweek. 1981, November 23. Anti-nukes, U.S. Style. pp.44-49.

Newsweek. 1982a, April 26. A matter of life and death. pp. 20-25.

Newsweek. 1982b, May 3. Fallout from ground zero. p. 24.

New York Herald Tribune. 1958, March 24. No contamination without representation. p. 9.

New York Times. 1957, November 15. We are facing a danger unlike any danger that has ever existed. . . p. 54.

New York Times. 1958, April 11. Nuclear bombs can destroy all life in war. p. 15.

New York Times. 1958, October 31. To the men at Geneva. p. 21.

New York Times. 1959, February 13. Mr. Eisenhower, Mr. Khrushchev, Mr. Macmillan, the time is now! p. 15.

New York Times. 1959, August 13. Humanity has a common will and right to survive. p. 17.

New York Times. 1960, February 8. Three out of four Americans favor a ban on testing. p. 8.

New York Times. 1962, April 16. Dr. Spock is worried. p. 30.

New York Times. 1962, July 5. Is this what it's coming to? p. 54

New York Times. 1963, April 7. Your children's teeth contain strontium-90. p. 10.

New York Times. 1965, July 22. The winner of World War III. p. 39.

New York Times. 1968, March 24. From the people who brought you Vietnam: The anti-ballistic missile system. p. 12.

New York Times. 1974, June 2. From the people who brought you inflation: Humane nuclear war. p. 23.

New York Times. 1983, March 26. FBI rules out Russian control of freeze drive. p. 1.

Nuclear Times. 1983. The next step: Acting on faith. *3,* 9-16.

Nuclear Times. 1985. The new face of the freeze. *3,* 7-8.

Nuclear Times. 1986. The freeze carries on. *4,* 14.

Nuclear Weapons Freeze Campaign. 1981, March. *Strategy for stopping the nuclear arms race.* St. Louis: Author.

Nuclear Weapons Freeze Campaign. 1982, December. *Summary of major decisions made by the national committee.* St Louis: Author.

Nuclear Weapons Freeze Campaign. 1983a, February. *1983 strategy proposal.* St. Louis: Author.

Nuclear Weapons Freeze Campaign. 1983b, December. *1984 strategy proposal.* St. Louis: Author.

Nuclear Weapons Freeze Campaign. 1984a. *Freeze focus.* St. Louis: Author.

Nuclear Weapons Freeze Campaign. 1984b, December. *Final draft for the strategy paper for 1985.* St. Louis: Author.

Nuclear Weapons Freeze Campaign. 1984c. *Decisions made by the fifth national conference.* St. Louis: Author.

Nuclear Weapons Freeze Campaign. 1985. *"Revised" decisions made by the sixth national conference on the nuclear weapons freeze campaign, November 15-17, 1985.* Washington, DC: Author.

Nuclear Weapons Freeze Campaign. 1985a. *Executive committee minutes, January 18-20.* St. Louis: Author.

Nuclear Weapons Freeze Campaign. 1985b, November. *Decisions made by the sixth national conference.* St. Louis: Author.

Oberschall, A. 1973. *Social conflict and social movements.* Englewood Cliffs, NJ: Prentice-Hall.

Olson, M. 1965. *The logic of collective action.* New York: Harvard University Press.

Paarlberg, R. 1973. Forgetting the unthinkable. *Foreign Policy, 10,* 132-140.

Parkin, F. 1968. *Middle class radicalism.* Manchester, UK: Manchester University Press.

Parsons, T. 1951. *Social systems.* Glencoe, IL: Free Press.

Parsons, T. 1951. *Theories of society.* Glencoe, IL: Free Press.

Patterson, D. S. 1973. An interpretation of the American Peace Movement, 1898-1918. In C. Chatfield (ed.) *Peace and justice: Pacifism in America, 1914-1941.* Knoxville: University of Tennessee Press.

Pauling, L. 1958. *No more war!* New York: Dodd, Mead.

Payne, K., and Gray, C. 1984. *The nuclear freeze controversy.* Boston: University Press of America.

Peck, G.T. 1947. Who are the United World Federalists? *Common Cause, 1*, 28-36.

Perkins, D. 1952. *The American approach to foreign policy*. Cambridge, MA: Harvard University Press.

Phillips, D. 1971. *Knowledge from what?* Chicago: Rand McNally.

Piccone, P. 1981-82. The role of the intellectuals in the 1980s. *Telos, 50*, 115-118.

Pickus, R. 1955. Speak truth to power. *Progressive, 19*, 5-8.

Price, H., and Pfost, D. 1983. *Resource mobilization theory and the movement for a bilateral nuclear weapons freeze*. Paper presented at the annual meeting of the Society for the Study of Social Problems, Detroit.

Pringle, P., and Spiegelman, J. 1981. *The nuclear barons*. New York: Holt, Rinehart & Winston.

Pringle, P. 1982, July. Putting World War III on ice. *Inquiry*, pp. 15-16.

Rabinowitch, E. 1951. Five years after. *Bulletin of the Atomic Scientists, 7*, 3.

Rabinowitch, E. 1956. Ten years that changed the world. *Bulletin of the Atomic Scientists, 12* (32), 2-6.

Rabinowitch, E. 1963. Eulogy for Leo Szilard. *Bulletin of the Atomic Scientists, 20*, 16-20.

Rabinowitch, E. 1966a. New year's thoughts, 1966. *Bulletin of the Atomic Scientists, 22*, 3-7.

Rabinowitch, E. 1966b. Open letter to Konrad Lorenz. *Bulletin of the Atomic Scientists, 22*, 2-3.

Ramsey, P. 1968. *The just war: Force and political responsibility*. New York: Scribner.

Rhodes, R. 1986. *The making of the atomic bomb*. New York: Simon & Schuster.

Robertson, I. 1988. *Sociology* (3rd ed.). New York: Worth.

Rose, P., & Laulicht, J. 1963. Editorial foreword. *Social Problems, 11*, 3-5.

SANE World. 1969. The story of an ad. 8, 3.

Schell, J. 1982. *The fate of the earth*. New York: Knopf.

Schneider, J. 1985. Social problems theory: The constructionist view. *Annual Review of Sociology, 11*, 209-229.

Schur, E. 1979. *Interpreting deviance*. New York: Harper & Row.

Schoefield, A.C., Meier, R.J., and Griffin, R.J. 1979. Constructing a social problem. *Social Problems, 27*, 38-62.

Schwartz, C. 1969. Scientists in politics. *Bulletin of the Atomic Scientists, 25*, 42.

Sheppard, N. 1984. Center for nuclear freeze setup in St. Louis. *New York Times*, March 23, A19.

Shils, E.A. 1964. Freedom of influence: Observations in the scientists movement in the United States. *Bulletin of the Atomic Scientists, 20*.

Shulman, M.D. 1987. Four decades of irrationality: U.S.-Soviet relations. *Bulletin of the Atomic Scientists, 43*, 15-25.

Simpson, J.A. 1981. Some personal notes. *Bulletin of the Atomic Scientists, 37*, 26.

Skocpol, T. 1984. *Vision and method in historical sociology*. Cambridge, UK: Cambridge University press.

Smelser, N. 1959. *Social change in the industrial revolution*. Chicago: University of Chicago Press.

Smelser, N. 1962. *The theory of collective behavior*. New York: Free Press.

Smith, A.K. 1965. *A peril and a hope: The scientists movement in America, 1945-1947*. Chicago: University of Chicago Press.

Snow, C.P. 1955. *The two cultures and the scientific revolution*. Cambridge, UK: Cambridge University Press.

Solo, P. 1988. *From protest to policy*. Boston: Ballinger.

Spector, M., and Kitsuse, J.I. 1977. *Constructing social problems*. Menlo Park, CA: Cummings.

Spiegelman, R. 1982. Media manipulation of the movement. *Social Policy, 13*, 9-16.

Stinchcombe, A.L. 1978. *Theoretical methods in social history*. New York: Academic Press.

Stone, P.H. 1982. The bomb: The last epidemic. *The Atlantic Monthly, 249*, 6-7.

Strickland, D.A. 1968. *Scientists in politics: The atomic scientists movement, 1945-1946*. West Lafayette, IN: Purdue University Press.

Szilard, L. 1947. Calling for a crusade. *Bulletin of the Atomic Scientists, 2*, 102-106.

Taylor, B. 1985. Learning electoral lessons. *Nuclear Times, 4*, 16-19.

Teller, E., and Latter, A. 1958. The compelling need for nuclear tests. *Life, 44*, 64-66, 69-72.

Telos. 1981-82. Symposium: The role of the intellectuals in the 1980s. *Telos, 50*, 115-160.

Teltsch, K. 1984. Philanthropics focus concern on the arm race. *New York Times*, A1, A42.

Tilly, C., and Tilly, L. 1981. *Collective action and class conflict*. Beverly Hills, CA: Sage.

Tilly, C., Tilly, L., and Tilly, R. 1975. *The rebellious century*. Cambridge, MA: Harvard University Press.

Time. 1958, April 21. How sane is SANE? *Time, 71*, 26.

Touraine, A. 1971. *Post industrial society*. New York: Free Press.

Touraine, A. 1976. From crisis to critique. *Partisan Review, 43*, 212-223.

Touraine, A. 1981. *The Voice and the Eye: An analysis of social movements*. Cambridge, MA: Cambridge University Press.

Touraine, A. 1983. From exchange to communication. In S. Aida (ed.), *The human use of human ideas*. pp. 115-140. New York: Pergamon.

Turner, J. 1981. *Just war tradition and the restraint of war: A moral and historical inquiry*. Princeton, NJ: Princeton University Press.

von Hippel, F. 1986. Finding common ground. *Nuclear Times, 4*, 19-20.

Walker, J.L. 1983. The origins and maintenance of interest groups in America. *American Political Science Review, 77*, 390-406.

Walker, P. 1979. *Between labor and capital*. Boston: South End Press.

Waller, D. 1987. *Congress and the nuclear freeze*. Amherst: University of Massachusetts Press.

Waller, W. 1936. Social problems and the mores. *American Sociological Review, 1*, 922-934.

Ward, B. 1966. *Nationalism and ideology.* New York: Norton.

Watson, R. 1963, January. Arms control: Now or never. *Newsweek,* pp. 14-21.

Weart, S., and Szilard, G. 1978. *Leo Szilard: His version of the facts.* Cambridge: MIT Press.

Wernette, D. 1985. *The freeze movement on the local level: Prospects for success.* Paper presented at the annual meeting of the Society for the Study of Social Problems, Washington, DC.

Wiltz, J.E. 1963. *In search of peace: The Senate munitions inquiry, 1934-1936.* Baton Rouge: Louisiana State University Press.

Wittner, L.S. 1984. *Rebels against war: The American peace movement, 1933-1983.* Philadelphia: Temple University Press.

Wood, P. 1982. The environmental movement. In J. Wood & M. Jackson (eds.), *Social Movements.* Belmont, CA: Wadsworth.

Woolgar, S., and Pawluck, D. 1985. Ontological gerrymandering: The anatomy of social problems explanations. *Social Problems, 32,* 214-227.

World Press Review. 1982, March. The new peace movement. p. 43.

Wright, T., Rodriguez, F., and Wartzkin, H. 1985. Corporate interests, philanthropies, and the peace movement. *Monthly Review, 36,* 19-31.

Yoder, J.A. 1972. The United World Federalists: Liberals for law and order. In C. Chatfield (ed.), *For peace and justice: Pacifism in America, 1914-1941.* Knoxville: University of Tennessee Press.

Zald, M. 1987. The future of social movements. In M. Zald and J. McCarthy (eds.), *Social movements in an organized society.* New Brunswick: Transaction Books.

Zald, M., & Ash, R. 1966. Social movement organizations. *Social Forces, 44,* 327-341.

Zald, M., & McCarthy, J. 1979. *The dynamics of social movements.* Cambridge, MA: Winthrop Publishers.

Name Index

191

Subject Index

About the Authors

Frances B. McCrea is Assistant Professor of Sociology at Grand Valley State University. She has published in the areas of social problems, social movements, medical sociology, theory, and women's studies. During the time this research was conducted, she was a Fellow of the Institute for the Study of World Politics, and she received a grant to participate in the Program on Nuclear Weapons and Arms Control at the Massachusetts Institute of Technology and Harvard University.

Gerald E. Markle is Professor of Sociology at Western Michigan University and was Visiting Professor of Science, Technology and Society at Cornell University. His research interests are in the sociology of science and knowledge. He is coauthor of *Science, Politics and Cancer: The Laetrile Phenomenon* and *Cigarettes: The Battle Over Smoking*.

Professors McCrea and Markle are currently working on a comparative study of the way East and West Germany have constructed the history of World War II.